HOOPS HEIST

A Slow Grind Media Publication

Books by Jon Finkel

The Greatest Stars of the NBA Series Vol. 1 – Vol. 12

The Dadvantage

Heart Over Height

Forces of Character

"Mean" Joe Greene: Built by Football

The Athlete

The Life of Dad

Jocks in Chief

Hoops Heist

Seattle, the Sonics, and How a Stolen Team's Legacy Gave Rise to the NBA's Secret Empire

HOOPS

HEIST

JON FINKEL

Foreword by ISAIAH THOMAS

For Seattle

SlowGrindMedia.com

Hardback ISBN: 978-1-63649-997-0
Paperback ISBN: 978-1-63625-484-5

Contents

Foreword

The story of basketball in Washington is more than just a collection of wins and losses by the Sonics and the Huskies and the high schools throughout the metro region. It's a story of kids on playgrounds in Pierce County, and at parks in King County, and rec centers and gyms and driveways in Snohomish and throughout the Pacific Northwest. It's a story of grandparents who cheered when pro basketball arrived in Seattle and who raised their kids on the feats of "Downtown" Freddie Brown and Slick Watts and Jack Sikma and Lenny Wilkens, and of the championship in 1979. It's a story of parents coaching their kids and bringing them to camps run by Doug Christie and Gary Payton and George Karl. It's a story of those kids who grew up idolizing Doug and Gary and Shawn Kemp, and who went on to make names for themselves in the game they love. It's Jason Terry's story. It's Jamal Crawford's story. It's my story. It's all of ours.

Basketball in Seattle is more than a sport; it's a brotherhood and sisterhood. It's family. It's everything. We don't think of it as a game. We think of it as a culture. It's a culture that, by way of the sheer amount of talent in our region, fills up the rosters of the best colleges in the country and puts dozens of players in the NBA. It's a culture that is based on giving back to our community. As you'll read in this book, every single one of us who has been lucky enough to make a career out of the game we love makes it a priority to pass our knowledge on to the next generation. It's just what we do.

And yes, for forty years it was a culture for which the centerpiece was the Seattle SuperSonics. And now they're gone. We all believe the team will return one day. Until then, I felt that it was important for the world to know the story of our town, our team and the individual dreams of those of us who are from here. The heart and soul of our city, the Sonics, was taken from us. But our basketball heartbeat is stronger than ever. Through the efforts of the NBA and college players from the region, and the high school coaches who keep the heritage alive, and the championships the amazing Seattle Storm keep bringing our city, we maintain our pride, our culture and our passion for this game.

Hoops Heist is the story of our past, our present and our future. We hope you'll enjoy reading about it as much as we've enjoyed living it.

— Isaiah

Introduction

The history of the Seattle SuperSonics franchise begins and ends on a thirty-mile strip of asphalt in Central Oklahoma known as the Tinker Diagonal. There, among the half-dozen churches, a handful of truck stops, the Grand Casino, and the highway's culinary anchor, Curtis Watson's Catfish Restaurant, the basketball story of promise and heartbreak in the Emerald City lives on. Let's start with the promise.

It's February 11, 1966 in Shawnee, Oklahoma. After temperatures reached a spring-like sixty-seven degrees earlier in the week they plummeted to zero on Friday, practically flash-freezing the entire campus of Oklahoma Baptist University. But nobody cared. Friday night was game night for the OBU Bison men's basketball team, and that meant nearly the entire campus would be crammed into the steamy Clark Craig Fieldhouse to watch the best basketball player any of them had ever laid eyes on: the 6'8", 190-pound, bespectacled and brilliant Al Tucker Jr.

"This was a different era," says John Parrish, OBU's then-director of public relations. "People didn't have the best teams in the country on television every night, so they drove from all over Oklahoma to watch Al play. It was a statewide attraction."

Tucker was the son of "Slick Al" Tucker Sr., a member of the Harlem Globetrotters in the early 1940s and the person most responsible for Junior's basketball talent, drive and IQ. On this particular night, underneath the high-arcing diamond latticework that framed the hardwood court inside the fieldhouse, the Bison hosted the Phillips University Haymakers, who they had lost to in January, 63-61.

Bison head coach Bob Bass wanted revenge. His 10-3 team was stuck in a tie for first place with Southeastern University atop the Collegiate Conference and a win would put them at the top of the league with only a few weeks left before the playoff tournament.

All year he had been teaching a championship style of play modeled after the gold (green) standard in the sport: the Boston Celtics, who were then seven-time defending NBA champions. Prior to the season, Bass had attended a breakfast meeting in Quincy, Illinois and Boston's Hall of Fame shooting guard Bill Sharman was the speaker. Sharman was an eight-time all-star and four-time NBA champion, and that morning he expounded on the philosophy of the Celtics' legendary coach Red Auerbach. In particular, he talked about Auerbach's belief that teams needed multiple offensive sets and, more importantly, that a coach had to make sure all five men on the floor were given specific individual assignments for the game. This gives a team options.

"A play without an option is not worth a dime," Auerbach famously said.

As Bass preached the gospel of Auerbach before tip-off, he had no way of knowing that on this night his team would realistically only need a single option, Al Tucker Jr., who threw haymaker after haymaker at the Haymakers for forty-eight minutes on his way to a team-record forty-six points (breaking his own previous record of forty-three points) and a 94-58 demolition of Phillips. Most impressive was Tucker's lethal efficiency. He was 18 of 26 from the floor and 10 of 12 from the free-throw line, and helped the team gain a rebounding edge of forty-nine to just seventeen—a stat line that even Auerbach's own best player, Bill Russell, would be proud of.

***

Thirteen hundred miles away, in the midst of a rare week in Los Angeles where it rained every day, former University of Southern California basketball player Dick Vertlieb and former classmate Don Richman were at the tail end of a half-decade quest to leave their respective careers and run a brand new National Basketball Association team. Not knowing which city they'd get to run a franchise in at the outset of their journey was beside the point. The goal was simply to get into the league.

Vertlieb would one day be recognized in NBA circles for his thick mustache, vintage pipe and big personality, but at this point he was young, clean-shaven and bored. After college he'd taken a job as a securities analyst at Merrill Lynch and it was as exciting as it sounds. He loved basketball and dreamed of running a team, but at the age of thirty his hoops leadership résumé was exactly one bullet point long: He spent a season coaching USC's men's freshman team. He had about as much chance of being an executive with an NBA franchise as your average stockbroker with no experience, which is to say, none.

Richman, in contrast, had a skyrocketing media and consulting career. He had formed a public relations firm with future Oakland Raiders owner Al Davis and his clientele included the Minneapolis Lakers (for whom he oversaw their move to Los Angeles) and the American Football League's upstart team in Los Angeles.

Among Richman's first assignments was to help find a name for the City of Angels' new pigskin squad. The team's owner was credit card magnate Barron Hilton, so Richman floated the name "Chargers," both as a nod to Hilton's business and because he liked the idea of a football team "charging down the field." He felt it was a nice double entendre. Unfortunately, the triple entendre never came to fruition as fans didn't really "charge to the stadium," leaving Hilton to quickly move his franchise to San Diego after just one season in LA.

After the team relocated, Richman stayed in Los Angeles and became a television writer. It was during this period of his career, while he was churning out scripts for *Gidget, Gilligan's Island, Green Acres* and *The Man from U.N.C.L.E.*, that his old college pal called him out of the blue to talk him into his scheme to run a basketball team.

Vertlieb's plan involved three steps: research, pitch and fund-raise. On the research side, he and Richman would study all the major cities that didn't have an NBA team and select the best one where a franchise could succeed. Then they'd pitch NBA Commissioner J. Walter Kennedy on selecting that city for expansion, after which they'd round up investors for seed money. The cost of an NBA franchise back then was roughly $3 million, which is just about a billion less than what a large-market team would cost now.

Their initial research pointed to Cleveland as the perfect spot for a new team, but when a deal fell through Richman suggested Seattle as their next best bet. He had traveled to Seattle a few times during his time working with the Trojan football team and never forgot the city's love for sports.

"The feel of the city for sports stayed with me," Richman said in a retrospective piece for *Sports Press Northwest.* "I just thought it would be an exceptional place for a professional basketball franchise."

Vertlieb agreed. Now all they needed was cash and a compelling argument to the NBA that Seattle deserved a team. It's important to keep in mind that this was the mid-sixties; this was long before the Seahawks, the Sounders, the Mariners, the Storm and obviously anything resembling the Sonics. There weren't any professional teams in Seattle and the NBA had never expanded into a city that didn't already have at least one pro football or baseball team. Vertlieb and Richman were undeterred.

They made nearly a dozen trips to Seattle over the course of several years and became more and more convinced that it was the ideal city in which to launch a new franchise. Then, late in the summer of '66, Vertlieb read that Richman's former boss Barron Hilton had just sold the San Diego Chargers to an entrepreneur named Eugene Klein for $10 million.

He had a hunch he'd found his moneyman.

In the span of seven days he set up a meeting, made a successful pitch, and got Klein, along with his partner Sam Schulman (who we'll learn a lot more about), on board. The final piece of the puzzle took the rest of the summer, the fall and the early winter to lock into place, as Vertlieb and Richman made a series of speeches to NBA suits extolling the virtues of Seattle as an NBA city. They showed the growing demographics, the projected attendance, the population charts—anything and everything that would whet the appetites of the Association's decision makers.

Finally, on December 10, 1966, their years of presentations and pitches and praying paid off when the NBA named Seattle the home of its newest franchise. Richman would be the team's general manager, Vertlieb would be the business manager, and Klein and Schulman would become majority owners, with Schulman being the "active" partner.

"I have a dream for this great city," Schulman said. "I intend to pull together some of the most talented men in this country. Together, we will bring the world championship to Seattle."

But there wasn't much time. With the SuperSonics' first game less than 10 months away, Richman quickly hired 35-year-old Al "Blinky" Bianchi to be the team's first head coach. Bianchi was born and raised in Queens, New York and had played for the Syracuse Nationals/Philadelphia 76ers for a decade before accepting the Seattle coaching job. Together, Richman and Bianchi filled out their roster from the NBA's expansion draft, with the prize pick being future All-Star Walt Hazzard from the Lakers. They also had the sixth overall selection in the 1967 NBA Draft.

It was a fairly loaded rookie class that would produce six Hall of Famers, including Phil Jackson and Pat Riley. The Detroit Pistons took Jimmy Walker out of Providence with the number-one overall pick and then the Baltimore Bullets took Earl Monroe from Winston-Salem State. Clem Haskins, Sonny Dove and Walt Frazier went off the board in quick succession, leaving the Sonics with a host of forwards and centers to choose from (positions they wanted to solidify). Kentucky's Riley was available, as was local star Tom Workman out of Seattle University. Center Mel Daniels from New Mexico was a reach as well. In the end, the new SuperSonics brass became enamored with a 6'8", 190-pound lanky scoring and rebounding machine from a small school in central Oklahoma. And so, with their sixth overall pick and their first in franchise history, the Seattle SuperSonics chose none other than Al Tucker Jr.

***

Forty years later in 2007, the Sonics were once again sitting at the top of the NBA draft (this time with the number-two overall pick), and once again they were considering a tall, skinny scoring savant: Kevin Durant. Durant was a 6'9", 185-pound, one-and-done University of Texas star who was the first player to win the coveted Naismith Award as a freshman.

In almost any other NBA Draft, Durant would have been the clear-cut number-one overall pick and the Sonics' drafting position would have been one slot too late. But this wasn't an ordinary year. Throughout the entire college season there had been a running debate as to whether Durant or star Ohio State center Greg Oden would be the first player taken. In the end, Oden was too much of a physical specimen (7', 250 pounds) to pass up, and the Portland Trailblazers took him first, leaving Seattle to take Durant.

The nineteen-year-old was the kind of player front offices built championships and careers around. He was a true-blue generational talent. (In his first twelve years in the league, Durant would be a ten-time all-star, league MVP and two-time Finals MVP.) The franchise was delighted. The fans, on the other hand, were devastated. They knew that Durant would not become a star in Seattle because the Emerald City was about to lose its beloved Sonics.

Clay Bennett, the businessman who bought the team from Starbucks CEO Howard Schultz in 2005, had been rumored to want to move the franchise to his hometown of Oklahoma City from the moment the ink was dry on the deal. (We'll take a deep dive into how all this went down later, but for now, just as when you saw the movie *Titanic* knowing that the ship sinks, you already know that Seattle no longer has an NBA team.)

Of course, Bennett went through the motions of making it appear that he had an interest in keeping the team in Seattle—but he never did. In April 2007, roughly two months before the NBA Draft and the team's selection of Durant, Bennett effectively gave up on the "staying in Seattle" charade when he couldn't strike a deal for a new arena in Washington. On November 2, 2007, one day after the Sonics' home opener and the debut of Durant, Bennett announced the team was leaving Seattle the moment it could legally do so.

Tom Carr, the attorney for the city of Seattle who had been hired to keep the team legally bound there, was livid.

"Mr. Bennett's announcement today is a transparent attempt to alienate the Seattle fan base and follow through on his plan to move the team to Oklahoma City ... Making this move now continues the current ownership's insulting behavior toward the Sonics' dedicated fans and the citizens of the city."

Carr wasn't wrong.

The Sonics played one final season in Seattle, and then on October 29, 2008, they played their first game as the newly minted Oklahoma City Thunder in the Ford Center. Kevin Durant, the Seattle franchise's final star draft pick, was on the floor for this game—a mere thirty miles from Oklahoma Baptist University, where the Seattle franchise's first star draft pick, Al Tucker, showed up on their radar.

And thus, the history of the Seattle SuperSonics franchise begins and ends on a thirty-mile strip of asphalt in Central Oklahoma.

In the forty years between Al Tucker putting on a Sonics jersey for the first time and Durant taking one off for the last time, Seattle formed an emotional bond with its franchise that infused the entire city, from its culture to its confidence. The team's logo with its famous shock of green and yellow became an emblem of the Emerald City, representing its style, its swagger and its status in the sports world and beyond. From Jack Sikma to Dennis Johnson, from Gary Payton, Shawn Kemp and Ray Allen all the way to Durant, the players, the teams and the coaches weren't just part of a basketball team in Seattle, they were a part of the city's identity. An entire generation of basketball talent in the Pacific Northwest was raised on that connection, leading to dozens of players who grew up idolizing the team and using it as inspiration to make it to the NBA—Doug Christie, Jamal Crawford, Jason Terry, Brandon Roy, Nate Robinson, Isaiah Thomas, and so many more. These men embodied the Sonics' character and charisma, and when the team was stolen away, they became the standard bearers of its legacy.

This is their untold story...and the story of their city.

Part I:
The Franchise

Chapter 1

Twelve Sonics Equal One Wilt Chamberlain

Kurt Cobain and Eddie Vedder brought grunge to the masses. Ken Griffey Jr. single-handedly made the backwards baseball hat cool for a generation of kids. Bill Gates and Paul Allen put Microsoft Word on desktops the world over, and Jerry Baldwin, Zev Siegl and Gordon Bowker put white coffee cups with a Starbucks logo on the side on those very same desks. Seattle, as far as modern pop culture is concerned, is an influencer—but in 1962, not so much.

When the city hosted the World's Fair, aka the "Century 21 Exposition," civic leaders were in search of an identity and a hook to draw people to the Pacific Northwest. The two most recent cities in the United States to host—New York City and San Francisco—had no shortage of iconic buildings and images and cultural touchstones with which to lure people. San Francisco even put its new (at the time) bridge in the title of its exposition, the Golden Gate International Exposition. Seattle, for its part, didn't have much to work with. After all, the reason it was hosting the exhibition in the first place was to put the city on the map and to provide a boon to the downtown area. It's difficult to promote your map highlights at the same time you're trying to build your map worthiness.

If Seattle were to host a World's Fair today, we could easily envision an original Pearl Jam or Macklemore song in an ad, or a Russell Wilson-led Seahawks 12th man-themed social media campaign, or even a giant building shaped like a Venti Macchiato, but when it came time to produce a short black-and-white cartoon in the early sixties to generate interest for families to pack up and travel to the Emerald City, the catch phrase at the heart of the campaign was:

"Let's skidaddle... to Seattle."

To be fair, this was 1962 and the cultural zeitgeist was different. In this case, one of the most popular shows on television was *The Flintstones,* which was a cartoon that ran in prime time and was mostly watched by adults. If you're reading this and you only know the Flintstones as a kids vitamin brand or Fred in particular as the guy on the Fruity Pebbles cereal box, that is where the name and characters came from: an adult cartoon from six decades ago.

All of this is to say that roughly four years before the NBA agreed to place a franchise in Seattle, the city was still very much in search of something—anything, really—that would anchor it in the minds of everyday Americans and lift it to its coveted status as a top-tier American city. To that point, the city's number-one recognizable name and brand was likely Boeing, an airplane company founded by William "Bill" Boeing. Today, Boeing is a $200 billion multinational corporation, but it started out in 1917 with a staff of twenty-eight people working to fulfill its first contract with the U.S. Navy for fifty planes.

By the end of World War I Boeing employed 4,000 people, and during the heart of World War II that number ballooned to nearly 100,000. For better or worse, the company's (and the city's) fortunes rose and fell with warplane production for much of the 1900s. After the company was forced to lay off 70,000 workers following World War II, it's possible that neither Boeing nor Seattle would have been able to get off the mat if not for the rise of the commercial jet airplane, which revolutionized air travel and reinvigorated the city.

Thanks to the "Boeing Boom," Seattle's population numbered nearly 600,000 citizens by 1970, roughly double what it had been in 1920, and one of every two working adults made their living with Boeing one way or another. The suburbs, flush with young families supported by parents with steady, solid-paying jobs, flourished and became the epicenter of daily life with theaters and schools and shopping and everything a community needs to thrive. Downtown Seattle, however, struggled. It had few attractions, a limping economy and no galvanizing cultural identity. These concerns had been top of mind for civic leaders for decades. In fact, it was all the way back in January 1955, inside the prestigious Washington Athletic Club, a 21-story Art Deco monument to fitness and social functions, that a group of Seattle's leading citizens hatched an idea to give the city, its urban center and the entire region a boost:

Seattle should host the next World's Fair.

After initially planning to host in 1959 with a theme that would "celebrate the American West," Seattle mayor Allan Pomeroy and his group of business and community leaders settled on the idea of focusing on space, science and technology to capitalize on Boeing's presence in the city and the United States' space race with Russia. They would officially call the fair the "Century 21 Exposition" and it would debut in the spring of 1962. The structures built for the Expo—from the Space Needle (featured on several of the SuperSonics' team logos) to the monorail to the Washington State Coliseum, which would eventually become the Seattle Center Coliseum, then KeyArena, all of which were home to the Sonics—would set the stage for Seattle's future and its future basketball team.

The very name "SuperSonics" is a nod to Boeing. After the British and French successfully launched the Concorde airplane, a jet that could travel up to twice the sound barrier (Mach 2) for fast trans-Atlantic crossings, Boeing decided to throw its hat in the ring and announced its own design for a commercial airplane that would break the speed of sound. The name they chose? The "Supersonic Transport."

When Don Richman, Dick Vertlieb, Sam Schulman and company decided to run a "name the team" contest, you can guess which name was most popular. Of the 5,000 entries submitted for the contest, there was a 163-way tie for people who all chose a version of "Sonics" or "SuperSonics" to be the team name. Schulman decided to have one name chosen at random to have an official winner, and the name pulled was Brent Schmidt, a ten-year-old who submitted the entry with his dad.

"At the time, there was a local band called 'The Sonics' and there was the SuperSonic Transport that Boeing was building," explains Schmidt. "We thought that the 'Seattle SuperSonics' was the name it should be."

They were right. Rarely has a name and a logo and the heartbeat of a city been captured so perfectly by a team in one fell swoop. And to think, without Boeing there'd likely be no tie to supersonic aviation in Seattle, the name SuperSonics would never have come up, the Space Needle wouldn't have been built, and Seattle may not have been able to host the World's Fair or build the future basketball arena. But because Bill Boeing's test pilot damaged the plane he was taking lessons on and he decided that he could "build a better plane himself, and build it faster," the rest is history.

In the end, the World's Fair accomplished nearly every single thing Seattle's leaders hoped it would. From April 21, 1962 to August 21, 1962, nearly ten million people attended the exposition, and when it was over the city had the cachet and the coliseum to house an NBA team, which is what had attracted Richman and Vertlieb to begin with.

Still, when the time came for the East Coast players selected in the NBA's expansion draft to head to Seattle, there was one question many of them had on their minds:

How far away is it?

***

If you owned a building in Detroit in the mid-1960s and you wanted an easier way to get from one floor to another, there's a decent chance that you called the Dover Elevator Company to see about getting an elevator. If you went ahead with the job, there's an even better chance that a 6'10" handsome and friendly man would arrive to install it. This man's name was Henry Akin, a gentle giant in his early 20s who was recently married and as happy as a guy could be.

He had a girl. He had a job. He was good.

Akin, from Troy, Michigan, was a solid high school basketball player who happened to grow eight inches between his sophomore and senior seasons, going from 6'1" to 6'9". He had been a quick-footed, smooth-shooting two guard before the growth spurt, and when the growing was done he was one of the lucky big men who maintained all of his guard skills at his new height. This dominance and dexterity led to a full scholarship to Morehead State in Kentucky, where he became a two-time Ohio Valley Conference first team selection, averaging 22.5 points and 12.5 boards his sophomore year and 18.5 points and 12.5 rebounds his junior year.

"The two attributes I had [were] I could run and I could shoot the ball," Akin said. "That's what we did at Morehead; we were a very high-scoring team."

Things were looking up basketball-wise for Akin heading into his senior year, but romance got in the way.

"I fell madly in love. I quit school, got married," he said. "Went to Detroit and started working with Dover Elevator Company and started installing elevators."

While married life and working life suited Akin just fine, he missed playing basketball. After a year in Detroit, Akin and his wife Diana moved to Hattiesburg, Mississippi where Akin could play basketball again for William Carey College, a small Baptist school. While he was warming up for the season, he took a spot on an AAU team that traveled all throughout SEC country—Alabama,

Georgia, Mississippi, Louisiana. The scenery changed, but wherever Akin went he was a beast. Then a phone call changed his life.

"About the middle of May, I got a phone call one day. I was in the gym shooting," Akin said. "The coach said, 'You got a phone call.' So, I go in and I answer the phone and it's a guy by the name of Eddie Donovan, who is the general manager of the New York Knicks at that time. He explained who he was, he explained that Red Holzman [then a scout, but who later coached the Knicks] had seen me play a couple times at Morehead and they were interested in me. I had no idea, nothing. These thoughts have never entered my mind. He said, the day after tomorrow we'll have a plane ticket for you at Jackson Airport in Jackson, Mississippi, and you'll fly to New York. I go 'OK.' So I go back home and tell the wife that I'm going to New York. Playing in the NBA had never entered my mind since I left school and got married; it was like it's not going to happen."

The Knicks ended up taking Akin 11th overall in the 1966 NBA Draft. He'd go on to average 3.8 points as a reserve on a squad that featured Walt Bellamy, a young Willis Reed and the number-one overall pick in the '66 draft, Cazzie Russell. At the end of the season, each NBA team could protect seven of their players and the rest were made available in the expansion draft, which was held so that the two new NBA teams, the San Diego Rockets and the Seattle SuperSonics, could fill out their rosters. Akin was left unprotected.

"I got a phone call from [Sonics general manager] Don Richman telling me I'd been selected by Washington—he called it Washington back then," Akin said. "I'm thinking, *Washington, that's only ninety miles down the road from New York, that's not bad.* He said, 'No, no, no. Seattle, Washington.' Then we get the map out and my wife and I look and see where Seattle is, and we say we'll never get there."

Of course, he did get there and he made the team and eventually found himself as the center, standing dead center in the first Seattle SuperSonics team photo in franchise history along with his fellow "expandables" and a smattering of rookies.

The photo itself is a thing of beauty, both dated and delightful. Akin is standing with his hands clasped behind his back, with the hint of a smile on his face and his back slightly to the left of a basketball hoop in the background. To his left in the photo is rookie Bob Rule, a center from Colorado State, and to his right is power forward Dorie Murrey, just one year removed from the Detroit Mercy Titans. Continuing down that side of the photo is George Wilson, taken from the Chicago Bulls; Tom Meschery from the San Francisco Warriors by way of Russia; Bob Weiss from the 76ers, and Walt Hazzard from the Los Angeles Lakers.

On the other side, moving on down from Bob Rule is Bud Olsen from the Warriors, then the Sonics' first-ever actual NBA draft pick; a beaming Al Tucker; Tommy Kron from the St. Louis Hawks; Plummer Lott, a hometown rookie from Seattle University, and future NBA executive Rod Thorn, also from the Hawks.

All the men are wearing white Converse sneakers, with socks pulled right up to the kneecaps and shorts that sit high on the thighs. The logo on the first uniform displayed the word "Sonics" across the chest in a thick cursive font, with a star dotting the I and an electric bolt jutting out from the last S and cutting under the name to act as an undercurrent and underline at the same time.

Of all the players on the team, notwithstanding Plummer Lott who played his college ball in Seattle, the only guy who had spent real time playing hoops in the city was Walt Hazzard, who competed against Washington while he was at UCLA.

Hazzard was, without question, one of the biggest college basketball stars of the early 1960s. After an otherworldly high school career in Philadelphia, where he was the city's player of the year as a senior and led his team to an 89-3 record when he was on the floor, legendary UCLA Coach John Wooden successfully recruited him to play on the other side of the country in Westwood, California.

As a sophomore, the 6'2" guard was a scoring and assist machine and helped lead UCLA to the Final Four. As a junior, he was named as a first-team All-American. His senior season, however, is when he earned true powder blue legend status as one of the captains on John Wooden's first championship team, which also happened to go undefeated.

During the 1963-64 college season, Hazzard, along with his backcourt mate and co-captain Gail Goodrich, had the Bruins number one in the polls by early January (they started off ranked sixth) and never let go, finishing the regular season 26-0 and blowing out their last four opponents by a total of 91 points. As fate would have it, Hazzard faced Seattle in the first round of the NCAA tournament and won in a nail biter, 95-90. The Bruins then beat San Francisco 76-72, followed by a win against Kansas State in the semi-finals, where Hazzard put together his tournament masterpiece, scoring nineteen points, dishing nine assists and grabbing seven rebounds.

The final against Duke was memorable for a variety of reasons that have all gone down in UCLA lore, but none more important than the Wizard of Westwood's "second best" speech. Just prior to the game, Coach Wooden, who was normally not accustomed to giving pre-game hype speeches, decided to deliver one of the best of all time, described perfectly in the book, *The Sons of Westwood*:

"You got here playing a certain way. We've rebounded. We've run. We've pressed. We've made this a 94-foot game," he said. Then he looked into the eyes of every player and asked, "How many of you remember who finished second last year?" No one raised a hand. "They don't remember who finishes second," Wooden said. "Now go out there and play."

Boom. The Bruins ran through the proverbial brick wall for their coach, going up twelve points at halftime and ultimately winning 93-83, giving Coach Wooden his first title and a perfect 30-0 record on the season. Walt Hazzard was named the tournament's Most Outstanding Player, and he finished his career with 1,401 points to become UCLA's all-time leading scorer.

Heading into the 1964 NBA Draft, Hazzard was a clear-cut favorite to be one of the top picks. Knowing this, the Los Angeles Lakers invoked the now-defunct "territorial rights" before the draft, meaning they would forfeit their first-round pick and instead select a player whose college team was within a 50-mile radius of their home arena. In this case, that home arena was in Los Angeles and the player they took was Walt Hazzard.

Unfortunately, Hazzard never had the success with the purple and gold that he had with the true blue and gold. Over the course of his three seasons with the Lakers, he averaged just nine points and three assists. He was constantly frustrated by the style of play and felt that he was never able to truly showcase his skills under head coach Fred Schaus. When the time came for the 1967 NBA expansion draft, the Lakers decided not to protect Hazzard, which was fine by him. When he was taken by Seattle, he viewed it as a fresh start.

"There was a conflict between my style and the Lakers," Hazzard said at the time. "Going to Seattle gives me an opportunity I haven't had in my three years with the Lakers. I have no ill feeling. I'm just determined to work even harder to prove myself. I want to establish my ability and this is my chance."

His coach, Fred Schaus, who moved up to be the Lakers' general manager after the season, gave Hazzard a vote of confidence on his way out the door.

"[He] will do a good job for them," he said. "His playing fits in well with the style used by Al Bianchi."

Of course, since Bianchi had never coached in the NBA and none of the players had played together or were very successful on their previous teams, nobody really knew what that style was going to be. But one thing for sure is that nearly every player selected by the Sonics had the same mindset as Hazzard:

"This is my chance."

"That team the first year," Henry Akin said. "I think was an opportunity for twelve people that had been role players on other teams. It gave them an opportunity to advance and expand their careers."

"When you're on an expansion team, the thing that's exciting is just that you get to play," said Bob Weiss, the point guard who had been selected from the Sixers. "You've got mostly guys who were the [number] seven, eight, nine guys on their team, and rookies, and guys who were [previously] not able to make the league. Then you've got a guy like Tom Meschery, an older veteran who sort of gets revived because he's caught up in the enthusiasm of the younger guys."

"I was just a wide-eyed rookie," Plummer Lott said. "You hoped it would be the beginning of a career. For some guys it worked out that way, and for others it didn't."

"When I walked into the first practice we had, it was an opportunity to be part of something," Akin said. "I had no idea what it was going to be. I think to a lot of us, it was something really special."

Special? Yes. High paying? No.

This ragtag crew of Sonics rookies, unprotected players, almost-starters and "guys with potential" didn't have a single highly paid star among them. The entire roster clocked in with a combined salary of roughly $240,000 that first year. That's about two games' worth of a paycheck for a current NBA star, but for a little perspective, the $240,000 cumulative number was small even for its time. Wilt Chamberlain, the star of the Philadelphia 76ers, had a yearly salary of $250,000 all by himself.

In effect, in 1967, according to the NBA's math, the Original Twelve Super-Sonics were worth just about one Wilt Chamberlain.

Chapter 2

It All Began at the Cow Palace

The Sonics' regular season NBA debut was on the road in Daly City, California, just outside of San Francisco, against the Warriors in the aptly named Cow Palace. For the members of the Original Twelve who had never been there, it was a sight to behold. From the front, it looked like a cross between a giant livestock pen and an airplane hangar, with a curved roof and a muted gray paint job. The only design was a darker gray, curved bar that sloped out from the center of the building, with straight lines shooting down to the awning above a string of doors leading inside. It looked, in no uncertain terms, like a monster-sized tractor grill. The main *Cow Palace* sign curved over the grill in huge red letters and an early arcade font. For players from big cities who were used to places like Madison Square Garden it was something of a culture shock.

Dorie Murrey, who played his college ball at the University of Detroit and spent a year with the Pistons before joining the Sonics, described it like this: "I'd never been to the Cow Palace, and it was, well, a cow palace. I was like, 'What the hell is this?' It was like a barnyard."

And that wasn't even the most unique aspect of the arena, which could hold up to 15,000 people, but on this particular night barely topped 5,000.

As if to attempt to offset the Old MacDonald look, Warriors owner Franklin Mieuli, known for having bizarre tastes and a colorful personality, hung an enormous chandelier that he had picked up in Italy inside the arena. J. Michael Kenyon, who covered the Sonics for the *Seattle Post-Intelligencer* at the time under the name Mike Glover, said, "It was this massive red thing, eight or nine feet across, and he had it suspended about fifteen feet above his owner's box at midcourt. You walked in there and the first thing you saw was this huge chandelier. It was surreal."

If that first visual impression wasn't enough, the Sonics' opening night continued into the theater of the absurd as both teams had their warm-ups cut drastically short due to a planning debacle during the pre-game festivities. Someone on the Warriors public relations team thought it would be a good idea to have local celebrities play miniature golf on the court before tip-off to draw people in for the game. But rather than putt on the parquet, they laid down a huge patch of artificial turf for the putt-putt competition. Nobody did a test run to determine how long it would take to restore the court before game time, so after the contest the Sonics and the Warriors sat around waiting to warm up while ninety feet of artificial turf was removed from the court.

Once that was cleared, the final act in the odd ball opening game took place as the San Francisco Warriors decided to honor one of their most popular players and former all-stars by retiring his jersey before the game. Seems normal, right? Only in this case, the player was 29-year-old Tom Meschery, who was standing on the sideline of the other team, wearing a Seattle SuperSonics uniform—the Warriors thought so much of Meschery that prior to the season they decided to leave him unprotected in the expansion draft. To add another twist, once Meschery was placed in the expansion draft, he told Seattle that he planned to retire and take a post in the Peace Corps in South Korea. Upon hearing this, Don Richman's staff asked him what salary he'd need to stay with the team, and Meschery apparently said $35,000, thinking there was absolutely no chance that Seattle would say yes...but they did, which led to Meschery, who should have been in South Korea, standing in northern California wearing a Sonics jersey while having his Warriors jersey retired in an oversized horse stall.

And while all of this was going on, our old friend, rookie Al Tucker, was stuck in the locker room with a nosebleed.

Then, finally, a basketball game was played.

The Warriors were the defending Western Conference champions and featured Hall of Famer Rick Barry, who averaged 35.6 points per game the year before, along with Hall of Fame center Nate Thurmond, who averaged 18.7 points and an absurd 21.3 rebounds per game. Not surprisingly, they demolished the Sonics, whose likely best player (Meschery) wasn't among the Warriors' top seven best, according to them. The final score was 144-116, but there were a few bright spots in the game. Walt Hazzard scored 30 points along with five assists and six rebounds, Meschery put up 26 points and grabbed 11 boards, and Al Tucker had 10 points and six boards in his NBA debut.

***

The game in the Cow Palace took place on October 13, and the way the NBA laid out the schedule the Sonics' second game, which was to be their home debut back in Seattle, wasn't set until a week later on October 20, giving the new team six full days to digest the butt-kicking it had just received.

Nevertheless, the city of Seattle was pumped for its first big time professional franchise, and when Friday night rolled around they literally rolled out the red carpet. As part of a promotion to mark the team's homecoming, a black-tie crowd paid $27 a couple to greet the Sonics and cheer them on against their fellow expansion team, the San Diego Rockets.

NBA Commissioner J. Walter Kennedy, who for years had listened to Don Richman and Dick Vertlieb's pitches to bring a team to Seattle, was one of the 4,473 fans in attendance that night, filling out less than one-third of the Seattle Center Coliseum. In the preseason, Kennedy had remarked during an interview how impressed he was with the off-season ticket sales for the team, although this premiere was slightly less than stellar. The Coliseum, which was a key to Seattle landing the franchise in the first place, felt cavernous that night. The bouncing of the ball and the sneaker squeaks on the floor seemed to echo around the mostly empty arena. And the play didn't help.

After the barn burner in the giant barn, the Sonics completely flipped the script in game two and lost in a low-scoring snooze fest, falling to the Rockets 90-82. Once again, Walt Hazzard was a dazzling scorer, pouring in 32. Rod Thorn dropped in 21 points, but the rest of the ten players on the team combined for a meager 29 points. The most exciting part of the game came in the second quarter when Meschery picked up two technical fouls and almost blew the buzz cut off the top of his head in anger. After arguing with the refs he was thrown out of the contest, giving him the honor of being the first SuperSonic to ever be ejected from a game.

The very next night, following a two-hour and forty-five-minute flight, both teams hit the hardwood down in San Diego and faced off in a rematch, this time with Seattle coming out on top in overtime for the first win in the history of the franchise. Rather than the two-man effort from the night before, the entire team pitched in for the win with Hazzard scoring 22, Meschery 19, Tucker 13 (with 11 rebounds) and Thorn and Dorie Murrey both having 12, with Murrey also grabbing 12 boards. Al Bianchi played ten of his guys, and even rookie Plummer Lott got the first points of his professional career.

After three games the Sonics were 1-2, and this was the closest they would get to .500 for the rest of the season. It was also the most stable part of their schedule. In order to drum up interest across the Pacific Northwest, Richman, Vertlieb and Schulman agreed to schedule nearly a dozen games at various towns across the region to give basketball fans a chance to watch their new pro team. Also, there were scheduling conflicts *with their own arena,* something most NBA teams didn't have to deal with.

"We are playing eleven of our forty-one home games away from Seattle," Hal Childs, the Sonics' first public relations man said in an early season interview. "First, we want to introduce the team to the Northwest, and second, we had to take some of them out of town because the Seattle Coliseum was booked for other events."

As part of this arrangement, the Sonics played three games in Tacoma, three games in Portland, one in Spokane, one in Vancouver, and one in a place that has absolutely nothing to do with the Pacific Northwest: Phoenix. The games played out to varying degrees of success from a win-loss standpoint, but attendance at random road cities was a struggle the whole year. For the first game the team played in Portland they drew just 1,533 people. The crowds at home in the Coliseum, at least in the early part of the year, hovered between 4,000 and 4,500 people. It was taking a little bit of time for the city to warm up to its new pro squad, but this was something the new owners, and even the NBA, anticipated from the revenue side and the attendance side.

"Sure, we were disappointed with the crowds," Childs said about the first month. "But we don't blame Seattle. The public doesn't owe us anything. It's up to us to give them a product they want. We're working on it. I think this team could make the playoffs, if it could improve about 5-10 percent in a couple of departments. It's early for basketball until December. And it should improve. There's a lot of youth on this club, rookies or near-rookies like Plummer Lott, Al Tucker, Bob Rule."

Childs, obviously, was being as optimistic as possible, even going on during this same interview to lay out some early season numbers and a path to the playoffs.

"We're getting beat just a little bit in a lot of departments. For instance, the opponents in five games have out-field-goaled us 236-222, out-free-thrown us 145-122, out-rebounded us 380-333, and we've had more fouls. If we get a little better here and there, we can be very competitive."

Perfectly said for a PR guy. Luckily, the owners had braced for a slow drip of interest and set up their salary cap and operating expenses accordingly to keep from losing money. They sold the radio broadcast rights to an oil firm for one million dollars and sold eleven home games to be televised on local television. Their back-of-the-napkin numbers worked out like this:

"We estimate that our first-year operating budget will be $750,000 for salaries, travel, equipment, office expenses and so on. If we draw an average gate of 4,500 people, we should crack that nut," Childs said.

In the early months of the season, the key to "cracking the nut" seemed to be hyping up Walt Hazzard and his newfound scoring touch that had been buried on the depth chart in Los Angeles. After averaging less than nine shots and eight points a game for the Lakers over three seasons, the first month of Hazzard's career in Seattle was a coming out party, in which he cruised to thirty or near thirty every night. More importantly, he was doing it with a smile on his face.

"Hazzard said when he rode the bench in Los Angeles it destroyed his confidence. He wasn't happy there," Childs said. "When he learned he'd be with the Sonics, he spent all summer with Wally Jones of Philadelphia working on his moves and his shots. He loves to play for Al Bianchi. He could be a superstar. He's taking only 20 shots a game and scoring 26. That's great efficiency, and he's also leading the club in assists."

But even with the rejuvenated Hazzard, the revitalized Meschery and the ridiculous acrobatics of Al Tucker, the team didn't get its second win until Halloween, and the third win wasn't until the week before Thanksgiving, when they beat the San Diego Rockets again. The 'W' put the team at 3-14, however two of its wins were against the other expansion squad, so over the course of the first six weeks of the season the only "veteran" NBA team the Sonics beat was the Chicago Bulls.

Still, the win was a catalyst for the most successful stretch of that first year. They followed up the victory over the Bulls by outdueling the double Daves of Detroit (Bing and DeBusschere) at home, led by 29 from Hazzard, 28 from the quickly popular and high-flying Al Tucker, and an impressive 31-point, 21-rebound game by Bob Rule. If there was an early-season game for Coach Bianchi to point to that gave him a glimpse of the team's potential, this was it. Detroit was several games above .500, had a few all-stars, and when the game went into overtime the Sonics never flinched. Technically, it was the team's first winning streak as well, which, for about 20 hours, gave the team a boost.

The very next night the two teams drove thirty minutes south to square off again in Tacoma, this time with Detroit winning 120-118.

After the loss to the Pistons, the Sonics traveled south to Los Angeles for the first game of their toughest back-to-back of the season against the Lakers, giving Walt Hazzard a chance to face the franchise that destroyed his confidence and discarded him in the expansion draft. The Lakers of '67 were a budding Western Conference dynasty, on the cusp of appearing in five out of the next six NBA Finals. It's important to note that they were a *Western Conference* dynasty and not an NBA dynasty because they lost all but one of those Finals, going down twice to the Celtics and twice to the New York Knicks.

The team was stacked, led by Hall of Famers Jerry West, Elgin Baylor and Hazzard's old UCLA teammate Gail Goodrich. While the Sonics wouldn't make their first Finals for over a decade, on this particular night the boys from the Emerald City played like studs. Hazzard dropped 34 and Tucker dumped in another 24, but it was Bob "Rule the Day" Rule who put up 47 points and 16 rebounds to beat the Lakers 137-132. The *Los Angeles Times* blared, "SuperSonics Stun Lakers as Rule Scores 47 Points."

Two nights later, the Sonics traveled 2,500 miles to face the only team in the NBA that had a more formidable roster than the Lakers, the Boston Celtics. Unlike the Lakers, who were on the brink of a dynasty in their conference, the Boston Celtics were smack dab in the middle of the most dominant stretch any professional team has ever had in any team sport. From 1957 to 1969, the Celtics appeared in every NBA Finals except for one. Of the Finals they appeared in, they won 11 of 12, and when the Sonics came to town they had already won eight straight titles. The names on the squad are all legendary: Bill Russell, John Havlicek, Sam Jones and Don Nelson. And the Boston Garden provided the ultimate home court advantage. The floor had dead spots that only the Celtics players knew about. The visitors' locker room was either stifling hot or freezing cold. Longtime Celtics coach Red Auerbach, who had recently moved up to GM and given the reins to Russell, made sure his team had every real and psychological advantage.

By any measure, the Sonics should have gotten creamed; the Celtics had lost only four games all season. The Sonics had won only five. And yet Seattle, despite the three-hour time difference, the cramped six-hour flight and the aforementioned drawbacks, opened the game with a blizzard of buckets and raced to a 35-17 lead after the first quarter and a highly unexpected but comfortable 75-31 lead at halftime. The Celtics answered with a 49-point third quarter, but it wasn't nearly enough. The Sonics kept pace and pounded the proud Russell and his squad 133-106, which led to some excellent national headlines:

"Supersonics (Would You Believe Supermen?) Rout Celtics, 133-106" – *Hartford Courant.*

"Celtics Stunned by Sonic Boom" – *Pittsburgh Post-Gazette*

"Red Hot Sonics Wallop Celtics" – *The Evening Times*

After the game, player/coach Russell admitted that he couldn't believe what he was seeing.

"I thought I was having a nightmare," he said. "We were flat and they were sky high. What else can you say? We took a lot of bad shots and you have to believe that the other team had a lot to do with that."

Russell was right on both accounts. His team did take a lot of bad shots and the Sonics were sky high, particularly coach Al Bianchi, who was gushing with praise for his team.

"My boys have come a long way since the exhibition season," he said. "They know now that every time they go out there they have a chance. They believe they can win. It showed them that if they hustle and put it all together they can beat any of them. They're not in awe anymore."

When asked what you tell a team that is up forty-four points at halftime, the excitable Bianchi replied simply, "I told them 'don't stop.'"

He extolled the virtues of Walt Hazzard and his 22 points and 14 assists, he raved about Rule's 26 points, and Bianchi, for a brief moment after defeating arguably the two best teams in the NBA in back-to-back games, had the attention of the entire league. It would be the highlight of the season.

The Sonics didn't win their tenth game until a few days before Christmas and had only fourteen wins at the All-Star Game, where Walt Hazzard proudly represented them at Madison Square Garden. Hazzard was nothing short of a revelation, scoring the second-most total points in the league at the break, with 1,119 to Dave Bing's 1,363 points. In fact, as teams considered who to protect moving forward with NBA expansion drafts, front offices made a mental note to not be so quick to give up on college stars too early. Call it the Hazzard Halo.

After the All-Star break the Sonics won two quick games and then bottomed out, dropping twenty-one more and losing nearly a dozen by twenty points or more. Their final record was 23-59. They were third in the conference in scoring, averaging 118.7 per game, but last in defense, giving up more than 125 points a game.

The one area where the Sonics dominated was with their rookie class. Al Tucker and Bob Rule both made the NBA's official All-Rookie team, along with Walt Frazier, Earl Monroe and Phil Jackson.

Tucker, the kid from the small school in Oklahoma that nobody had heard of, was brilliant. He averaged 13 points and 7.5 rebounds per game. He could dunk from anywhere inside of the foul line, and as one of the co-creators of the alley-oop (allegedly) along with his brother, he loved to show off his hops and electrify the crowd when he could.

His old director of public relations at Oklahoma Baptist University, John Parrish, followed the box scores in the paper closely and watched Tucker on television whenever he could, which back then wasn't often. Looking back, he says it's a shame that Tucker didn't get to play in the modern era.

"He could shoot from three-point range," he said. "If we'd had a three-point shot then, who knows? He was a great long-range shooter. He could have played later on for sure."

In addition to Hazzard, Rule and Tucker, there were a few other bright spots as well. Tom Meschery became a fan favorite and regained his passion for the game, averaging a double-double on the year with 14 points and 10 rebounds a game. Rod Thorn averaged over 15 points per game and Tommy Kron, Bob Weiss and Dorie Murrey all averaged nine points.

All in all, despite barely keeping their heads above water attendance-wise and a second-half swoon in competitiveness, the season was a success. They had eight more wins than their sister expansion team the San Diego Rockets, and finished one place ahead of them in the standings. Most importantly, they existed.

"Before the Sonics' existence, Seattle sports consisted of fewer attractions than today," wrote Sean Quinton for the *Seattle Times* on the 50th anniversary of the team's first season. "Husky football and basketball were draws, along with hydro racing, rowing and a minor-league baseball team called the Seattle Rainiers, which later became the Seattle Angels. With the Sonics in the fold, Seattle had a major pro team for the first time."

And in a unique twist of fate, two days after the Sonics' season ended Boeing announced that delivery of the airliner the team was named after, the SuperSonic transport, was going to be delayed a year for design reasons. The flaw: the plane would be far too heavy to attain the necessary speed, which was the reverse problem of the squad named after them that was far too light on veterans to gain the necessary wins to reach the playoffs. Both teams (the engineers behind the plane and the front office behind the team) needed more time to fly.

Chapter 3

Haywood vs. The National Basketball Association

Spencer Haywood's 1971-72 Topps Basketball Rookie Card is classic and confusing and sanctioned by seven United States Supreme Court judges. The word "Seattle" graces the headline of the card in bright yellow hippy bubble letters with a heavy drop shadow. Underneath it, framed on a green square background, Haywood stands half-turned, looking off the card to what would be your right shoulder. He's got a hidden grin on his face and he's holding the ball with two hands just below his hips. His yellow Sonics uniform pops off the cardboard. Everything appears to be normal and in fact, to the untrained eye, the entire card is, until you notice that the number 24 on the jersey is a little high and that, instead of reading *Sonics* on the front, it reads *Haywood*, which means only one thing: The jersey is on backwards.

Nevertheless, the card would not exist if it had not been for Sam Schulman suing the NBA along with Haywood, which subsequently led to the case reaching the Supreme Court and changing the NBA landscape forever. At first glance, Schulman, the 61-year-old owner of the Sonics, and Haywood, the 20-year-old basketball phenom from Detroit, seemed to be a strange legal tag team. Schulman had a Harvard MBA, was an executive producer in Hollywood, and then owner or co-owner of the Sonics and the San Diego Chargers. Haywood was originally from Silver City, Mississippi and was one of ten kids. At age 15 he moved to Chicago to live with his brother and get away from the highly charged segregated south. Then, in about a three-year span, he won a Michigan Class A Championship at Pershing High School, spent a year at Trinidad State Junior College in Colorado, won a gold medal with the USA basketball team in the 1968 Olympics, transferred to the University of Detroit (where he averaged 32 points and 21 boards) then quit school to play for the American Basketball Association's Denver Rockets. And this is where his path collides with Schulman's.

Beginning in the late 1960s, the NBA and the ABA had danced around the idea of a merger. Even as Schulman was buying the team and entering the league, discussions were taking place over what a league with both sets of teams combined would look like under one roof and how it would work. Despite the public rhetoric from each league about competition and wanting to beat the other league, the fact was that a merger ultimately made too much sense geographically and economically to not happen. And yet, every year negotiations failed, and Schulman put the blame squarely on the NBA's commissioner, J. Walter Kennedy.

"I'm continually frustrated by his weakness when he has to make decisions," Schulman said. "His deportment depends on who the owner is."

By the end of the decade, Schulman's relationship with Kennedy was straight up combative.

After a failed attempt to get Kennedy fired, Schulman turned his attention to challenging the NBA's long-standing rule that forbade NBA teams from signing a player until his college class had graduated. This particular rule was near and dear to Kennedy's heart, so Schulman knew that by attacking it he was also provoking Kennedy. However, he wasn't going to do it just for political reasons. There were strong basketball and moral reasons to attack it. On the basketball side, the rule prevented the NBA from signing college stars who left school early, thus handing big names like Haywood over to the other league and limiting the talent available to teams that needed young, impact players—teams like the Sonics. On the morality side, Schulman thought the rule was completely unfair and un-American.

"It was a matter of principle," Schulman said. "I couldn't see any logical reason for keeping a man from making a living. I thought it was unconstitutional."

As part of the lawsuit, Haywood challenged the decision to keep him out of the NBA by commencing an anti-trust action against the league. He argued that the conduct of the NBA was a group boycott and a violation of the Sherman Antitrust Act. The focus of the lawsuit was about whether the NBA draft policy was a restraint on trade and therefore illegal in accordance with the Sherman Act. The NBA, represented by legal counsel and future commissioner David Stern, strongly disagreed.

The official case was filed in the United States District Court for the Central District of California, which then issued an injunction in Haywood's favor. The language read:

> If Haywood is unable to continue to play professional basketball for Seattle, he will suffer irreparable injury in that a substantial part of his playing career will have been dissipated, his physical condition, skills, and coordination will deteriorate from lack of high-level competition, his public acceptance as a super star will diminish to the detriment of his career, his self-esteem, and his pride will have been injured and a great injustice will be perpetrated on him.

Kennedy and the NBA, of course, appealed right away to the famous Ninth Circuit Court of Appeals, which stayed the injunction. Haywood then appealed to the Supreme Court.

While all of this was going on, Haywood attempted to play with his Sonics teammates, but because of the sporadic nature of how the case wound its way through the court system, he had no idea what would happen from one night to the next. He was like a ping-pong ball caught between the league and the legal system. He'd be eligible to play one night, and then the following night there was the possibility while shooting warm-ups that he'd be served papers that said he wasn't allowed to play.

"They would wait until I got on the floor to jump ball and then an announcement would come on, 'Spencer Haywood is being served right now,'" Haywood said. "I would have to leave the gym and maybe sit on a cold bus until the game was over."

Even on the nights he wasn't given a subpoena before tip-off, several NBA teams said they wouldn't play against him because he wasn't eligible to be on the court. Teams even filed protests with the league.

Eventually, the case worked its way up to the Supreme Court where the justices ruled 7-2 in Haywood's favor, effectively eliminating the NBA's rule about a player having to wait four years from his high school graduation to join the league. With the case behind him, Haywood made a triumphant return to the court in mid-January. The scene was captured perfectly at the end of a *Time* magazine feature explaining the Haywood vs. Supreme Court case, in a vivid Web Editor's note:

> Probably the loudest cheer in Seattle's Sports History—certainly louder than anything generated by Seahawks fans—was heard on the evening of January 14, 1971, as Coach Wilkens motioned to Haywood that he was coming in. Spencer stood up, dropped his sweats, and Seattle—both those in attendance at the UW's Hec Ed (not the normal Seattle Center Coliseum) and the tens (hundreds?) of thousands listening to Bob Blackburn over KOMO stood and cheered ourselves hoarse. Seattle was playing the Baltimore Bullets and won the contest by a close score of 114-110. Haywood had started his career with the Supersonics 10 days earlier on January 5, playing against the same Bullets in their home court in Baltimore.]"

While Seattle fans enjoyed the immediate on-court impact, there was still a price to be paid for going against the league. Schulman always believed the owners treated him differently after the court battles, even though he had to pay a $200,000 fine in an out-of-court settlement to officially end the dispute that March (in addition to the $500,000 in legal fees). For Haywood's part, he felt that the league did its best for a long time to tamp down his legacy.

"The players today, many of them are under this ruling," Haywood said. "I go up to shake their hand, 'Hey, I'm Spencer Haywood.' They look at me blank and tell me I didn't do it. At least, I thought they would respect me for doing it."

One player who understood perfectly well what Haywood meant to the league was Kobe Bryant, who was interviewed about Haywood shortly after his first year in the league.

"He's not getting nearly all the praise he should because some players don't want to speak out," Bryant said. "The owners might not be too happy about it. It's a [delicate] topic. I know who [Haywood] is. I think it is important for what he stood for. He wanted to walk a different path, to follow his heart. He set the standard for years to come. All the hype about us skipping college has made people wonder. But first and foremost, Spencer is the first to do it."

Haywood rewarded Schulman's loyalty and support by making four straight all-star games for Seattle from 1972 to 1975. In 1973, he averaged 29.2 points and 12.9 rebounds per game. He was an All-NBA First Team selection twice and an All-NBA Second Team selection twice, while finishing top ten in MVP voting two times as well.

As for Schulman versus the NBA, let's just say that taking the league to the Supreme Court wasn't the last time the Sonics owner found himself in litigation with the association.

In 1969, forward John Brisker was drafted by the Pittsburgh Condors of the ABA. When Brisker decided to leave the ABA after the Condors disbanded following the 1972 season, Kennedy had warned NBA owners to not sign him and instead allow Brisker to enter the regional draft, essentially handing him to Philadelphia, the worst team in the NBA. Kennedy made it clear that contacting Brisker in any way would be a violation of the NBA draft rules, despite Brisker's attorney stating that the NBA Board of Governors said he could sign with any NBA team he wanted. Schulman agreed with the board and took the double opportunity to sign Brisker and piss off Kennedy, a win-win for him. The commissioner responded with a swift $10,000 fine and also the loss of Seattle's 1973 first-round draft pick (given to Pittsburgh for compensation).

"I will fight this with every effort at my disposal," Schulman said at the time. "[The ruling] is outrageous, discriminatory and totally unfair."

Schulman, who was very comfortable with litigation, took the issue to the courts and U.S. Judge John H. Tenney ruled that "Kennedy had usurped the authority of the NBA's Board of Governors and was guilty of misconduct because he failed to hold a hearing or consult the board before making a decision."

But Schulman's victory was extremely short-lived. Prior to the 1973 NBA Draft, Kennedy called a meeting of the 17-member board, and following a nine-hour meeting he got their backing, nullifying the judge's ruling and officially levying the penalty against him. Schulman took his medicine and turned his attention to a much more important matter: landing his dream head coach.

Chapter 4

An Offer Bill Russell Couldn't Refuse

Seattle in the mid-1970s was a city on the come-up. The worst of the Boeing recession, when the company laid off 70% of its workforce, was in the past. The snarky-but-famous sign a couple of realtors put up in 1971 that read, *Will the last person leaving SEATTLE turn out the lights*, was no longer there. The city had recovered from mourning and burying music icon and local hero Jimi Hendrix in 1970 and its adopted son, action star Bruce Lee, in 1973. (Hendrix was born in Seattle; Lee lived in the city for five years, attended the University of Washington and taught martial arts before leaving to pursue his destiny in Los Angeles.)

By 1974, rather than a sense that the city was experiencing a mass exodus and downturn, a renewed energy seemed to pump through the region. The construction of the Seattle Kingdome, which broke ground in 1972, was halfway completed and on schedule to open in 1976. Accordingly, the National Football League granted Seattle an expansion team, the Seahawks, which would open play in the Kingdome that same year. Major League Baseball would soon follow suit, approving its own expansion team, the Mariners, to begin play in 1977. The Seattle Sounders of the North American Soccer League would play there as well. The days of Seattle being a one-team pro sports town were over and Sam Schulman knew it. By the end of the decade, he would be competing for the hearts and minds and wallets of Seattleites with every other major sports league, as well as a huge increase in entertainment options for people in the city. Aerosmith, Led Zeppelin, the Major League All-Star Game, the Pro Bowl and more would soon be taking place in Seattle. The Sonics, who were sitting alone at the head of the local sports table for a decade, would soon be elbowing away other teams for space. Schulman was aware of all of this during the deplorable 1973 season, and in order to pull the team out of the basement and into the headlines he decided to forget about going fishing for his coaching search. Instead, he was going whale hunting.

***

Imagine if Michael B. Jordan reeled off eleven Oscar wins for Best Actor in less than a decade-and-a-half, and then instead of starring in Ryan Coogler's next big-budget masterpiece he took a four-year break and then decided to direct a film with an indie producer in Washington. That's kind of what it was like when Bill Russell went from the Celtics organization to the Sonics organization.

When Russell's career as a player/coach finally ended in Boston, his team had just come off the single most successful run in professional sports with eleven championships in thirteen years. Even the New York Yankees, with their 27 World Series wins and complete dominance of baseball across several decades, never won eleven titles in thirteen years (the closest they got was eleven in sixteen years, from 1936 to 1952). And when it came to Russell in terms of importance to the sport, he was untouchable. He was dominant in whichever aspect of the game you choose as a measuring stick. He was the smartest player. He was the most successful player. He was the highest-paid player for a while. He was Biggie and Tupac and Jay-Z rolled into one. He was a two-time All-American at the University of San Francisco, a two-time NCAA Champion, the NCAA Tournament's Most Outstanding Player, an Olympic gold medalist, an eleven-time NBA champion, a five-time MVP, a twelve-time all-star, and a member of the NBA's 25th, 35th and 50th anniversary teams.

The Sonics franchise as a whole, after six years of existence, had produced four all-star players with a combined six appearances. The team had zero playoff appearances, zero playoff wins and no championships. The Celtics, via Red Auerbach and Russell, had absolute franchise stability whereas the Sonics ran through four coaches in six years. Al Bianchi lasted two seasons, then Lenny Wilkens, in his first stint with the team, did a good job as player/coach for three seasons before leaving to coach Portland. The following year Tom Nissalke coached a disastrous first half of the 1972-73 season before being replaced by Bucky Buckwalter for an almost equally disappointing second half.

Aside from a dip in the second season, attendance at Sonics games had been slowly rising, from just over 6,000 people per game in year one to just over 11,000 per game in 1972-73 (year five). But in year six the attendance dropped down to around 9,000—and Schulman wasn't happy. He had backed up the Brinks truck to bring in ABA all-stars like Spencer Haywood, John

Brisker and Jim McDaniels in the hopes that their talents would bring quick titles to Seattle. That wasn't happening. Without playoff wins as evidence that the experiment was working, they were just a cast of free spirits with big egos who played well individually but weren't gelling as a team.

After the Nissalke/Buckwalter duo combined for a measly twenty-six wins in the 1972-73 season (just three more than the team's inaugural year), Schulman, with his Hollywood background and appreciation for spectacles, wanted to make a splashy hire that would give the franchise two things it desperately needed: a winning culture and star power.

Enter Russell.

Russell's last season in Boston ended successfully, albeit somewhat acrimoniously and abruptly. In fact, for the most part, it was downright weird. During the 1968-69 regular season, Russell, after taking his team to the Finals for over a decade straight and bearing the pressure of being the team's leader, best player and hardest worker on defense, was running on fumes. Add in that he had also absorbed the role of head coach the previous year, and Russell's fumes were running on fumes. He gained fifteen pounds throughout the year, became apathetic about his schedule, missed coaches' meetings, and seemed to be down in the dumps and depressed.

Russell was also a highly involved social activist, and the onslaught of social unrest, discrimination and the Vietnam War made him feel that maybe playing basketball wasn't the best use of his time. This was a man who once, in Lexington, Kentucky when a restaurant wouldn't seat him and his black teammates prior to an exhibition game, decided to boycott the game, which was a completely new concept. Up to that point, black athletes were just expected to swallow and suffer such indignities. Not Russell. He made a conscious choice to be on the forefront of social change, and the toll was exacting. Following the assassination of Robert Kennedy, who was looked upon as a leader of the civil rights movement, Russell said, "We foolishly lionize athletes and make them heroes because they can hit a ball or catch one. The only athletes we should bother with attaching any particular importance to are those like [Muhammad] Ali, whom we can admire for themselves and not for their incidental athletic abilities."

What Russell was surely aware of was that he himself was one of the "lionized" athletes along with Ali. In fact, he and Ali were friends, and Russell attended the famous Cleveland Summit in 1967 to support him while he awaited his draft dodging charges, along with Kareem Abdul-Jabbar (then Lew Alcindor), Jim Brown and other high-profile black athletes. When it was over, Russell famously said, "He has something I have never been able to attain and something very few people I know possess. He has an absolute and sincere faith. … I'm not worried about Muhammad Ali. He is better equipped than anyone I know to withstand the trials in store for him. What I'm worried about is the rest of us."

Add it all up and the 1960s had physically and emotionally beaten Russell down. It all came to a head after a game against the Knicks, when he complained of pain all over his body. He was later diagnosed with acute exhaustion. Even so, Russell rallied, and the Celtics finished 48-34, beat the 76ers and the Knicks in the east, then faced down the Lakers in an epic seven-game series to win their 11th title on the road in Los Angeles.

All's well that ends well, right?

Nope.

A few days after the Celtics hoisted the trophy, the team returned to Boston to celebrate the championship with their fans and, they thought, their best player/coach. John Taylor, author of *The Rivalry: Bill Russell, Wilt Chamberlain and the Golden Age of Basketball*, described the scene wonderfully in his book:

> …on a cool and drizzling Thursday morning, 30,000 people gathered four and five deep along a parade route that ran from the Commons down Tremont Street and then up Washington Street and ended at City Hall, where Mayor Kevin White waited to hand out silver trays and Boston rockers to the members of the team. A flatbed truck, its sides lined with red, white and blue bunting, pulled the Celtics slowly through the cheering, waving crowds. Auerbach wore a khaki raincoat and jovially scattered cigar ashes on his players. They were all there, the heroes of the series: Havlicek the team captain, Sam Jones the savior of game five with his off-balance final-seconds shot, Little Em Bryant,

> Satch Sanders, Bailey Howell...all of them that is except Bill Russell. It was the first time in their eleven championships that the city had honored them with a parade, but Russell—the man who played for the Celtics not for Boston, who said he owed the public nothing, who never heard the boos because he never listened to the cheers—declined to attend. Although no one knew at the time, he was gone.

Russell, who felt that Boston was a deeply racist city with a prejudiced sports media, who refused to sign autographs and once said, "I refuse to smile and be nice to the kiddies," was done. When he initially told Red Auerbach of his decision to quit, Auerbach didn't believe him and was sure he'd be able to convince him to keep playing—but he was wrong. Russell was through with basketball and Boston and the beat writers—so much so that rather than make his retirement public through a writer from the *Globe* or any of the journalists who had covered him for his entire career, he sold his announcement to *Sports Illustrated* for $10,000, which angered nearly everybody. To many, it looked like he had quit on the team for a magazine payday. And to the writers in Boston who loathed his aloofness and churlishness off the court, it was all they needed to say good riddance. But Russell, as always, didn't care. He got into his Lamborghini in Boston and didn't stop until he hit the Pacific Ocean in Los Angeles, where he got a place, took up golf, became a vegetarian, re-examined his views, and in no uncertain terms tried to figure out what to do with the rest of his life. It would be decades before Bill and Boston would reconcile.

***

Cut to four years later and Bill Russell's phone was ringing. Again. He had a feeling it was Sam Schulman. Again. Schulman had been calling a lot throughout the late winter and early spring of 1973, and the two men had some version of the same conversation over and over and it went something like this:

Schulman: "I'd like to hire you to be the next head coach of the Seattle SuperSonics.

Russell: "No."

Each call was different and each pitch from Schulman was different, but the gist was the same. Russell was simply not interested. By his own count, in the four years since he had left Boston, he had been offered seven different head coaching jobs and turned them all down, and Seattle was just another job in the rejection pile. He'd grown comfortable in his new life. He was a public speaker, an activist, had a radio show and a nice gig as a color commentator for ABC's NBA Game of the Week.

What the hell did he need the headache of coaching for?

Schulman, however, was relentless. He wanted a winner in Seattle and his goal was to sign nothing short of the biggest winner in the history of the sport to lead his team. The very idea that Russell said "no" each time drove him to push harder the next time. He hated hearing "no," but he also felt that, eventually, Russell was going to say "yes" to *someone* and he couldn't live with himself if he hadn't done everything he could to make that someone Seattle.

"What do you need to coach?"

"What would it take to get you to sign?"

"Just name it. Tell me and we'll work it out."

Eventually, Russell decided to have a little fun with Schulman, and on one of their calls he laid out a string of demands that would make a hostage negotiator proud. He asked for a contract north of $500,000 over five years. He wanted absolute control of the franchise from the top down, going so far as to ask that nobody else in Sonics management speak on behalf of the team without talking to him. He asked for bells and whistles like a fancy rental car in every town and anything he could think of to make Schulman blush.

"When I finished, I was surprised that Sam was still on the phone," Russell said in his book, *Second Wind*. "But he didn't give me the slightest excuse to back out; he simply said, 'Okay'. Which is how I let myself be maneuvered [into the coaching job]."

Shortly after the call, both sides announced that Russell would be taking over the roles of head coach and general manager. In his official statement accepting the job, channeling *The Godfather,* Russell said, "Sam made me an offer I couldn't refuse."

In a separate appearance, he laid out why he chose Seattle.

"The last four years that's where I've gone on my vacation. I like that part of the country. And there were only four cities that I would consider staying—Los Angeles, San Diego, San Francisco or Seattle," he explained. "Now, my friend K.C. Jones is in San Diego, Bill Sharman is here, and Al Attles and the guys are with Golden State. So that left only Seattle and they didn't have a coach and their general manager quit last week."

As for how he felt it compared to Boston, Russell was impressed with how forward-thinking Seattle had been when it came to civil rights. He was aware of the city's commitment to integration and how aggressively it went about desegregating neighborhoods, schools and places of business. He also was keenly aware of how the city had embraced Walt Hazzard and Lenny Wilkens in his brief time as a player/coach. For a man who believed deeply that Boston in the 1950s and '60s was a city rife with underlying bigotry, the switch to Seattle was a fresh start and a chance to heal. With words that would ripple across the country and rile up Celtics fans, he stated, "I'm going to try to erase the scars and a new day begins."

Schulman was in need of a new day for his franchise as well, and if the city was going to be the home of the Bill Russell Revenge Tour on the way to eleven Sonics titles, then he was all for it. He had total faith in Russell and gave him the keys to the franchise. "He'll have full reign over the team," Schulman said. "I hope it produces a winning team and does for Seattle what I've been striving for all these years."

In addition to the on-court strategy, Russell had a vision of how the team and the citizens of Seattle could grow together. "I want the Seattle SuperSonics to become an integral part of the community," he said. "I want every section of the community to meet the players on a very personal basis."

First, he had to mold the players.

***

"I'd go into the gym with a carrot in one hand and a baseball bat in the other. A month later I'd come out with a team, or a bunch of bodies."

"I have this thing about winning and...if the players survive training, we will win."

"Most of the guys can run, and those who can't run will walk to the unemployment office."

"I intend to teach...the hard way."

"We'll work together, or we'll die together."

"I'm not a miracle man or a genius. But I'll be very tough, you can be sure of that."

These are just some of the quotes Bill Russell gave to the media when asked how he was going to whip his new team into shape.

What does he mean we'll die together?

He's going to have a baseball bat in his hand?

If we survive camp?

What the hell?

Sure, Russell was a bona fide basketball deity, and yes, the Sonics players heard he was a hard ass, but was he trying to turn them into better basketball players or Marines? Nobody knew. And between Russell, his coaching philosophy and the roster he inherited, this was uncharted territory for everybody in Seattle.

Other than Walt Hazzard, who returned to Seattle for the 1973-74 season after stints with Atlanta, Buffalo and Golden State, not a single member of the Original Twelve was still with the team. In their place were talented ABA stars like Spencer Haywood and John Brisker, as well as young guys like "Downtown" Freddie Brown, Kenny McIntosh, Dick Gibbs, John Hummer, and rookies Vester Marshall and Slick Watts.

Watts was the biggest long shot of the bunch. He had an exceptional college career at Xavier University, but despite talk that he would likely be selected in the 1973 draft, the day came and went and it never happened. Fortunately, he had one ace in the hole. His college coach Bob Hopkins just so happened to be Bill Russell's cousin and he made a phone call on behalf of his young player.

"We got a little kid here, he plays with a lot of heart, he plays great defense, he's not afraid to stick his nose in there," Hopkins told Russell on a phone call from the team's training room. "Let me talk to the boy," Russell said.

"Boy, I heard you can play."

"Yes, sir," Watts said.

"How tall are you?"

"Six-foot-one," Watts said.

"That's mighty small," Russell said in his deep voice.

"But I got long arms," Watts said.

"But can you play?"

"Can you coach? If you can coach, I can play," Watts snapped back.

"Boy, you got a big mouth. Let me speak to Coach Hopkins."

Hopkins got on the phone and Russell said, "Get the boy on the plane and get him up here."

When Watts arrived, he learned very quickly where he was in the pecking order. Russell was from the generation of players who believed that on the hierarchy of a basketball team there were starters, subs, bench warmers, uniforms, shoes, socks, dirty socks...drafted rookies and then undrafted rookies. Watts was literally and figuratively looking up at every other person in a Sonics jersey.

During a meeting before the start of rookie camp, Russell sent his former teammate and now assistant Em Bryant to meet with the rookies and give the opposite of a pep talk. It was more like a "please quit" talk. "Personally, I don't even know what you all are doing here, because I have twelve contracts already," Bryant began with disgust in his voice. "I guess the team just needed a tax write-off. If you make it, it's a miracle. I have twelve guys already and no cuts. Maybe I can find one or two guys who can help us."

The rookie practices, which were a precursor to the ones Russell would run with the full team, were exactly as he said they'd be. He roamed the court with a bat on his shoulder, mocking players and laughing at them for his own amusement.

"Look how funny he looks," he'd cackle to one player. "You can't play no basketball, boy, look at you," he'd say to another.

"He would talk about you like a dog," Watts once said.

Spencer Haywood, the team's highest paid player and captain, wasn't spared. Nobody was. Haywood, who openly admitted that Bill Russell was his favorite *man* in basketball, was taken aback by the verbal tirades. From day one, Russell blasted players for mental mistakes, for physical mistakes, for not giving effort, for missing assignments—for even breathing. He wouldn't tolerate errors on any level, and he was vicious. "Do you know how to play this game?" he'd shout. "How can you be so stupid?!"

In Haywood's book, *The Rise, The Fall, The Recovery,* he wrote, "That kind of stuff is hard to take from any coach. Coming from Russell, the God of basketball, it cut right down to your heart. It's one thing to be berated by a Tom Nissalke; you can laugh that off. But when Bill Russell belittles you, you stay belittled."

And there was a boatload of belittling. Russell told the media that his team had "tragic fundamentals," and he was shocked that "some of these players were giving out clinics on their own." He got so fed up that one day during training camp he ran two four-hour sessions that he dubbed "junior high fundamentals," where he worked on the very basics of the game of basketball, treating his pros like a group of seventh-graders. And in another nod to high school tactics, if the Sonics lost a game, the next day at practice the team had to run a lap for every point they lost by. He held to this rule for scrimmages too. His goal was complete control and, for the most part, he got it.

***

Eleven thousand people showed up to the Seattle Center Coliseum for each of Bill Russell's first two home games as Sonics head coach, general manager and, as the press began calling him, "dictator." After dropping his first game on the road to Phoenix, the Sonics beat the Bullets (now Wizards) and the Milwaukee Bucks to jump to a 2-1 start. It was the only time that year they'd have a winning record, but Russell, in effect, had two objectives for his first nine months on the job. In addition to being tasked with winning games he was in charge of slashing the Sonics payroll as well, which ballooned to the second highest in the NBA the previous season despite the team not winning thirty games. Over the course of the first half of the season, he destroyed the confidence of Jim McDaniels to the point where the once-promising center seemed to no longer enjoy playing and his performance suffered.

Russell traded him.

John Brisker, the second-highest paid player on the team, got on the wrong side of Russell in the preseason due to his penchant for fighting. In one practice, Brisker dropped Joby Walker with one punch then turned to Russell and screamed at him like a madman. Despite Brisker's all-star-caliber talent, Russell refused to even talk to him after that incident, ignoring several of Brisker's attempts to reconcile with the coach and resurrect his career and reputation. Ultimately, Brisker was shipped out too, and whether either move was right or wrong didn't matter. Russell successfully dumped two of the highest three salaries on the team.

That left Spencer Haywood, who Russell had taken a liking to. The two men were the same size and Russell had admired Haywood's play ever since he saw him in the Olympics years earlier. Despite the losing season, the two formed a bond, and after his career was over Haywood made a point of visiting Russell every time he was in Seattle.

Of course, no fan in the history of sports ever bought a ticket to watch their favorite team because they were impressed with how much salary the general manager was able to cut. They wanted wins, and short of that they wanted exciting, charismatic players they could root for. The backcourt duo of Slick Watts and "Downtown" Freddie Brown filled that role nicely.

Let's start with the nicknames.

Brown, who won two state titles for Lincoln High School in Milwaukee and was twice named all-state, was given his nickname as a teenager by opponents on the wrong side of his never-ending barrage of long-range shots. After high school, Brown went to Iowa where he averaged 27.6 points per game before becoming the sixth overall pick in the 1971 NBA draft by the Sonics. By the time Russell arrived, Brown went from scoring just four points per game, up to 13 and on his way to 16.5 as the starter for his new head coach. The NBA didn't officially have a three-pointer yet, but Brown shot nearly 50% from the floor while relying on a variety of twenty-foot jumpers. Fans loved his pump fakes, double pump fakes, grins, winks and smiles that he'd let loose before draining a shot from deep. He also had a knack for steals, which were always a crowd pleaser.

Watts, his backup, had all the ingredients necessary to become a local legend: a cool name, a trademark look, off-the-charts charisma, exciting play and, most importantly, a megawatt smile. Born Donald Earl Watts, the self-described "man of the people, player of the people" got his trademark baldness after a head injury from playing football in middle school. The injury required doctors to shave his scalp, and when the hair grew back it came in patchy, so he decided to keep his head shaved. This was long before Kareem Abdul-Jabbar or Michael Jordan intentionally shaved their heads and made it a fashion statement. At the time, his buddies just thought it looked strange. Without any hair to mop up his sweat it poured all over his face, so he went in search of a headband and, in his words, "he found the only one that wasn't on Wilt Chamberlain's head." Again, unlike today, when players routinely wear headbands as part of their carefully selected Instagram-ready game ensemble, Watts didn't know of any pro players other than Chamberlain who wore them. He also had a penchant for wearing the headband at three different angles, all of which had their own carefully crafted meaning, according to Watts.

"When I was shooting well, I would put it back straight," he explained. "If I tilt it, I had a tendency to shoot it whichever way I tilt it. I had a philosophy that if I started it over to the right, and I was shooting the ball right, I would bring it back to the left. If I was shooting left, I would bring it back to center. If I started it right, and I was going good, I wouldn't mess with it. I had a little more style when I cocked it a bit."

The nickname itself, Slick, came after a string of other nicknames referring to his dome, such as "Shine," "Head," "Eagle" and "Bald Eagle," never stuck. After one game at Xavier in which Watts had twelve steals, Sister Mary Francis told him in class the next day, "you are so slick." Students picked up on it. Then the cheerleaders picked up on it and started chanting "Deal Slick, Deal. Deal Slick, Deal!" and the name went viral.

Bill Russell, as you'd probably guess, did not care one bit about nicknames. He cared about winning, and during the first part of the 1973-74 season Watts barely left the bench. As the losses piled up, the Seattle fans became fixated with Watts and his shiny head and his headband sitting on the bench. "Slick! Slick! We want Slick! We want Slick!"

The chants would rain down through the arena and Russell, whose sense of humor was as sharp as his insults, would stand up and chant along with the fans, "Slick! Slick! We want Slick!" He'd then look at Watts, who was on the end of the bench, and say, "The fans want you to get in there, better get in there." Watts would jump up, excited, only to watch Russell cackle and say, "Sit down, boy."

"I thought it was funny," Watts said. "It became a little game. He would hear the fans, and he'd start chanting with them. Soon I laughed, because I knew he wasn't going to put me in."

By the end of November the team was 9-17 and capped off the month with a 34-point loss to Milwaukee. The next game, against Atlanta, Russell decided it was time to give Watts his shot.

"Boy, you been walking around practice, talking all this trash and telling me you can play. I am going to see if you can play tonight," Russell said.

The match-up was a nationally televised game against one of Watts' idols, "Pistol" Pete Maravich, who he thought of as a "white Globetrotter." Watts shined. He scored 21 points in just seventeen minutes of playing time and dazzled not only the crowd, but also his new coach and his old coach, Bob Hopkins.

"I hadn't seen Slick since he talked to Bill Russell in my office that day," Hopkins said later. "And the next time I saw Slick he was going against Pistol there in Atlanta. He came in and took the ball from him three straight times. And two times he stole it. I mean, Slick did something that you rarely ever see. He did something we called the reverse move, where you fake one way, then turn the other way, and when you turn, he's got the ball. Pete didn't know what hit him."

After the game, Russell told Watts, "You're doing things I haven't seen since K.C. Jones."

"I idolized K.C. Jones," Watts said in his memoir. "It was one of the proudest moments of my career."

***

The 1973-74 season ended with the Sonics in third place in the Western Conference's Pacific Division and a grand total of thirty-six wins, a ten-game improvement from the year before. Spencer Haywood averaged 23 points and 13 boards, Dick Snyder dropped in 18 points per game and "Downtown" Freddie Brown scored 16 per game. Slick Watts led the team in assists and was second in steals.

"All things considered, it's been a good year," Russell said after the last game. "Our last six games were very good for us. We really played as a team in tough situations."

For many of the players, the tough situations they experienced weren't from the games but from Russell himself.

"I think it's safe to say that Bill Russell and I had a love-hate relationship," Watts said. "Most players had a hate-hate relationship with Russ."

In addition to the insults and constant berating, Russell had a way of antagonizing his guys so that they'd really loathe him. From small things, like banning alcohol on the road, to annoying tweaks like picking the players' shoe colors and their roommates on the road, all the way to being a straight-up jerk. One of his most egregious habits was intentionally benching players on nights they were playing in their hometowns. If you had your mom and dad and sister and fifty members of your extended family in the arena to see you play...you can be guaranteed you'd sit.

"If you had the most tickets, you might not play at all," Watts said. "He just loved to do it."

From the outside looking in, the Bill Russell honeymoon was still in full swing. Fans bought into the idea that he was building "Celtics West" and that he needed to ship out some bad apples who weren't *his guys* in order to succeed. Brisker, Snyder and Jim McDaniels were out by the end of the '74 season; Archie Clark and Leonard Gray were in. As the '74-'75 season got under way, Brown and Watts stepped their games up and Haywood was still a mostly dominant big man, despite a slight dip in his production. More importantly, from a community perspective the Sonics, still the only professional sports team in town, were visible. The squad held its regular practices at the Sand Point Naval Air Station, but per Russell and Schulman's plan, the team also practiced and scrimmaged at local high schools to build a bond with their fans, especially the young fans. High school students throughout the Seattle-Tacoma area never knew when their principal was going to call an assembly, only to show up to find the great Bill Russell running a practice with the hometown team.

Nevertheless, the Sonics were three games under .500 at the all-star break and as late as March 23 still hadn't improved. The team had been under the tutelage, aka the dictatorship, of Russell for almost two full seasons and they were about three weeks from ending another year with more losses than wins and no postseason to show for it. Then, they got hot. In quick succession they beat the Lakers by twenty-one at home, the Warriors by four, the Trail Blazers by ten, and won the next four games to end the season with a shocking seven-game winning streak and their first-ever postseason appearance.

Russell, for a brief moment, let down his guard and (gulp) hugged his players. *Who is this guy?* they thought. It was a proud moment for the fans and for the organization. Ten years earlier Dick Vertlieb and Don Richman were pitching their hearts out to NBA brass about why Seattle deserved a team; now, they were contending for a championship with an opening-round series against the Detroit Pistons. Not only that, but the efforts to endear the team to the community paid off. The Sonics broke their total season attendance record by attracting 524,692 fans to the Coliseum and broke their per-game attendance record with an average of 12,797 people at each game. They even had fifteen regular-season sellouts. Vertlieb and Richman were right: The Great Northwest in general, and Seattle in particular, was primed for an NBA team and the Sonics had, little by little, found their way into the hearts of the Emerald City's citizens. The fans even presented Schulman with a plaque prior to game one, essentially telling him how great he was. There were victory laps happening all over the city—from the fans, from the organization, from the head coach. Everyone seemed to be saying the same thing: *See! You just needed to have a little faith!*

Still, a playoff basketball series needed to be played.

"I'm confident," Russell said when asked about the series against Detroit. "I did like the way we ended our season. If Tommy [Burleson] plays well and Spencer is good, we can really be tough up front against Detroit."

He was right. In game one the team put up "the best defensive effort of the season," according to Russell, and beat the Pistons 90-77. Detroit then won game two, setting up a winner-take-all game three (back then first-round series were best-of-three). The Sonics' 7'3" rookie center Burleson had a huge first half with 17 points, and Watts came off the bench like a bolt of lightning to energize the squad and lead them to their first playoff series win in franchise history. But there was no time to celebrate. Forty-eight hours later they were on the floor ready to tip off against the heavily favored Golden State Warriors and their nearly unstoppable scorer, Rick Barry.

As expected, the Sonics got smoked in the first game, 123-96. In the post-game press conference, when asked if there was anything his team did right, Russell mocked, "Let's see now. Well, we showed up on time. And we were in the right uniforms." He then went on to sarcastically say that the poor play "was a team effort. Nobody was moving without the ball... The Warriors just ran us out of there."

Spencer Haywood and "Downtown" Freddie Brown combined for 54 points in game two to lead the Sonics to a one-point win and a coveted 1-1 series tie heading back to their home court. Game three was marked by a series of fights and a completely flat effort that led to the Sonics losing by nine on their own floor. Burleson went for 25 points and 11 boards, but the rest of the team didn't show up. In game four, Freddie Brown went to town, scoring 37 points, including a truly unconscious 17 straight points in the middle of the game to lead the team to a win. "I wasn't conscious of my offense," Brown said after the game. "I was just trying to come out with more points on the board than they had."

With the series tied 2-2, the Warriors suddenly found themselves in a dog fight and buckled down. They won by twenty-four points in game five and then never trailed in game six en route to the series win, despite a heroic 24-point, 11-assist, four-rebound effort from Slick Watts that even Bill Russell had to acknowledge. "He played one of the great games ever played in basketball," Russell said. "He did everything he could possibly do for us to win."

Watts, who played all forty-eight minutes, was spent and admitted it after the game. "I'm mentally worn out. They hit me, knocked me around all night. When we started to play with intensity at the end it was too late."

Wrapping up the season, Russell remarked, "I'm not disappointed. Sure, I'd like to have gone much further, but you try to take life as it comes. This is a game of physical talent, intelligence, will power and heart. The players gave me the best they could. We just lost to a better team. But what we accomplished this year was very important. We established that we are a winning team and we will take up from there next season."

***

The 1975-76 Seattle SuperSonics season under Bill Russell followed almost the exact blueprint from the year before. Step one: Ship out a bunch of productive players (goodbye Spencer Haywood, Archie Clark and Jim Fox). Step two: Watch Freddie Brown and Slick Watts continue to improve and become the team leaders. Step three: Be three games under .500 in early March. Step four: Finish strong, win seven out of ten games to wrap up the year and secure a second straight playoff berth. But while step five in 1975 was to win a playoff series, in 1976, that wasn't the case. After winning their opening game against the Phoenix Suns in the Western Conference semi-finals behind Brown's 34 points, the Sonics dropped four of their next five to lose the series. Their season was over before May 1 again.

Sam Schulman brought in Russell to build a winner, and after three full seasons his record was 122-124 and he was 1-2 in playoff series. Yes, the playoff appearances were a step forward, but "Celtics West" this was not. The aura of the great Bill Russell, which had already worn off with his players, was slowly wearing off with the fans. In fact, an argument could be made, and *was* made in national headlines, that the face of the franchise shifted that year from being Russell to, of all people, the happy-go-lucky Slick Watts. Ralph Barbieri, a writer for *Sport* magazine, drove to Seattle from the publication's iconic San Francisco headquarters during the season and spent four days with Watts, driving around with him, hanging with him, and getting an idea of how the city felt about him. His conclusion: Seattle was Slick's town. In an excerpt from the piece, he wrote:

> Bill Russell is still the coach and general manager of the Seattle Supersonics, but the Sonics no longer sell tickets on his name and reputation. The Sonics sell more tickets now. They sell them on Slick Watts's name and reputation. In Seattle, Slick Watts not only towers over Bill Russell; he's bigger than the Puget Sound. He's the most popular athlete in the history of the state. He's the most famous unknown who ever lived.

Russell was livid when the article was published and wouldn't speak to Watts. "Daddy put me on ice for a week or two," Watts jokingly said in his memoir about the write-up. It was a petty, ego-driven response by the legend. Any fair-minded observer knew who Seattle's favorite son was in the mid-seventies. Look at any poll; check out any survey. The answer always came back the same: Slick Watts.

Watts did the most community events.

He was the most accessible player.

Hell, he even broke up a fight after a traffic accident just by getting out of his car and asking if he could help. When *Sports Illustrated* jumped on the media bandwagon and finally sent a writer to cover Watts, Bob Walsh, who worked in Seattle's front office, said, "It's impossible to calculate Slick's worth to the team. He puts at least 1,000 people a night into the Coliseum, and those are just the people he's met in the past week or kids he's met who demand that their parents take them to the game. Even if he couldn't play, he'd be worth an awful lot to us. If we ever traded him, we'd all have to leave town."

On the heels of his popularity and legitimate on-court success, Watts, who was one of the lowest-paid players on the team, asked for a contract that would pay him what he was worth—somewhere north of the bench guys but below the superstar big men. He and his agent asked for a five-year deal starting at $120,000 per year. For a frame of reference, Spencer Haywood was making $302,000 per year and Tommy Burleson was pulling down $325,000 per year. Frank Oleynick, whose face not a single person outside of his family would recognize, played twelve minutes per game and was making $100,000 a year.

Russell, ever the hard-ass, offered Watts a three-year deal starting at $70,000 per year and Watts had to take it. A player like Watts simply had no leverage back then, even though, when the city opened the Kingdome, guess who was invited along with Seattle's mayor, the state senators, the governor of Washington and other luminaries? Yup. Watts. And guess who got a five-minute standing ovation from the near 60,000 people in attendance? Watts.

"I felt like the Beatles for a hot minute," Watts wrote in his memoir. "I had to move twice. After games, people were sitting around my house with posters. I was in Kirkland on Bridle Trail. My wife finally said, 'We have to move. I can't take this anymore'. Then they named me SeaFair Grand Marshall. Twice. Bob Hope was once a SeaFair Marshall!"

As Watts' stature in Seattle grew, along with that of "Downtown" Freddie Brown to a lesser extent, Russell's shrank. The 1976-77 season was a complete failure. The team finished 40-42 and missed the playoffs, and Russell, for the first time in his career, regularly heard boos at home. He'd lost the locker room and he'd lost the fans. When the season ended, Schulman had grown tired of "The Dictator" and decided it was time to overthrow him. In the offseason, he chose not to bring Big Russ back for a fifth season.

"Bill Russell has always given me 110 percent, just as he gave the Celtics and NBA fans 110 percent as a player," Schulman said in a prepared statement announcing the end of Russell's tenure.

Overall, it was an amicable separation.

"Sam Schulman has a dream, which I know he will fulfill to bring the NBA Championship to the wonderful people of Seattle," Russell said in his own statement. "I have mixed emotions about leaving the Sonics, but I feel I have reached a point in my career where I want to pursue other activities. I find Sam Schulman to be an extremely good man, civic-minded, with a goal which I wished we had realized together."

The Great Bill Russell Experiment was over.

Chapter 5

Lenny Wilkens Wins, Wins, Wins No Matter What

If you're the type to believe that there are no coincidences, then the cosmic forces in charge of pulling the strings in our universe must've had it in for the city of Seattle in late November of 1977. In the same week, the Concorde passenger plane landed for the first time in New York City and the SuperSonics basketball team hit rock bottom. The Concorde landing in the Big Apple was a stick in the eye of Boeing, who years earlier lost the contract to build, and subsequently canceled, their prototype for a supersonic plane (the very plane the Seattle SuperSonics were named after). Several days after the Concorde's NYC debut, the Sonics lost their 17th game before December 1, which had fans wishing the season, like their namesake plane, would also be canceled. After parting ways with Bill Russell, Sam Schulman promoted Russell's assistant (and cousin) Bob Hopkins to be the new head coach. Hopkins, unlike Russell, was a personable guy and popular with the players; in a way, Schulman felt that he was the antidote to the ex-Celtics legend.

He was wrong.

Although Hopkins had a strong hoops pedigree of his own, with an excellent college playing career at Grambling and a short NBA stint with the Syracuse Nationals, his hiring was a complete disaster. Inside of twenty-three games the locker room became a refuge of listless losers looking for answers. Hopkins had none.

After a particularly gut-wrenching loss to Cleveland during this futile stretch, co-captain Freddie Brown said, "I've asked the players to consider what's going on, to take a personal inventory. I want the public to know we want to win. I want the public to know we are actually trying to do something."

Recently acquired NBA veteran Paul Silas, who won two championships with the Celtics in the mid-1970s and was a two-time all-star, was equally flummoxed. "I don't think it has anything to do with the physical," he said. "It's just an attitude on this ball club that prevails. We don't have the mental attitude to gut it out. I've never encountered this before. I think everybody is at a low ebb. It's a total negativism."

Damn. Aside from that, Paul, how do you think the season is going?

"[At] some time we have to start thinking about how to win," he continued. "How to communicate, how to bust out of this."

Even the ever-ebullient Slick Watts was down. "I'm drained, man," he said in a post-game interview. "Emotionally and physically." Brown, for his part, was open to any and all options. "I don't know what the solution is," he said. "I'd try anything."

Five days after Thanksgiving, following an embarrassing loss to Denver, Schulman and his director of player personnel (and the Sonics former player/coach) Lenny Wilkens gave Hopkins the hook. Enough was enough. Despite their horrendous record (the second worst in the league) the Sonics front office believed they had a decent team with a nice mix of veterans like Silas, Brown, Watts, Mike Green and Gus Williams, along with promising young guys like Jack Sikma out of Illinois-Wesleyan and Dennis Johnson from Pepperdine. This was not going to be a lost season, and for the second time in seven years Schulman turned to Wilkens, who was now 40, to run the team.

"For all of us, it was a very difficult thing," Wilkens said at the time. "I want to change our mental attitude immediately. Sometimes we've been playing with what looks like a defeatist attitude. We will change some things we do on the court, but it's nothing that will show up as fast as [the next game]."

Hold that thought.

***

Neither Russell Westbrook nor James Harden nor Chris Paul nor Steve Nash nor John Stockton nor Magic Johnson nor any other player in the history of the NBA was an all-star while leading the league in assists and *also* being the head coach of their team. Isiah Thomas wasn't. Oscar Robertson wasn't. Jerry West wasn't. All those men nailed two-out-of-three (league assist leader and all-star), but the third leg of the trifecta is the most difficult and was achieved by only one man: Leonard Randolph Wilkens, aka Lenny, who accomplished the feat as the 32-year-old player/coach of the Seattle SuperSonics during the 1969-70 NBA season. This is an even more astonishing feat when you consider that fourteen years earlier the number of colleges interested in offering Wilkens a basketball scholarship was zero.

Growing up, Wilkens was the pride of Bedford-Stuyvesant and a bona fide Brooklyn playground hoops prodigy in the late 1940s and early 1950s. He attended the famous Boys and Girls High School, the oldest public school in Brooklyn, and although he made the varsity basketball team as a freshman, he chose not to play the next two years because he thought he wasn't good enough. In fact, basketball wasn't even his favorite sport. "My first sport was baseball," he said in a retrospective interview. "The Dodgers were the thing, and I loved Jackie Robinson. I knew Gil Hodges and Pee Wee Reese and Duke Snider."

In a unique twist of sports history, Wilkens worked as a grocery store delivery boy and one of the houses he regularly delivered to was Jackie Robinson's house. "I had a little part-time job and I got to meet him [Jackie]," Wilkens told SonicsRising in an interview. "The thing that I saw is that he was such a fierce competitor on the baseball field, but he was also very intelligent. And he used a lot of that. No matter what anyone said, it didn't deter him from what he wanted to accomplish."

Wilkens wasn't quite sure which sport he wanted to dedicate his time to, so he split his efforts evenly between his two favorites. "We played a lot of baseball, and as far as basketball, you had to make your name on the playground. I remember I did that one day against Vinnie Cohen, who was a great player at Syracuse. I was able to stay with him, and I had made it," he said.

Rather than potentially ride the bench for his school team, Wilkens spent the bulk of his high school basketball career working on his quick passes and quick-release shot on the playgrounds and for a series of Catholic Youth Organization leagues. It wasn't until his good friend (and future Dodgers star) Tommy Davis pushed him to try out for the basketball team again as a senior that he played for the school. Unfortunately, he was slated to graduate in the middle of the season, so despite playing well, he missed out on the number one high school hoops showcase in the city, the Brooklyn city tournament.

With no spectacular postseason feats to build buzz and no daily limelight with a deep run in the tournament, Wilkens' basketball future was up in the air, if not potentially over, after his last midseason game. In stepped Father Thomas

Mannion, one of his CYO coaches who happened to have a relationship with Providence College coach John Mulaney. Mannion convinced Mulaney to offer Wilkens a scholarship and the Hail Mary paid off. Wilkens led the freshman team to an undefeated 23-0 season—and he was just getting warmed up.

As a sinewy, silky smooth guard who barely filled out the skin-tight T-shirts the Providence hoops team played in, Wilkens averaged 14.9 points and 7.9 rebounds per game (they didn't keep track of assists). By the time he finished his Providence career, the kid who needed a priest's letter to get a scholarship led his team to its first NIT tournament, and its first NIT Finals appearance the following year. He was also a two-time All-American. There were no personal appeals that needed to be written to NBA general managers to take a flyer on the great Friar, and the St. Louis Hawks selected him as the sixth overall pick in the 1960 NBA Draft. He made five all-star appearances with the Hawks alongside future Hall of Famer Bob Pettit, and the team regularly made the playoffs. After the 1967-68 season, Wilkens finished second in league MVP voting behind Wilt Chamberlain. A few months later, Seattle gave up Walt Hazzard to acquire Wilkens, who earned three straight all-star nods with his new team. After his first season, the Sonics fired head coach Al Bianchi and the team approached Wilkens about taking over as player/coach.

"They let the coach go and Dick Vertlieb, who was the general manager, wanted me to be a player/coach," Wilkens explained. "I told him he was crazy. He said, 'No, you're like a coach anyway on the floor. You know what to do, you run the show'. We went around and around. I told him 'no' at first. I finally decided, what the heck, I had nothing to lose. I'd try it and see if I liked it."

The move paid off, with Wilkens improving the team's win total from 30 under Bianchi to 36 in his first year, 38 in his second year, and 47 wins his third year. After the third season Wilkens was spent, as the self-described "novelty" of being a player/coach was wearing off.

"I began to realize that I had to do a lot more to coach successfully," he told *HOOP* magazine. "After a while, we had started to do more things within the league, with trapping and double-teaming becoming more sophisticated. And we were finding that young players were coming in and they didn't really know the game. So that required a lot of teaching and helping them to understand situations, and I began to realize after a while that I couldn't do both."

The Sonics hired Tom Nissalke to coach the team for the 1972-73 season, and in one of his first moves he shipped Wilkens off to Cleveland. This ticked off Wilkens and, to a more important extent, the Sonics season ticket holders, 200 of which signed a petition that stated, "If Lenny goes, I stay home."

Well, Lenny went, and the season ticket holders (and a lot of other ticket holders) stayed home as the team struggled to a 13-32 record before Nissalke was fired midseason. For his part, Wilkens spent two years in Cleveland and one in Portland as player/coach before taking a break from the hardwood to work in Seattle's front office.

And now we're caught up to the firing of Bob Hopkins in 1977 and Lenny Wilkens taking over the Sonics coaching duties for a second time.

"I still remember when I took over that team," Wilkens recalled in 1994. "I had heard general managers and other people say it was the worst team ever."

It was a combination of the rumblings of those GMs and the team's abysmal record that led to Wilkens' statement that, while he planned on turning things around, there was no magic bullet strategy he could implement to reverse course right away. The only thing he knew for sure that he *could* do was (cue random sports cliché generator) take it one game at a time and make sure his players were giving 100%.

***

All I do is win win win no matter what
Got money on my mind I can never get enough
And every time I step up in the buildin'
Everybody hands go up
And they stay there
And they say yeah
And they stay there
'Cause all I do is win win win
And if you goin' in put your hands in the air

Make 'em stay there

These are the opening lyrics to the 2010 song "All I Do Is Win" by DJ Khaled featuring Ludacris, T-Pain, Snoop Dogg and Rick Ross. The song went triple platinum and about a half-dozen NBA teams mixed it into their starting lineup introductions the year it came out, including the Nuggets, Blazers, Pacers, Raptors and a few others. But if there was one team in NBA history for whom the anthem would have been perfectly suited for its mid-season starting lineup intros, it likely would have been the Lenny Wilkens-led 1977-78 Seattle SuperSonics.

Really? Yes.

Despite taking over a team that was ranked twenty-one out of a then twenty-two NBA franchises, a team that, as Paul Silas put it, was cloaked in negativity, and a team that most GMs thought was hot garbage, Wilkens took the reins and began one of the all-time greatest in-season turnarounds in the history of sports.

In Wilkens' first game the Sonics beat the Kansas City Kings 86-84. No big deal, just a nice two-point squeaker to get his second coaching run in Seattle off to a good start. Three days later they smoked the Boston Celtics 111-89, behind 24 points from Dennis Johnson and 23 from Gus Williams. The next night they beat Buffalo 102-95, and over the next week they reeled off easy wins against Atlanta and Milwaukee before blowing out Houston 116-84. That made six wins in a row. Something strange and wonderful was happening to the team.

Spokane Chronicle sportswriter Merle Derrick wrote, "Chalk up another flub for your reporter. In a recent column, I noted that it was probably a lack of talent that was hurting the Sonics, not the coaching of a deposed Bob Hopkins. So, what happens? Well, the Seattle club suddenly comes to life and begins winning in impressive fashion. The bubble may burst and the Sonics may drift back to their previous futile struggling, but right now, however, the club is performing as though there were new players in the lineup—not just a coaching change."

Wilkens chalked it up to his players' renewed positivity and their willingness to help each other out. "Our good shooting is because of our increased confidence," he said after the game. "I want them to shoot when they're open eight to ten feet from the hoop because they're good shooters. This is the most unselfish team I've coached."

On December 19, the winning streak came to a halt with a loss to Cleveland. Oh well, all good things come to an end. What more can you ask of a team that was 5-17? They had to come back to Earth at some point, right?

Wrong.

The Sonics won their next five in a row, capping their second-longest winning streak of the season with a pummeling of the Boston Celtics, 132-99. In an ode to the new unselfish mantra running through the team, eight players scored in double digits and all ten men on the roster played and scored. The team then dropped two games before winning seven in a row and ultimately going 11-2 heading into the all-star break. Remarkably, amazingly, incredibly, the team that two months prior had the "worst lineup in the league" and was sitting twelve games below .500 was now five games *above* .500 with a 27-22 record. They also didn't have a single player selected as an all-star.

After the break, the team-first attitude continued. "Downtown" Freddie Brown was rolling and having a career year. "The Wizard" Gus Williams was on the cusp of becoming a scoring machine. "The Human Eraser," center Marvin Webster, had the best year of his life, averaging 14 points and 12 boards a game. Jack Sikma was averaging nearly a double-double as a twenty-two-year-old. Dennis Johnson was running the floor and showing flashes of greatness. All in all, Wilkens was getting the absolute best from each of his players, and the Sonics turned in a 20-13 second-half record and finished the season an impressive 47-35, good for third place in the Western Conference Pacific Division and a playoff berth. The only real casualty of the season was the city's former biggest star, Slick Watts, who had lost a step and lost playing time to the younger Gus Williams and Dennis Johnson. During the year, Wilkens traded him to New Orleans. Aside from that one tough move, the starless Sonics managed an out-of-nowhere 42-18 record under Wilkens, surprising absolutely everybody, including the coach himself.

"I didn't think we'd be in the playoffs, let's be honest about it," Wilkens said after the regular season. "Our first goal was to be competitive and we did that.

Our second goal was to reach .500 and we did that. Our last goal was to reach third place and get the home-court advantage (in the first round of the playoffs)."

Done, done and done. But now that the team actually made the playoffs and secured home court in the first round, the miracle season had an open ending. Rather than waiting for the other shoe to drop and wondering when the unselfishness and team chemistry and "luck" would run out, Sonics fans began to let their minds wander to other more pleasant thoughts, like, exactly how far can this "no-name," no all-star team go? And, can they actually beat all-time greats like Kareem Abdul-Jabbar in a series with their season on the line? In a word, 'yes.'

In the first round the Sonics beat the Lakers in a best-of-three series, winning games one and three. Gus Williams, Marvin Webster and Freddie Brown handled the scoring, with Webster putting up a terrific 17 points and 14 boards per game against Abdul-Jabbar to match his numbers as best he could. This set up a Western Conference semifinals against one of Wilkens' old teams, the No. 1-seeded defending NBA Champion Portland Trail Blazers, coached by the legendary Jack Ramsay and led on the court by Bill Walton, Maurice Lucas, Lionel Hollins and Tom Owens. The Blazers won fifty-eight games that year and in some ways were a mirror image of the Sonics, with a deep bench, steady big men and a knack for spreading the scoring around to six or eight players.

After jumping out to a 3-1 series lead, the Sonics were blown out in game five behind 31 points from Owens. This set up one of those classic game six matchups where a young, underdog team has a shot to close out the series at home, wanting no part of a game seven in hostile territory against a playoff-hardened opponent. A sellout crowd of 14,098 fans showed up at the Seattle Coliseum and the Sonics didn't disappoint. Dennis Johnson scored 20 points, Marvin Williams put up a 19-and-11 double-double, and Freddie Brown poured in another 19 to give the team a win and its first ever trip to the Western Conference Finals.

"It looks like we're in a groove again," Wilkens said after the game. "If we are, there's no telling how far this team can go."

"We were all in tune for the game," Brown said. "We were not going to be denied."

By this point even the most superstitious fans in the Emerald City had to let their guard down a little bit. *We just beat the defending NBA Champions. Could this team actually do it? Could they make it to the Promised Land?*

With the Lakers and Blazers now vanquished, the last Western Conference opponent was the high-scoring, high-flying Denver Nuggets, who dropped nearly 112 points per game during the season behind All-NBA first-teamer David Thompson and seven-time all-star and former NBA scoring champion Dan Issel. Just like in the previous round, the Sonics grabbed a 3-1 series lead, were beat up on the road in game five, and once again a sellout crowd of 14,000-plus showed up for game six. This time, however, a trip to the NBA Finals was on the line. Pressure? Nah. Nerves? Nope. The Sonics blasted out of the gate with a 39-point first quarter and never looked back. They were up 62-54 at the half and then dumped another 31 on the Nuggets in the third quarter to put the game out of reach. And as if the game was pre-ordained by the basketball gods, it was the longest-tenured and most beloved Sonic, Freddie Brown, who led the team to its first NBA Finals appearance with 26 points.

"We scored 39 points in the first quarter, and from then on it was history," Brown said. "I knew we were going to have a big game tonight because everybody felt great. When everybody plays well there's no telling what we can do."

"We knew we had to play the kind of defense we're capable of and get our running game going, and we really got it going," Wilkens said.

After the game, Paul Silas, the man who bluntly stated that the team back in November was a cesspool of negativity, revealed that during the Christmas party the team tried to speak success into existence with a toast to each other.

"We had our Christmas party and we made a toast to the world champion Seattle SuperSonics, and that's when the seed was planted," he said. "We've always believed, and then Lenny came along and jelled things together."

For Sam Schulman, the man who had been pulling the strings behind the scenes since year one, Wilkens was everything he could have asked for. "No one in history has stepped in when a team was in the depths, the second-worst team, and done what he's done," Schulman gloated.

In a year full of statistics reversing themselves as if from an alternate universe, the Sonics' win against the Nuggets was their 20th straight victory on their home court in the Coliseum. Long before the Seahawks had their twelfth-man advantage, the Sonics had their own version, the sixth man, and it was fourteen thousand strong night and in and night out. Now, the only thing standing in the way of the team's wishful Christmas toast becoming a reality were the Eastern Conference Champion Washington Bullets.

"I don't make predictions," Wilkens said. "It's going to be a hell of a series."

***

The familiar CBS eye logo is sitting beneath the red, clown-nosed style microphone in 40-year-old Brent Musburger's hand. Musburger is wearing a beige sports jacket and his shaggy, '70s-style hair is parted on the side. The fourteen thousand fans at the Seattle Center Coliseum are howling louder and louder as tipoff to Game 1 of the 1978 NBA Finals between the Seattle SuperSonics and the Washington Bullets approaches, causing Musburger to practically scream in order to be heard. Over his right shoulder, a fan raises a giant white poster with *SONIC BOOM IS BULLETS DOOM* written in thick black marker. The atmosphere feels more like a title fight than a basketball game.

"Never in my wildest dreams did I think I would stand before you on this Sunday and say, 'For the championship, we've got Washington and Seattle,'" Musburger shouted. "Two amazing turnarounds by these ball clubs coached by Dick Motta and Lenny Wilkens, and I'll promise you one thing: You are about to see some of the toughest basketball you have ever viewed on television, particularly underneath. Wes Unseld. Elvin Hayes. Marvin Webster. Paul Silas…"

As the pregame intro wound down, the teams shook hands before the opening tip. The row of press seats behind them was wrapped in a bright yellow banner with the words *Seattle Center Coliseum* printed across the length of the court. The floor was a plain, light wooden color with the midcourt circle in white. The starting lineups were Dandridge, Hayes, Unseld, Henderson and Grevey for Washington; and Johnson, Sikma, Webster, Williams and Dennis Johnson for Seattle. Sikma was the only rookie starting for either team.

"Keep in mind that Seattle has not lost at home in twenty games," Musburger said. "Washington was the last team to beat them."

Washington started the game with two quick jump shots, quieting the fans a little bit until the next possession, when Marvin Webster hit a sweet little eight-foot jumper and the crowd roared to its feet: The Seattle SuperSonics had tallied the first NBA Finals points in the history of the franchise.

The crowd. The team. The arena. This is what Dick Vertlieb and Don Richman envisioned over a decade earlier. *Seattle was a great basketball town. They knew it. And now the entire sports world was getting to see it.*

As for Sam Schulman, the Hollywood showman who finally had his team in the NBA's signature showcase, it was not a time for humility. "It's a miracle and I deserve it to happen to me," he said of his team being in the Finals. "This is the highlight of my life. This is the most extraordinary, special year for any sports team ever. Way down deep I have felt this is our year."

For the first three quarters of game one, Schulman's belief was put to the test. The Bullets had a 19-point lead deep in the second half when "IO," Mr. Instant Offense himself "Downtown" Freddie Brown, got cooking with an onslaught of jumpers, leaners and swishes. When they got the lead under nine, he pulled up for a quick two at the elbow: boom. Then he hit a leaner at the foul line that drew contact for a three-point play and caused Musburger to gush, "Lordy, lordy mother of mercy, ball please go in the hole! And it did for Freddie Brown!"

Brown hit his free throw and then the Bullets got a quick bucket to go back up by four, before Marvin Webster smoked a put-back jam after a Brown miss to put the game back within two. The next time down the court the Bullets, unbelievably, played off of Brown about twenty feet from the hoop and he calmly hit another jumper to tie the game 88-88 with 6:24 to go.

One minute later Brown grabbed a tough rebound, took the ball out, slid along the baseline, knocked down an impossible lefty floater (with his head and body actually behind the rim) and was fouled, setting up yet another three-point play, which he converted to tie the game at 91-91. The Sonics faithful were roaring by this point. The Coliseum sounded like a jet engine behind the announcers as Washington was forced to take another time out.

With his men getting a much-needed breather on the bench, Wilkens sat down in front of them, pen in hand, and drew up another play for Brown, who was officially NBA Jam-level on fire. "Fred, I want you to split out to here [the top of they key], and DJ, as you come off, hesitate there for a second, start back and see if you can reverse that underneath, alright? Now just read it. If he's open, give it to him. If not, continue on back and find whoever is open."

Marvin Webster, the second option on the play, leaned in and said, "Fred, if you're open I'm gonna give the ball to you for a pop shot right away." It was all Brown at this point. He had already scored 12 points in the quarter and the team was determined to ride him to the finish. With the crowd screaming and banging cowbells and chanting after every bucket, the teams traded scores for a few possessions and the Sonics found themselves down by three with two minutes left. As had been the plan all quarter, they gave the ball to Brown and he worked around a Paul Silas screen to knock down a twenty-two-footer to bring Seattle to within one. After a few sloppy possessions, Dennis Johnson was fouled and sank two clutch free throws to put Seattle up 103-102. The Bullets air balled their next shot, and following a rare Freddie Brown miss, Paul Silas came up with the most important rebound in Sonics history and kicked the ball back out to Brown with about thirty seconds left. Brown, as he had done all night, calmly backed down his defender and felt his way across the floor. At the twenty second mark he waved to his teammates to clear out and he dribbled with his left hand to the top of the elbow. With six seconds left on the shot clock and fourteen in the game, he made a lightning quick stop and rose up just to the left of the top of the key. The ball hung in the air for a beat and then...swish.

"Fred Brown! The fourth quarter man! Has done it for Seattle with a three-point lead!" Rick Barry, Musburger's broadcast partner, shouted above the cheers.

And with the bucket, the Seattle SuperSonics took another step into uncharted territory, winning the first NBA Finals game in franchise history.

"I thought it was a super comeback," Wilkens said of the team's 21st straight home victory. "One thing about these players, and they have done it all year long, is that they don't give up. They don't win all the time, but they fight to the end."

Bullets Coach Dick Motta had nothing but praise for the Sonics and Brown. "He [Brown] can miss his first twenty shots and still win the game for you. He doesn't get discouraged. His shots are going to be in the hole from an unlimited range."

How important was the game to Seattle fans? Well, one man came back from the dead to watch it. The following story was picked up by the Associated Press and ran in hundreds of papers across the country with the headline, *Seattle Fan Dying to Know Score.*

> SEATTLE (AP) — The man had a heart attack and was taken to the hospital. His first request in the coronary care unit was to watch the first game of the NBA championship playoffs between the Seattle SuperSonics and the Washington Bullets. Then his heart stopped beating. Doctors worked feverishly to revive him and succeeded, but had to insert a tube into his windpipe. "He couldn't talk," said Dr. Scot Linscott of Virginia Mason Hospital, "but he motioned for a piece of paper and a pencil. He wrote that he wanted to know what the Sonics' score was. This was from a guy that had been dead. Then he pleaded (in another note) with the nurses to let him watch the rest of the game on television. They were hesitant, but the guy kept pleading. Finally, the nurses let him watch the game. The man was reported to be resting comfortably—after the Sonics won.

Because the series was played in a bizarre 1-2-2-1-1 format, the next two games were played on the Bullets' home court at the Capital Centre in Landover, Maryland. In game two, Elvin Hayes and Bob Dandridge combined for 59 points and the Bullets won easily 106-98. The win was especially important for the Bullets, who had lost a record nine straight Finals games after being swept in their previous two appearances (plus the loss to the Sonics in Game 1). Game three was a defensive battle, led by point guard Dennis Johnson blocking seven shots and Paul Silas grabbing fourteen boards. The Sonics had six players in double digits, and they won 93-92 to give them a 2-1 series lead.

In game four, Seattle's past futility came back to bite the Sonics in the form of one of the most unique scheduling conflicts and game situations in NBA history, let alone NBA Finals history. To illustrate the point, imagine a scenario where, let's say the home of the Dallas Mavericks, the American Airlines Center, was so confident the Mavericks wouldn't be in the Finals that they scheduled another event on one of the NBA Finals potential game dates prior to the season. Now fast forward through the season, and perhaps the Mavs miraculously make the Finals behind Luka Doncic, but because the arena is booked for Game 4's home date they have to go play the game at AT&T Stadium. That's basically what happened to the Sonics in 1978. The schedulers at the Seattle Center Coliseum gave the date of Game 4 to a mobile home expo, so rather than play in the arena where they'd won 21 straight games the Sonics were hosting Game 4 at the Seattle Kingdome (the new home of the Seahawks and the Mariners), where, as fate would have it, they were planning to permanently move the following year.

"I believe in our home court advantage," Dennis Johnson said. "We're tough at home. I'm pretty sure we're going to end the series in Seattle."

"You can't say we're unbeatable," Marvin Webster added. "But we feel we're going to wrap it up at home."

Regarding playing in the Kingdome, Wilkens made sure that it "felt" as much like the Coliseum as possible. "Every court is the same," he said. "We'll actually be using the same floor we normally use. But instead of having 14,000 fans screaming for us, we'll have 40,000. Tell me that's not going to get a team up."

When the Sonics announced the game's location at the Kingdome and opened up ticket sales, they sold 29,000 tickets inside of two hours. Remember, this was before StubHub or Ticketmaster or SeatGeek, where you can just tap open an app on your smartphone and see if tickets are available. In order to sell 29,000 tickets inside of 120 minutes back in 1978, hundreds of thousands of people had to jump on the phone, call the box office, and hope someone picked up who could process their order and mail them the tickets. The demand outpaced the supply by about a hundred to one. To try and pack as many people into the stadium as possible, the franchise made an additional 15,000 seats available for $3 and called them "distant viewing" seats. These were nosebleeds even for a football game, so they were in another zip code for a basketball game. The goal, aside from winning the game, was to shatter the attendance record for an NBA game. At the time, Cleveland held the record for an NBA playoff game at 21,564 fans, and the regular season record was 35,077 for a game at the Louisiana Superdome. However, these records all depend on if you include a rare double header in the Houston Astrodome in 1969, which saw a total of 41,165 people attend.

"I think it's going to be fantastic playing before 40,000 or more," Seattle forward Jack Johnson said. "We're going to be up for this one."

A few members of the media suggested that the game was more of a neutral site, since the Sonics weren't able to technically be on their home floor, but Bullets Coach Dick Motta called BS. "I don't see how anything in Seattle can be considered neutral," he said.

The obvious game plan inside the Sonics' locker room was to sweep the two games in Seattle and win their first title at home. The idea of flying all the way back across the country after a split—or worse, back-to-back losses—put a pit in the bottoms of their stomachs. Nobody in the league had ever been through what they had as a team. In November they were as dead as the turkeys being served for Thanksgiving. They were dismissed and disrespected, and they had to fire their coach. Now, here they were, two home wins from the franchise's first ever title. *They could taste it.*

"I've seen a lot of things happen with this club," Freddie Brown said, reminiscing about his tenure with the franchise. "There were times I felt we would never have a winner here. Now that it's within reach, I want it. I feel this deeply, very deeply. What I do individually doesn't matter. I could shoot 0-for-10, 0-for-20, I wouldn't care as long as we won. We're on the verge of making history here. The Seattle SuperSonics—NBA champions. Winning is something everyone is going to enjoy."

In the end, 39,457 Sonics fans crammed into the Kingdome to watch their team handle the Bullets fairly easy for three quarters. Dennis Johnson was having an all-time great Finals performance and it looked like 40,000 people were about to have the biggest party in Seattle sports history. Then DJ took a shot to the ribs and had to leave the game for a bit—and the Bullets pounced, charging all the way to a 103-101 lead with three minutes to go. In what should have been remembered as a return for the ages, Johnson came back to the game, instantly hit a shot to tie it up, then blocked a shot, grabbed a board and hit a foul shot to put his team up 104-103. Dandridge then converted on a three-point play to put the Bullets up by two points before old faithful Freddie Brown hit a jumper to tie it back up. After a few missed shots, the game went into overtime, where instant Washington legend Charles Johnson hit three buckets to put the game out of reach. The Sonics lost. The series was tied 2-2.

By now you know this particular Sonics team would never let a single deflating loss derail their dreams. They bounced back solidly in game five with a combined 50 points from Dennis Johnson and Freddie Brown and won 98-94 while staying in the driver's seat the entire time. Next came the 2,750-mile trip back to Maryland with a 3-2 series lead. All they had to do was win one of the next two games. They could win on the road or win at home. It didn't matter. They just needed one. And they all believed they'd get it in game six.

But in the words of college football's legendary analyst Lee Corso, the Bullets said, "Not so fast, my friend." They blew the doors off the Sonics in game six, 117-82. Elvin Hayes, Wes Unseld and Greg Ballard combined for 41 rebounds and the Sonics, despite leading after the first quarter, couldn't get anything going, so it was back to Seattle for a game seven.

Elvin Hayes hoped the knockout punches they threw in Maryland would stay in the minds of the Sonics players when they returned to the west coast on their long, frustrating flight. "Losing the way they did has got to be in their minds," he said. "It's going to be very difficult for them to shake it so quickly."

"It's easy to snap out of a game like this," Wilkens countered. "Our players have pride. They didn't like what happened and it won't happen again."

There was no reason for a prolonged back and forth. Forty-eight hours later, at 6 PM on June 2, 1978, with the entire sports world watching, we'd find out whether Wilkens or Hayes was right. Could the Sonics shake off the blowout and bring it home for their fans, or would the pressure be too great?

Despite playing at a near hall of fame level for the entire series to that point, guard Dennis Johnson tightened up and had a disastrous outing, missing all fourteen of his shots. Gus Williams felt the stress as well. He hit only four of twelve shots, meaning the star guards shot a combined 4-for-26 from the floor in the biggest game of their lives. Freddie Brown was his usual spectacular self, shooting 50% from the floor and scoring 21 points. The two bright spots were rookie Jack Sikma, who dropped in 21 points and grabbed 11 boards, and Marvin Webster, who had a monster game with 27 points and 19 rebounds. We're leading with the positive for Seattle fans here because, despite these three strong efforts, the Bullets took the lead in the first quarter and held on like a boa constrictor slowly and methodically choking out its prey. They were up three after one quarter, up eight after two, up thirteen after three and, despite some tough play by Silas and some clutch shots from Brown and Webster, the Bullets held off the Sonics on their home floor and won the 1978 NBA Championship by a score of 105-99 in game seven.

Pick your analogy: Gut punch. Groin kick. Sucker punch. Body blow. All of them apply. The Sonics players, and their fans, were devastated.

"No one except those involved knew how far we came," Wilkens said after the loss, trying to frame the season. "A lot of the people around the country looked past us, even when we were winning. We proved to them we are a good ball club."

"There's no reason for anybody to hang their heads," Gus Williams said. "We had a great season. One we can be proud of."

Of that there was no doubt. When the team returned home the following Thursday, thousands of fans greeted them downtown to show love and pay respect. The loss, as much as it hurt, still capped off the most successful season the franchise, and the city, had ever had on a basketball court. Not only that, the team was young and had been improving all season. Johnson, Sikma, Webster, Williams…these guys were just getting started. When the emotion and sadness of the loss faded into the offseason and the fans and players had time to process it, they all came to the same realization: *There's no reason we shouldn't be back in the Finals next year.*

Chapter 6

"Downtown" Freddie Brown, the Wichert Wonder, and DJ Deliver

Twenty-two-year-old Jack Sikma sat at a table with his coach Dennie Bridges, holding a few playing cards. Sikma was nearly seven feet tall, platinum blond and lanky. Bridges stood about chest-high to Sikma, had a broad smile with narrow eyes and looked like every dad in every 1960s black-and-white television show. They were at Bridges' house along with a handful of Sikma's close family and friends. Neither Sikma nor Bridges was paying attention to the hands they were dealt. Sikma was fidgeting. Bridges was fidgeting. They were trying to pass the time with the cards and some small talk, but it wasn't working. Time wasn't passing. It was frozen solid.

The phone should have rung by now. Something must be wrong. What was happening?

It was June 10, 1977 and the two had come a long way since Bridges, the head coach of Illinois-Wesleyan University's men's basketball team, first laid eyes on Sikma five years earlier. Sikma was a senior at St. Anne High School in Kankakee County, Illinois, and as Bridges described him in his book *A Dunk Only Counts Two Points,* "Jack was as tall as I'd heard he was, and actually looked maybe taller than 6-foot-9 because he definitely was as skinny as I'd heard. He looked a little like the Dutch Boy on the wrapper of the paint can with a mop of floppy blond hair. The next morning when I got to my office, I told Coach [Jack] Horenberger about seeing Jack play. I told him that if I could recruit Jack that 'he would be the greatest player in Illinois-Wesleyan history.'"

Although Sikma was recruited by much bigger schools after scoring 100 points during St. Anne's playoff run, he chose to sign with Bridges because he promised him a starting job as a freshman. "In recruiting me, Coach said that the issue of me being seen and recognized was not going to be a problem, and I agreed with him there," Sikma said in an interview with his alma mater. "Back then you could schedule majors a lot more easily, so we played a lot of the major schools in the area. We usually took a trip over Christmas break and played a couple majors then as well… I was a late bloomer and I wanted to play right away. I knew I was going to get a chance to get on the floor and play, and the competition in that league was pretty good. There were some good players there, so early in my career, the fact that I got to play was a big plus. As time went on and I became more recognized, things opened up for me even though I played ball [at a smaller school]."

The recognition came from leading his team to three straight conference championships and totaling more than 2,200 points and 1,400 rebounds while playing for IWU. In fact, it was Bridges who helped Sikma develop his patented "Sikma Move" that served him so well throughout his college and pro careers. The move was a quick reverse pivot away from the basket with the ball already up and in shooting position. It was kind of like an inverse fadeaway. It was an awkward move, but Bridges stayed with Sikma after every practice and made him take 100 shots from each side of the basket until the move was fluid...and unstoppable. By the time the '77 NBA Draft rolled around, Sikma was on several teams' radars. Unlike today, there were no trips to New York City for his selection. No wearing a goofy suit. No meeting the commissioner. Back then you gathered with your friends and family at your house or your coach's house and you waited for a call. Again, there were no smartphones and Google and Twitter and texting weren't invented yet. The exact way that Sikma was going to find out when, or if, he got drafted was as follows:

Illinois-Wesleyan's sports information director, Ed Alsene, spent the evening of the draft at the publishing office of the local newspaper so he could follow the draft selections on the Associated Press newswire. The plan was for him to call Bridges' home after every pick. He called after the number one overall pick, Kent Benson, went to Milwaukee. He called after the Kansas City Kings selected Otis Birdsong. He called after Marques Johnson was taken. And then he stopped calling. First, ten minutes passed. Then twenty. Then thirty. Nothing. Bridges' nerves finally got the best of him and he put down the cards and called the newspaper office.

Did Sikma drop out of the first round? What the hell was going on?

Actually, nothing like that at all. The AP wire had simply gone down. At first, relief, then back to anxiety. They still didn't know if Sikma had been taken.

"I don't know if it was forty-five minutes, an hour, maybe an hour and a half later. It was probably forty-five minutes. It seemed like it was a couple hours. The AP wire came back up and I had been drafted," Sikma recalled.

The Seattle SuperSonics selected him with the eighth overall pick in the draft. Lenny Wilkens (the director of player personnel prior to taking over as head coach later that year) had seen Sikma play in the NAIA tournament and was convinced he'd be a great pro. When he called Jack to tell him the news officially, Sikma was brutally honest about going to the (then) down-and-out Sonics. "Well, it's not my first choice," he replied to Wilkens when asked if he was excited to be in Seattle.

On the other side of the coin, the questions Sonics fans had about Sikma were: *Who is this guy? He played where? He's supposed to replace Spencer Haywood? Come on!*

"Seattle took some flak for taking me that early," Sikma recalled. "It was a bit of a surprise."

And yet, inside of twelve months, Sikma would be the second-best player on the Sonics and starring in game seven of an NBA Finals as a rookie. After that crushing loss, one comforting factor for both the Sonics franchise and their fans was the idea that Sikma was just scratching the surface of his potential. He was likely going to be even better in the 1978-79 season. There was reason to believe.

***

Along with Sikma, the other breakout star of the miracle '77-'78 run was Dennis Johnson, who was drafted one year earlier and remarkably had an even more unlikely road to the NBA than a seven-foot Dutchman from a Division III school. Johnson was born in Compton, California as the eighth of sixteen children. His dad was a bricklayer; his mom was a social worker. Neither were great basketball players. By now we're all familiar with the story that Michael Jordan was cut from his high school basketball team, but Johnson can do that about three times better. He was cut from his seventh- and eighth-grade teams. He barely made the varsity squad as a junior and senior at Manuel Dominguez High School and he rode the bench nearly the entire time. In his own words, he played "maybe a minute or two each game." He stood 5'9" his senior year and had just about the same chance of playing ball in college as the average high school benchwarmer whose only time on the floor was during mop-up duty and blowouts. Which is to say, he had zero chance.

After Johnson graduated from high school he took a job as a forklift driver for $2.75 an hour. Deep inside, he still dreamed of playing basketball in college. When he laid in bed at night, like millions of other kids who were too short or too slow or just not talented enough, he thought about what it would be like to play in the NBA. In his mind, the only way the dream would die is if he stopped playing basketball—so he kept playing. After eight-hour days on the forklift, he'd take a bus to the courts to play in Summer League games with his brothers. He held his own. Always. Even when he was fighting for his measly two minutes a game in high school, he was a gamer. Tough. Scrappy. Overly confident.

As that first summer wore on and he continued to play into the fall and winter, Johnson grew. And grew. Before he knew it, he was standing nearly 6'3" with muscles on his frame and what some of the guys he played with dubbed "rocket launcher" legs. Now Johnson isn't holding his own anymore—he's dominating. One day Jim White, the coach of Harbor Junior College in Los Angeles, spotted Johnson on a playground court and asked him to enroll, which Johnson happily did. Two years later he averaged 18.3 points and 12 rebounds per game and led Harbor to a state junior college championship. His performance got him noticed by a few local Southern California schools, and Pepperdine University in Malibu offered him a scholarship.

In Johnson's only season with the Wave, he averaged over 15 points per game, played voracious defense, had the team ranked in the top 20, and led them into the NCAA tournament for the first time in fourteen years. They beat Memphis in round one and then gave UCLA all they could handle in round two before losing. It was an astonishing rise for a kid who had been seven inches shorter and working construction just three years earlier. But Johnson's basketball story was still being written. In a move that shocked even him, the Seattle SuperSonics selected him 29th overall in the second round of the 1976 NBA Draft and offered him a four-year deal. During his rookie year (Bill Russell's last), he backed up Slick Watts and Freddie Brown and didn't see much playing time. The same pattern continued under Bob Hopkins in the '77 season, until Hopkins was fired. When Wilkens took over, he gave "DJ" more and more playing time, and we already covered how that turned out for the miracle '77-'78 season. Like Sikma, the Seattle faithful believed that Johnson could only get better, which meant the team could only get better too. As the wounds from the crushing game seven loss to the Bullets healed, a sense of optimism hung around the franchise.

***

If you were a die-hard Seattle sports fan at the start of the 1978-79 season and you wanted to lay down a bet on one of your teams to win a title that year, the only reasonable wager you could make was on the Sonics. The Seahawks, led by the arm of quarterback Jim Zorn (who threw 15 touchdowns and 20 interceptions) and the legs of running backs David Sims and Sherman Smith, went a respectable 9-7 in 1978 but were still far from being Super Bowl contenders. The fledgling Mariners completed their second season in 1978 and lost 104 games, good for seventh place in a seven-team league and a spot 35 games out of first place. That meant that the Emerald City's hopes and dreams for a professional sports championship were still firmly placed on the Sonics' shoulders, as they should have been. The team had nearly every important piece from the previous year's Finals run returning: Sikma, Johnson, John Johnson, Gus Williams, Freddie Brown and Paul Silas all came back. The only major contributor the team lost was the Human Eraser, Marvin Webster, who became a free agent and signed a $3 million deal with the New York Knicks.

Lenny Wilkens, who most people forgot was just an "interim coach" when he took over, signed a three-year deal to remain the head coach, and also to stay on as director of player personnel for another two. Sam Schulman was "very excited" to sign Wilkens and said, "his story last year was like a Cinderella story that I'm sure will be told for many years to come!" Wilkens was energized too, but he knew all too well the heavy expectations that lay ahead for his team and he didn't want to feed into those, so he opted for mostly humble responses. "I'm happy to be part of this organization," he said. "If we can stay healthy we should have another fine season." If by "fine season" he meant "win a championship," then yes, he was dead on about what most people in Seattle were expecting. After all, the gang was back together and the sky was the limit.

The only major change heading into the season involved the team's address. They were saying goodbye to the Seattle Center Coliseum and moving into the "King County Multipurpose Domed Stadium," mercifully shortened to "Kingdome." Whereas the Sonics regularly drew around 12,000 fans per game at the Coliseum, the Kingdome could hold 40,000-plus for basketball, and the team expected to top at least 18,000 per game with the success carrying over from the previous season. All the Sonics had to do was win.

***

In almost every way the beginning of the Sonics' 1978-79 campaign was the exact opposite of the previous year. Long gone were the endless losing streaks and the overwhelming negativity and the feckless coach and the 5-17 start. Instead, this season saw a string of winning streaks with excellent camaraderie and positivity, led by a confident coach, and a 17-6 start en route to a 34-16 record at the all-star break. Rather than having no all-stars in the game like the previous year, in 1979 the Sonics had two, Jack Sikma and Dennis Johnson, who went a combined 9-12 from the floor in the game and scored 20 points off the bench. Johnson ended up playing the third-most minutes in the game for the Western Conference behind David Thompson and Kareem Abdul-Jabbar. After the break, the Sonics wobbled for a brief moment, losing nine of twelve before righting the ship and finishing 14-4 for a final regular season record of 52-30 and first place in the Pacific Division. All in all, aside from losing Tom LaGarde to an injury, the season had largely been a breeze, with the Sonics locking up a first-round bye and the number one seed in the West.

Their first real test of the year was slated to come against the Los Angeles Lakers in the Western Conference semifinals. The Lakers had just beaten the Nuggets in the first round, 2-1, and the NBA media was hyping the series as a sort of Ali vs. Frazier title bout between the star centers, Abdul-Jabbar and Sikma.

"Sikma, Kareem to Do Battle" the AP headline blared before game one.

"We have to be ready for him…because he's coming," Silas said of Abdul-Jabbar, as if he was a bad guy set on revenge in a Bond movie.

The pole position of first place was new territory for the Sonics, and they basically had a week off while the first round played out. They scrimmaged and practiced endlessly to keep their edge, but nobody knew how the layoff would affect the team. "We haven't been in the physical aspect of it for a week," Dennis Johnson said before game one against the Lakers. "Their adrenaline will still be flowing." Paul Silas agreed. "We have been off eight or nine days now and they have been playing. They will be a lot [fresher] competition-wise than us."

The Lakers' Norm Nixon went with the Schadenfreude approach, saying, "Usually, when we have a layoff, we have a slow start afterwards. I hope that happens to them."

Coach Wilkens just wanted to get the series underway. "We've had enough of each other," he said, referring to the scrimmages. "We're ready for someone else." At the end of the day, the coach was right: They were ready, and the Lakers really never stood a chance. The Sonics took game one easily with 72 combined points from Gus Williams, Dennis Johnson and Sikma. Then they won game two with 38 points from Williams and a near triple-double (10-8-10) from Sikma. Abdul-Jabbar put the team on his back with 32 points when the series returned to Los Angeles for game three, and the Lakers were finally victorious, 118-112. That was the only game they'd win the entire series.

Seattle won game four with three players scoring twenty-plus points (Williams, John Johnson, Dennis Johnson) and won game five to seal the deal behind another 30-point effort from Williams. *Los Angeles Times* staff writer Ted Green perfectly summed up the final game and the series in his morning-after wrap-up, writing, "The Seattle SuperSonics did not let their guard down Wednesday night. Nor did their guards let them down. And that, in a nutshell, was their series against the Lakers. With Fred Brown and Dick Snyder, a couple of cagey, old guards, complementing Gus Williams and Dennis Johnson, the young colts who killed the Lakers throughout, Seattle won Game 5 106-100 to take the Western Conference Semifinal series 4-1, and end the Los Angeles season on the same court where it ended in the first round a year ago."

The win set up a Western Conference Finals against the 50-32 Phoenix

Suns, who were led by Paul Westphal, Walter Davis, Alvan Adams, Don Buse and Truck Robinson. The Suns were the second-highest scoring team in the NBA, averaging 115.4 points per game, and they were almost unbeatable at home with a 32-9 record at the Arizona Veterans Memorial Coliseum. Heading into the playoffs, they'd lost only two games on their home floor since January.

Lenny Wilkens and his boys were unfazed. They won games one and two by a combined 21 points and appeared to be in complete control of the series. Spoiler alert: They weren't.

***

During a hard-fought playoff series in 1970 between Los Angeles and Phoenix, legendary Lakers broadcaster Chick Hearn nicknamed the Arizona Veterans Memorial Coliseum the "The Madhouse on McDowell," combining the intensity of the Suns' die-hard fans with the street where the building resided. Nine years later, as the Suns returned home down 0-2, the madhouse was about to turn into a house of horrors for the Sonics. Underneath the occasionally leaky and ominously looming tension-cable roof, game three of the series got underway on May 6, 1979, and through the first half the series seemed to be going as it had the first two games. The Sonics were up 61-60 and all was relatively well from their perspective. In fact, things seemed to be downright rosy. One of the Suns' best players, Alvan Adams, the man responsible for guarding Jack Sikma, went down with an ankle injury and couldn't return. Joel Kramer, a 6'7" rookie out of San Diego State, was suddenly given the task of trying to contain Sikma, despite giving up five inches in height and about ten feet in talent. This was the kind of mismatch that championship teams exploit, and to Seattle fans, it seemed like the perfect time to feed Sikma, step on the gas and put the series away quickly. The opposite happened.

In an odd twist, Kramer, who over the course of his five-year NBA career would barely average 4 points and 3 rebounds a game, used his main (only) attribute, his physicality, to his advantage and squirrelled his way into Sikma's head with a barrage of herky-jerky arms, elbows, chest bumps, hip shoves and every other erratic movement he could think of. He was like a younger brother in a driveway using sheer annoyance and borderline fouls to get his big brother flustered. But it worked. Just like some boxing matches are wholly about style, Kramer's style, or lack thereof, completely and totally threw Sikma off his game. First, he missed one shot, then another, then his entire rhythm went to hell and the whole team seemed out of sync. The Suns went up eight after the third quarter and never looked back, winning the game 113-103.

"I just tried to crowd him [Sikma] as much as I could," Kramer said after the game, suddenly finding himself the center of attention. "I bumped him a little—not enough for a foul—but enough to give him some trouble and maybe knock him off balance."

Despite the effort he gave as a substitute, even Kramer's own teammate, Truck Robinson, acknowledged that Kramer likely stood no chance against Sikma once the series resumed in a few nights. "Joel is really overmatched with Sikma," Robinson said. "I'm sure Sikma is going to see the ball a lot Tuesday night."

So, Tuesday night came, and Sikma did see the ball a lot, but the ball didn't see a lot of the net. For the second time in as many games, the man who was known as the "Wichert Wonder" was left wondering what in the world had happened to his offense. In game three Kramer was absolutely stifling, holding Sikma to just two baskets in the entire game, despite him taking thirteen shots. His shooting percentage, which had hovered near 50% for the much of the season, had plummeted to 15% and dragged the Sonics' offense down with it. Almost the entire team struggled, and for the first time in the series they didn't break 100 points, losing 100-91 and finding the series tied 2-2.

Surely the performance by Sikma in game four was a fluke and he, along with his teammates, would bounce back from two disappointing losses with a little game-five home cooking back at the Kingdome with 28,000 of their closest friends cheering them on. They had to. The alternative was frankly unthinkable. There was simply no way the Sonics were going to go from being up 2-0 to down 2-3 after how easily they dispatched the Lakers and then the Suns in the first two games. That is, unless Kramer truly was kryptonite to Sikma's Superman, which appeared to be the case, because in game five bizarro Jack was still on the floor, shooting a measly 23% and hitting only three of thirteen shots. The rest of the Sonics played ably for the first half, ending the second quarter with a lead before falling apart in the fourth quarter and giving up 33 points, and the game, to the Suns.

With the series headed back to the madhouse, and the Sonics now one game away from elimination, it was, officially, time to be concerned.

"Right now we've got our backs against the wall," Wilkens said. "We've got to go down to Phoenix and win."

Wally Walker, a reserve small forward who would one day become the Sonics' president and general manager, could not believe what he was witnessing. "You lose game five at home and you're like, 'Really?'" Walker said. "But I don't remember any sense of panic or anything. We were a calm team, and Lenny (Wilkens) was a calm coach. But obviously there was lots to worry about. The odds weren't good for us." Forget odds that "weren't good" for the Sonics—they were historically bad. To that point, teams that were up 2-0 had a 262-20 playoff record. Not only were the Sonics on the verge of joining those twenty sad teams but they had just lost game five to go down 3-2. Teams that won game five in best-of-seven series in the NBA playoffs typically had an 83% chance of winning. The number represented a disastrous swing. In about six days the Sonics went from 90% favorites to win the series all the way down to 17%. Ouch. Add in the fact that Phoenix had won sixteen straight home games, and a statistician could argue that the Sonics were dead men walking from the moment they deplaned in the desert. Even their hometown paper, the *Seattle Times*, sounded grim in its game day assessment of the match-up: "A near miracle is necessary today to avoid the end."

Walker wasn't sure about a miracle or how to manifest one, but in the locker room before the game he witnessed 35-year-old veteran Paul Silas mentally preparing for war. Silas was battle-hardened, having gone through playoff campaigns with St. Louis, the Celtics and this Seattle team. He knew what was going to be needed that night as he sat in his locker clenching and unclenching his fists, channeling a reserve of energy he knew the team would need.

"I still have this visual of him in the locker room," Walker said. "He was just kind of sitting in this chair in the middle—the locker rooms were tiny in those days—and he's not saying a word, but he's breathing audibly, his eyes are blood shot and he's just doing this thing with his hands. He used to use Stickum, which wasn't legal, but he hid it under his wrist. So he had his hands going, breathing heavily. And the rest of us were kind of looking around like, *OK, this is what intensity looks like when you are getting ready for an elimination game.* There is a guy who has been there, has won championships. I think it had a big impact on everybody like, *OK, get yourself ready because here is what needs to get done, and this is how you do it*."

To borrow a line from *The Usual Suspects*, Silas was about to show men of will what will really was. He played thirty minutes that night and attacked the basket, tying the team lead in free throws with eight. He scored 10 points to go along with 9 rebounds in an attempt to pace his teammates, and it worked... for a bit. Seattle went into the half up 55-50 and came out for the third quarter full of confidence—a confidence that was quickly shattered. Paul Westphal and Walter Davis had been rolling all night and were on their way to combining for almost 60 points, and they got particularly hot to start the second half. Before the Sonics knew it, the Suns had 35 points in the third quarter and went up eight with only fifteen minutes left in the game.

On the bench before the start of the fourth, Coach Wilkens told his team to keep attacking the boards and to keep pushing. Freddie Brown, who had been through every single up and down with the franchise, implored his teammates, "Let's go right at them." Dennis Johnson refused to contemplate losing. His mindset was, "We have to win. We're not going home losers."

One positive they had going for them was that, over the previous three quarters, Sikma had finally solved the Kramer conundrum and was back to having one of his typically strong games. Entering the fourth quarter, he was getting to the line regularly, hitting his signature shot and pulling defenders to him. Most importantly, along with Silas and Lonnie Shelton, he crashed the boards to give his team second chances and take them away from the Suns. They outrebounded the Suns 11-5 in the fourth and held them to 28% shooting. By the time there was 1:22 left, Gus Williams calmly hit two free throws to put the Sonics within one point, 105-104. On the very next possession, after a Suns turnover, Williams sank a clutch 18-footer to give the Sonics their first lead of the fourth quarter, 106-105, with less than one minute left. After the teams traded missed shots, the Suns wound up with the ball and sixteen seconds left to win the game. The ball went to Walter Davis, who was immediately smothered by Lonnie Shelton. Davis got the shot off practically sandwiched by Sonics and missed. In a scrum for the rebound the ball skimmed off Sikma's hand, giving the Suns possession of the ball with one second left—just enough time for a final shot to sink the Sonics' season and save their own.

Don Buse was in charge of inbounding the ball, and the number one and number two options on the play were Westphal or Davis, but both were covered. With time ticking down and his teammates scrambling all over the court, Buse hit Gar Heard, who somehow broke open. Sikma stretched every cell in his body to alter the shot, and from the second it left Heard's hand nearly everyone in the arena thought it was going in—especially the Sonics. "I contested it, but you just never know," Sikma said. "I thought it was good," Silas said.

Time stretched like silly putty as the ball slowly made its way to the hoop and the sold-out crowd stood up and watched every rotation as if it was in the Matrix. At the end of its arc, the ball bounced off the rim and the audible "Ooooohhhhhhhh!!!!" of Suns fans echoed throughout the cavernous madhouse.

"When it went over the basket, I was the happiest man in the world," Silas said.

The Sonics and Suns were headed back to Seattle.

***

"Freeze your teeth and give your tongue a sleigh ride!"

This was the signature call (bellow, actually) of the most famous beer vendor in all of sports. His name was, fittingly, Bill the Beerman (Bill Scott) and he checked all the boxes of what a man who cheerfully and loudly sold beer at sporting events should look like. He had an absolute keg of a chest; burly forearms; a thick, heavy beard; a full face; a big mouth with a giant smile; and loose, floppy hair that unfurled from his classic, eight-inch tall hat that read *$1.25 COLD BEER* in big block letters. Bill the Beerman was a staple at the Kingdome from the late seventies all the way into the nineties, and he went to the arena to do two things: sell beer and lead cheers. By the end of the Sonics' first season in the Kingdome, the building had gained the reputation as the noisiest arena in basketball, and possibly all of sports. This achievement was due in no small part to the Beerman, who often whipped the crowd into a frenzy with his cheers and by using his self-described skill as a "synergy facilitator."

When the Sonics returned home for game seven against the Suns, the loud, boisterous Kingdome was packed with 37,552 fans, the second-largest crowd ever to watch a playoff basketball game. The sheer number of fans and the sound they were capable of making seemed to swing the momentum in the favor of the Sonics during warm-ups. When the game got set for the opening tip and Jack Sikma lined up opposite Alvan Adams on the forest green Kingdome logo at center court, the floor was practically vibrating from the yelling. As Sikma got ready for the official to toss up the ball, his long, lanky right leg seemed to jackhammer against the ground, feeding off the energy the crowd was infusing into the court. After a high-scoring first quarter that ended with the Sonics down one, Sikma, Dennis Johnson and Gus Williams took over the game. The three-headed monster joined forces for 88 points, 5 blocks, 7 assists and 23 rebounds. Sikma led the way with a relentless effort under the basket, sinking shots and drawing fouls on his way to a career-high 33 points and 11 boards. After trailing in the first quarter, the Sonics cruised to a 100-85 lead with just six minutes left in the game, at which point they made the mistake of trying to milk the clock and slow the game down. The Suns hit a few shots and then went on an 8-0 run to cut the Sonics' lead to 105-101 with two minutes to go. The atmosphere in the Kingdome went from frenetic to frantic in what felt like no time at all. *Were they going to blow a 15-point fourth quarter lead? At home? In game seven?*

Not if the kid who was 5'9" as a senior in high school and played "barely a few minutes a game" had anything to say about it. Pressure wasn't being up four in a game seven; pressure was driving a forklift at the age of 18 and wondering whether this was going to be the job you'd have for the rest of your life. So, when the Suns started fouling Dennis Johnson to stop the clock and see if he'd have any nerves on the foul line, well, they were fouling the wrong guy. He sank seven straight free throws to put his team up 112-104. The Suns kept charging but it was too little, too late, and the Sonics held them off for a final score of 114-110 to earn a second trip to the Finals.

"Wow, what a nightmare that would have been if we lost it," Sikma said after the game. "I think we can win the NBA championship. I thought we could win it last year. I think these last two games may spur us on and carry us over the hump in the Finals."

In the locker room, Dennis Johnson, quickly becoming one of the most clutch, pressure players in the NBA, raised a glass and toasted, "For all those who thought we couldn't make it!"

Well, they made it. Now they had one more mission to complete: to take home the title against the team that took it from them the year before, the Washington Bullets.

***

Elvin Hayes was ready to defend his title. So were Bobby Dandridge and Wes Unseld and Kevin Grevey. As far as the Bullets were concerned, they'd beaten the Sonics once in the Finals already, so there was no reason they wouldn't do it again. And this time, they had home court advantage and the series would be starting at the Capital Centre in Maryland.

"Seattle wants us because of last year," Grevey said. "But we'll just have to be sure to play our game."

The Bullets' game was based on one thing: physicality. Their goal was to bully you, push you, and wear you down and grind you up so that by the time the fourth quarter hit you were either already behind or didn't have the energy to stay ahead. They were a lineup of bruisers, and from Coach Dick Motta's perspective, when his men squared off against the Sonics they were looking at another team full of guys who wouldn't feel out of place in a boxing ring. "If this isn't the most physical series in NBA playoff history I'll be surprised," he said. "Compared to last year, Seattle is more physical, and that's our best game too. They don't have that shot blocker they had last year in Webster, but they're more muscular."

In game one, the added muscles didn't matter because the Sonics were almost run off the floor. They were down nine points at the half and then trailed 91-73 early in the fourth quarter. Just like in game one of the Finals the year before, they were able to stage a comeback, but unlike in that game (in which they came back to win from down nineteen), they fell short this time. Despite scoring 23 points on 20 Washington turnovers, they lost 99-97. Seattle then won a defensive battle in game two, 92-82, to get the split and head home to the Kingdome.

Games three and four were the Gus Williams, Dennis Johnson and Jack Sikma shows, with Williams and Johnson each putting on scoring displays and vying for series MVP. In game three Gus Williams had 33 while Johnson just missed a triple-double with 17 points, 9 rebounds and 9 assists. Sikma went for 21 and 17 and the Sonics won easily. In game four, Williams scored 36 and Johnson scored 32, but added 4 blocks and 10 rebounds to go along with it. The Sonics won both games to give them a 3-1 lead as they headed back to Baltimore for Game 5.

If ever a kids book were to be written about the 1979 Sonics season, a potential title could be *Sikma and the Great Guards*, because in games two through five, they were the story every single night. Yes, "Downtown" Freddie Brown was still a stellar shooter and pitched in 12 or 14 or 16 nightly off the bench, and yes, Lonnie Shelton and John Johnson gave the team the defensive toughness they needed to shut down other team's frontcourts. And of course Paul Silas was the guts and grit of the whole operation, but when it came to the players the Bullets had no answers for, it was Sikma and the great guards, Dennis Johnson and Gus Williams. Or Gus Williams and Dennis Johnson, depending on whom you felt was the headliner on a given night.

In game five, DJ had 21 points, 4 rebounds, 5 assists, 2 steals and a block. Gus had 23 points and 3 steals. Sikma had 12 points and 17 rebounds. The game was close through three quarters, and Washington even led 69-66 going into the fourth, but Sikma scored six straight after the whistle. When the game got tight, as per the new normal, DJ hit a shot, then Williams hit a shot, then Williams sank a few free throws down the stretch.

As the night unfolded, fans all over Seattle were beginning to realize that they might actually have a title in their grasp. A waiter at a popular Seattle restaurant said, "Fans screamed constantly until the end of the game. I think they drink much more when they're winning." In the state's capital of Olympia, a special night legislative meeting had been scheduled to put important matters of state to bed before the end of their session. Whatever those "matters" were, however, they weren't nearly as important as the Sonics being on the cusp of a championship, so they were put off for several hours while the politicians watched the game. At the Sonics' home building, the Kingdome, about 4,000 fans were in attendance to watch the Seattle Mariners beat the Toronto Blue Jays, but by far the loudest cheers of the night came when the stadium cut into the action to show the final fourteen seconds of the Sonics game. As the clock wound down to 0:00 and the final score read 97-93 and the reality sunk in that the once-lowly Sonics had finally won a championship for the city of Seattle, bedlam struck the town.

Cars clogged every major intersection as fans got out to celebrate all over downtown. Emerald City citizens let off fireworks and danced and cheered in the streets. Kurtis Mitchell, who was 26 at the time, screamed, "I knew they were going to do it tonight!" and danced between cars, kickstarting a celebration wearing nothing but green shorts and running shoes. Everywhere you looked, from First Avenue to Fifth, from Pioneer Square to Belltown and Cherry Hill, fans were going ballistic. In Pioneer Square fans flooded the streets, hugging each other and high-fiving and smashing beer cans together. Alcohol flowed in the streets and smiles spread across everyone's faces. A local auto parts chain spent $50,000 to print full-color posters that said, "Seattle SuperSonics – NBA World Champions" and paid a van to drive through the mayhem to pass them out to as many people as possible. It was glorious, and the party was just getting started.

Back in Maryland, the Sonics players themselves were relieved and elated and ecstatic. At the moment the buzzer sounded, Sonics assistant coach Les Habbeger jumped up and raised his arms in triumph. "Downtown" Freddie Brown pumped his fist and, in a photo captured a split second after the clock wound down, Dennis Johnson and his "rocket launcher" legs are caught about forty inches in the air in celebration.

"We were the Rodney Dangerfields of the NBA," John Johnson said afterward. "But if they don't respect us now, we don't care, because we're world champions. Even when we won fifty-two games in the regular season, nobody wanted to give us credit. But we climbed the mountain and we're at the top."

For many around the league, including the Sonics' own owner Sam Schulman, the title was proof that a team didn't need a "star system" with big-time free agents to win. "I was inexperienced when I got into basketball," he said. "This thing was a toy and an ego trip. I thought all it takes to win a championship was to go out and buy players. I found out that's not the way to do it. Sports is a business and that's how you have to attack it to make it go."

One of his key "business" decisions was putting Lenny Wilkens in charge, and in the moments after the game was over, the coach and one-time Sonics player was grinning ear to ear. "This is the most satisfying experience of my life," he said. "I think we proved with our players that we were fighting as a unit. We felt confident going in because no series like this is won by one man. It makes the thrill even greater to play, and beat, the Bullets, the defending NBA champs."

Forgotten amidst the storylines during the 1979 Finals was Dennis Johnson's game seven collapse in the 1978 Finals, a poor performance he rectified throughout the '79 playoffs, culminating with him winning the Finals MVP. "I never allowed myself to think about last year," he said. "But I do know I didn't go 0-14 this time. The future is now and our championship is now."

The hometown celebration, however, would have to wait a few days until the team returned to Seattle to attend their victory parade, which began promptly at noon on June 2. Over a quarter of a million people crammed themselves into every nook and cranny of downtown Seattle to get a glimpse of their new champions. Under a dark gray sky, the motorcade that featured all the coaches and players and Sam Schulman, and even Seattle's mayor, made its way to University Plaza, where there was a makeshift stage set up for Wilkens to accept a key to the city on behalf of the team and raise the trophy for all to see. In addition to the 250,000 fans cheering along the motorcade, another 100,000 were said to be in University Plaza itself. After Wilkens thanked his players and coaches and did the humble move of giving everyone else the credit, the old showman Sam Schulman took the microphone.

"They said that the celebration in Seattle was the greatest since World War II," he said, talking about the parties that broke out all over town the night the team won the title. "I am forever grateful to all of you. You are without a doubt the greatest sports fans in America. I said it twelve years ago. I'll say it today. God bless you all."

Representing the fans, Bill the Beerman even got his turn at the mic, booming, "The Sonics are more powerful than a locomotive, able to leap tall buildings in a single bound and faster than a whole crowd of speeding bullets!"

Every Sonics player had a chance to address the crowd, with each of them getting their own standing ovation, including role players like Dick Snyder, who, although he barely played, said, "I'm smiling. I'm going to be smiling for months."

Ultimately, it was team captain and Mr. Sonic himself, "Downtown" Freddie Brown, who stole the show. Brown had spent his entire career with the Sonics and was as much a part of all the downs as he now was with the ultimate "up." When it was his time to speak, he succinctly stated with a big smile on his face, "It's been a long time coming."

Chapter 7

Sam Schulman Has Left the Building

Here's a short story about how Butch Cassidy, Ferris Bueller and James Bond are to blame for Sam Schulman selling the SuperSonics in 1983:

Throughout the early 1980s the David Mamet screenplay for *The Verdict* was one of the hottest films in production in Hollywood. At first, Robert Redford was attached to star, but when he tried to find a new director behind the studio's back he was fired. Following that, every single big-name, middle age-ish actor was rumored for the movie: Frank Sinatra, Dustin Hoffman, Cary Grant, William Holden and Roy Scheider were all after the lead role, which ultimately went to Paul Newman, who nailed the part of Frank Galvin. The movie made $54 million (a lot for a drama in 1982) and was nominated for five Oscars. A year later, a movie inspired by the Cold War and Stephen Hawking and computers and hacking, starring Matthew Broderick and called *War Games*, was released. The movie was an immediate hit and turned Broderick into a star three years before *Ferris Bueller's Day Off*. What does any of this have to do with the city of Seattle or the Sonics?

Both of those films were financed by Sam Schulman, and their combined critical and box office success (over $120 million domestically) led Schulman to believe that if ever there was a time for him to take over Hollywood, this was it. He also had a financial interest in the 13th James Bond film, *Octopussy*, which grossed $187 million worldwide. Despite attending nearly every Sonics home game, Schulman still lived full time at his house in Beverly Hills and continued to be the chairman of two production companies in Los Angeles during his tenure as an NBA owner (the second longest tenure in the league at the time behind Franklin Mieuli of the Warriors).

"We have some tremendous plans for this business, which is going to consume tremendous amounts of my working time," he said. "If they materialize, we will become a tremendous factor in the movie business."

He'd been thinking about selling the team to focus on his Hollywood ventures, but even as the deal was being finalized, he admitted some regret. After all, he considered the 1979 championship to be "one of the major highlights of [his] life." When he spoke to the media to announce that the team was no longer his, he said, "Selling the Sonics has been, and is, a very traumatic thing for me. It's been part of my existence and life. Even the scotch I drank last night couldn't penetrate the separation trauma I felt... But I had to get rid of something to ease the onus and the workload."

As far as a financial and emotional investment, Schulman's stewardship of the team paid off. He was part of the group that bought the rights to the expansion team for $1.75 million in 1966 and seventeen years later was selling it for $21 million. Where there had been no major professional sports teams in Seattle and no early success, Schulman built a winner on the court and in the seats. Not only did the team win the title in '79, but the franchise set an NBA attendance record the next year, averaging 21,725 people per game during the 1979-80 season. The team, as he'd planned since day one, had woven its way into the hearts and minds of the city.

"I leave with some sense of enthusiasm and glory," Schulman said. "We showed the prudence and wisdom to start the first pro team in Seattle. As a result, the people now have the Dome and some other teams. I think I said Seattle was going to be a sports mecca per capita, and it's arrived."

Schulman was selling the team to Barry Ackerley of Ackerley Communications, a company based in Seattle that owned 11,000 billboards all over the country and had advertising franchises at more than 80 airports. It also owned three television stations.

"I think I found an outstanding Seattle citizen," Schulman said of Ackerley. "He's going to be dedicated to winning and doing it on a sound basis."

This last sentence was the most important of all the statements Schulman made about the sale, because following the back-to-back NBA Finals appearances in 1978 and 1979, the Sonics had mostly continued to win. The year after they took home the championship trophy, they set the franchise record for wins with fifty-six and advanced to the 1980 Western Conference Finals before running into the budding buzzsaw that was the new Lakers dynasty, led by first-year phenom Magic Johnson. The 1980-81 Sonics had seven players average double digits on the season, including old standbys Jack Sikma, Lonnie Shelton and Fred Brown, but they took a big step back in wins and defensive production, going 34-48 and missing the playoffs for the first time in four years.

Over the course of the next four seasons (Lenny Wilkens' last four as coach), the team had three first-round playoff exits and one second-round playoff exit. The Sonics hovered around fifty wins from '82 to '84 before the bottom dropped out in the 1984-85 season, when they won only thirty-one. At that point, it was time for Wilkens to leave the sideline and head back to the front office as general manager, where he would help the team find its next coach. "We want to bring a winning professional basketball franchise back to Seattle," owner Barry Ackerley said. "That's what we're working towards. All decisions concerning this franchise are difficult. I take full responsibility for this one."

Realistically, if Ackerley could see into the near future, it's unlikely he'd have wanted to take responsibility for what was about to happen to the once-proud franchise. Even though the team was barely five years removed from its title, the only player left from the championship roster was Jack Sikma and Gus Williams. To be fair, he did have some decent players around him like Tom Chambers and Gerald Henderson, but overall the team and the attendance was in decline. Long gone were the days of 20,000-plus in the Kingdome every night. By the end of 1984 that number was cut in half, down to a nightly average of 10,900 fans per game. By 1985, they'd lost another 25% of their attendance, plummeting to 7,300 people a night, a number that hadn't been that low since 1970 (the team's third year in Seattle). The Sonics were back playing their home games in the Seattle Center Coliseum at this point, and despite the lull in attendance new coach Bernie Bickerstaff was putting together a competitive team.

Fittingly, one of the last great members of the iconic 1970s teams, the Wizard, Gus Williams, was traded during the 1984-85 season, leaving only Jack Sikma to carry on the memories of the team's stellar recent past. Fans went into mourning upon hearing about the Williams trade, even circulating a petition to convince the team to keep their beloved star. Alas, the appeal didn't work, and after a sendoff of nearly 3,000 people outside the Seattle Aquarium, a going away party of sorts, Williams officially left as part of a trade to the Washington Bullets. After winning only thirty-nine games in 1987, the Sonics made a surprise run to the Western Conference Finals, led by Dale Ellis, Tom Chambers and the new most-popular Sonic, the X-Man, Xavier McDaniel. All three of them averaged over 20 points per game.

Although they were swept by the Lakers, the season started a three-year playoff streak under Bickerstaff. Chambers, Ellis and McDaniel each picked up an all-star nod during this mini run of respectability, but after another .500 season and early playoff exit, Bickerstaff was let go after the 1990 season. K.C. Jones was brought in as his replacement, and after a mediocre season and a half (when Jones went 41-41 in 1991 and then started 1992 with another even-Steven record of 18-18), he was fired as well. By the end of the '92 season, however, the Sonics had the three pieces in place that were primed to launch the second most successful (and singularly most iconic and popular) era in franchise history. Of course we're talking about Head Coach George Karl, power forward Shawn Kemp and point guard Gary Payton.

Chapter 8

A Brief Interlude with The X-Man

All six feet, seven inches and 225 pounds of Xavier McDaniel is staring at you. He's wearing jeans and a sleeveless denim jacket that shows off his jacked biceps. In his left arm sits a silver basketball he's holding snug against his hip. His right hand firmly grips the thick black leash of a Doberman pinscher that has lit up, green lasers in its eyes. Behind McDaniel, amidst a cloud of smoke, are two yellow lasers forming his signature "X." This is the poster thousands of Sonics fans and young NBA fans had in their rooms across the Pacific Northwest and the entire United States. The caption read: *The X-Man Cometh.* To a ten-year-old or twelve-year-old, it might as well have been a poster for a horror movie. The thing was terrifying. Then again, that was how the X-Man played. He was bold, brash, bruising, and for six years he was the Emerald City's resident enforcer and scoring machine.

The Sonics selected McDaniel fourth overall in the 1985 NBA Draft after becoming enamored with him during his senior year at Wichita State. As the star of the Shockers and the MVP of the Missouri Valley Conference, he accomplished a feat many thought wasn't possible by leading the nation in scoring *and* rebounding (27.1 points per game and 15 rebounds per game). In his first season in Seattle, he averaged 17.1 points per game and finished second behind Patrick Ewing in the Rookie of the Year voting. More importantly, he became an instant cult hero in Washington. Like the former unofficial "most popular Sonic" before him, Slick Watts, X-Man rocked the shaved head before it was a major fashion trend in the league. Unlike Watts, however, he wasn't known for wearing a happy-go-lucky smile on his face. In fact, he was known for the opposite: bone-chilling intensity and an all-time great mean mug before there was even a term for mean mugging. Hell, back in the '80s, mean mugging might as well have been known as X-Manning, because when he was on the floor he had complete and utter disdain for his opponents. He was strong and intimidating and the exact kind of guy you wanted in the proverbial trenches on your team. "Xavier is pretty much the definition of a pro's pro," Bob Ryan of the *Boston Globe* said.

He had every tough guy move in the book: hard fouls, questionable bumps, vicious swats, insults—all of it. If a Sonics teammate got into a scrape, there was zero doubt about the first teammate who'd arrive to back him up: X-Man. But unlike other hoops heavies whose main function was to start fights, finish fights, dish fouls or draw fouls, McDaniel was a legitimately talented scorer and rebounder. From 1986 to 1990 he had scoring averages of 17.1, 23, 21.4, 20.5 and 21.3, all while averaging about 7 boards a game. He made the 1988 all-star team and probably should have made a few more. "If you look at my first five years, I had Hall of Fame numbers," McDaniel told Vice.com in a story about the 30th anniversary of the 1985 NBA Draft. "I was right there with any forward in the league except Larry Bird, and he's *Larry Bird*."

While not recognized for All-NBA selections or as many all-star nods as he may have deserved, he was given the honor of representing Seattle in pop culture during his run in the city. He had a famous cameo in the movie *Singles* (although he wasn't with the team when the movie came out) and appeared in an episode of *Married... with Children*. Sandwiched between the title in 1979 and the glory years of the 1990s, the peak years of X-Man's time in Seattle have been somewhat overlooked as time has passed. His best playoff performance was even in a loss, when he went toe-to-toe with James Worthy in game three of the Western Conference Finals. Worthy had an impressive stat line of 39 points, five rebounds and five assists while X-Man matched him all the way with 42 points, 10 rebounds and four assists.

"I'll never forget that game. He couldn't stop me, I couldn't stop him. Late in the game, we call time out and Coach calls a play for Dale Ellis, because 'he got us here,'" says McDaniel. "I said, 'This is bullshit. I'm hot. Give me the ball, I guarantee I'll score. Post Worthy up, drop a turnaround on his ass.' I was so pissed, I walked out of the huddle. Dale's shot got blocked. We lost."

In early December of the 1990-91 season, in the midst of averaging 20 points per game and mentoring the Sonics' young star Shawn Kemp, X-Man was unceremoniously traded to the Phoenix Suns for Eddie Johnson and two first-round picks.

"Xavier has definitely been a big plus for the Sonics organization," former GM Bob Whitsitt said at the time. "On the basketball court, we're giving up offense and getting offense, plus two number-one picks in return. But in the community, X has been wonderful for us and we wish him the very best."

Unfortunately, McDaniel would never have it as good as he did in Seattle. After barely a year in Phoenix he was traded to the New York Knicks, where he only stayed a year before signing as a free agent with the Boston Celtics. He spent three years in Beantown, putting up respectable numbers, but he was past his prime. In a few more years he'd retire and move to South Carolina to run a construction/janitorial company, appropriately named 34 X Man LLC, after the number he wore with the Sonics. Apparently, his post-playing days wouldn't be complete without a nod to his time in the green and gold, and no Sonics story would be complete without at least a quick nod to the great and powerful (and underrated) X-Man.

Chapter 9

Reign Man

Six-foot, three-inch shooting guard Chandler Thompson had the stop-start explosiveness of a speedy slot receiver. He could dribble within inches of a defender, shimmy, hesitate and blow right by him for an easy bucket. This move worked for him all season and he sure as hell wasn't going to abandon it in the biggest game of his life. With his team down a few points early in the second quarter, he took the ball across the three-point line, surveyed his teammates and, as he hugged the elbow, gave the slightest stutter to his defender, pounced right, broke free, coasted to the baseline and soared into the air for a highlight-reel dunk that would force the 17,000 fans on hand to explode out of their seats.

Except he never dunked the ball.

The defender in question was 6'11" with a 7-foot wingspan and the speed and quickness of a full-grown gazelle. For a brief moment, Thompson had him beat, but with two slide steps and a jump stop, this lanky, springboard of a human, Shawn Kemp, caught up with Thompson, leapt, met him at the basket and blocked the dunk above the rim with two hands. Yes, two hands.

This epic swat did not take place in an NBA or college basketball game. It happened in the 1988 Indiana high school state finals at Market Square Arena, home of the Pacers. Kemp was the star of Concord High School and a finalist for Indiana's coveted Mr. Basketball award. He was also the biggest high school sports attraction in the state, selling out gyms across the region, including his home gym, which added 770 seats in an end-zone-type balcony to push the capacity to 3,500-plus. During Kemp's playing days, the team had 3,200 season ticket holders and, taking a cue from professional arenas, they invested in a "Scream Machine" that measured the noise level in the gym, with a green light at the top that flashed like a police siren when the Concord faithful were roaring at peak volume. They even had radio stations covering their games. On the road, some teams were forced to change locations to accommodate his rabid following.

Earlier in his senior year, when Concord played rival St. Joe's on the road, St. Joe's head coach Steve Austin realized their home gym was far too small to handle the monsoon of hoops fans who would be showing up to watch Kemp play. "I went to my principal five times to ask him to change the venue," Austin said. "He thought I was crazy." Austin's idea was to play the game on Notre Dame University's basketball court, and he was willing to give up a home game to do it. And it still almost wasn't big enough.

"When we got there for the JV game, the arena just had the padded seats down below open," Jim Hahn, Kemp's head coach at Concord said. "Before the JV game ended it was completely full. Then they started pulling out bleachers in the upper section, and as soon as they'd pull them out they would fill up."

The arena eventually filled to capacity and the Shawn Kemp show was officially underway. In no uncertain terms, what the paying customers wanted to see was an onslaught of soaring dunks, ceiling-level lobs, half-court alley-oops, put-back jams and vicious blocks by the 18-year-old, seemingly bionic Kemp. On this night (and really on any night during his high school career) Kemp did not disappoint. From leading the varsity team to a sectional title as a freshman to selling out NBA arenas as senior, night in and night out, he toiled in the spectacular. During this particular game on the Fighting Irish's home court, Austin recalled a play that took his breath away. "There was a lob dunk where my center was in perfect position to defend Shawn," he said. "As the pass came in, my center's hands were maybe at the rim, and all of a sudden you saw Shawn… and all you saw was probably his waistline at my kid's head and he had to be at least box-high on the backboard if not higher and just dunked it on him. My kid turned around and I just… You know… What can you do? You can't stop that."

Kemp's cousin Kerry Ellison swears that some of his dunks were electrifying in a completely literal sense. "He dunked the ball so hard that sparks flew off the metal chain in the basket," he said. "I realize things tend to get exaggerated over time, but you had to be there. And if you weren't there, you don't want to hear about it because you don't know what you missed."

Kemp dunked so hard and so often that Ellison became concerned that his cousin might do permanent damage to his hands. He'd often look at the scars and scrapes and bruises on Shawn's hands after games and tell him to back off. *Don't be so…thunderous.*

"When I dunk, I just want to tear the rim down," Kemp would say.

While the dunks drew in the fans, it was Kemp's effortless jumper, defensive presence and ability to win that helped attract the nation's top college recruiters and curious NBA scouts. He averaged 25.5 points, 14.4 rebounds and 4.5 blocks per game as a junior. The team was much better overall his senior year, and while his dominance remained the same, his numbers dipped slightly. Still, the team won twenty or more games every year Kemp was in the lineup, and he made the McDonald's All-American Team, the Parade All-American team twice, and was named to a slew of other national high school lists. As a product of Indiana state basketball, he received the typical full-court press from all the usual suspects when it came to college: Purdue, Notre Dame and the big dog, Bobby Knight's Indiana. He was also heavily recruited by Eddie Sutton of Indiana's arch-rival Kentucky, which is where he opted to sign.

"The thing that attracted me was the tradition," Kemp said in his press conference at the time.

The decision to spurn Indiana, coupled with his difficulty passing the SAT, made him public enemy number one in every gym except his own. Fans of the opposing teams tried to rattle Kemp by taunting him with chants of "S-A-T! S-A-T! S-A-T!" while his Concord fans countered with their own comeback: "N-B-A! N-B-A! N-B-A!" And sadly, as one of the only black standout athletes in a mostly white conference, he heard horrible slurs from racists in the crowd.

"There were ignorant fans," Coach Hahn said. "They were throwing things at him and saying bad words, and some of the things that were said were disheartening."

Kemp, for his part, internalized most of the pressure and shrugged off the crass comments. The one thing he couldn't let go of then, and still can't now, is that he believes (as do many others) that Bobby Knight was so furious about Kemp choosing to be a Wildcat over a Hoosier that he tanked his chances of earning the one thing Kemp coveted as much as a state championship: the title of Mr. Basketball in Indiana.

"Coach Knight would come to the gym a lot to watch me practice and we had a lot of meetings around this area," Kemp said in a visit at his alma mater. "He was the kind of guy who let you know right away, if you go blue, there's no Mr. Basketball of Indiana."

"It was a disgrace," Coach Hahn said. "He was by far the best player in the state. In my opinion he was the best player ever in the northern part of the state."

As fate would have it, Mr. Basketball or not, Kemp never actually played for Kentucky. He failed to score a 700 on his SAT, which entangled him in the web of the NCAA's Proposition 48 and made him ineligible until he scored higher. This posed a real problem for Kemp, who was now stuck on a campus without any athletic outlet or team to be a part of. His inner circle was worried.

"To have Shawn in a college environment without basketball, the one thing he loves, was, I felt, a big mistake. It even crossed my mind to advise him to go right into the NBA, and the only thing that stopped me was the fact that so few players had done it," Coach Hahn said.

His concerns turned out to be valid, and Kemp found himself embroiled in controversy when he was caught selling two gold chains for $700 to a pawn shop. The chains reportedly belonged to Kentucky Head Coach Eddie Sutton's son Sean. The Suttons didn't press charges, claiming they couldn't confirm whether the chains in question were actually the ones taken from Sean's dorm room. Kemp, who never denied that he sold the chains, said that he was selling them on another player's behalf, and for thirty years has never named the player.

"At the time, I couldn't see why Shawn decided to take the blame," his mom said. "Now I can support what he's done, because he was leaving Kentucky anyway. What good would it have done to name other people? He was young, and kind of drawn into the situation. He was asked to do something, which he did, and the other person never stepped forward."

Following the incident, Kemp transferred to Trinity Valley Community College in Texas. He didn't play basketball there, and after one semester he made the controversial decision to declare for the NBA Draft as a 19-year-old whose last game was in high school.

"The odds against Shawn Kemp are astronomical," NBA Scout Marty Blake said at the time. "Most guys out of college can't play at the pro level; most can't even play at the college level anymore."

Blake wasn't just being a hater. He had the numbers to back him up. Of the 161 players who declared for the NBA draft early, either as "hardship" cases (after the landmark lawsuit won by Sam Schulman and Spencer Haywood) or later as "early entry cases," a vast majority did not pan out: 72% were actually drafted, 62% earned a paycheck from an NBA team, and 34% had what were considered to be "productive careers."

And then there were people who were against the decision on its merits, claiming that Kemp somehow needed the full college experience before he could really become a professional. His coach and his agent would hear none of it.

"People go to college to get a degree and to use that degree to enter a profession," Hahn said. "Shawn's profession was going to be basketball. What did he need to get a college degree for?"

"I'm surprised at the question," Kemp's agent Arn Tellem said back when he was asked. "I think the reasons are rather obvious. Basketball was going to be his profession anyway, he was ready and able, and the alternatives weren't good."

There was also this important fact: NBA teams were interested in Kemp. Like, really interested. So interested, in fact, that many lied about their interest to try to keep other teams off their scent. Some scouts, like those for the Orlando Magic, claimed that they could only get grainy high school footage to evaluate him. Others spread rumors about his problems at Kentucky in an effort to keep teams at bay. But perhaps the most egregious attempt to hide Kemp came from none other than Magic Johnson and the Lakers, who, according to Kemp's story on the *Sonics Forever* podcast, effectively stashed Kemp away in Los Angeles for a month. Over the course of four weeks, Kemp worked out with Magic at UCLA, got to know the team and the city and prepared to live there. That is, until one fateful day when he got a visit from Barry Ackerley's son, who had been sneaking into the pick-up games to scout Kemp. He convinced Shawn to take a visit to Seattle to meet with his dad and the coaching staff.

The reason for the subterfuge was that Kemp's individual workouts with teams often left front offices drooling. After all, this was a kid who at age sixteen had already bested an NBA player mano-a-mano.

"I remember when the Indiana Pacers ran a camp at my high school my sophomore year," Kemp recalled. "They brought one of their players to the camp. We were in our gym and I ended up beating him in a game of one-on-one to ten."

That match-up had been three years, five inches and about forty pounds ago. Kemp was no longer a man-child playing against boys. He was a man ready to play against men, and that was plain for all to see. "Their main concern wasn't about Shawn's ability to play in the NBA," Tellem said about the teams spreading rumors. "But how to keep him hidden from other teams."

The SuperSonics' head coach heading into the 1989 NBA Draft, Bernie Bickerstaff, wholly agreed with Tellem's assessment. "You had a lot of guys telling you things, perpetuating rumors," Bickerstaff said. "They were saying all kinds of things because they didn't want you to take him. They wanted Shawn for themselves."

When the night of the draft finally arrived, the SuperSonics had two picks in the first round, the 16th and 17th selections. They knew they were too far back to take any of the headliners in the draft like Louisville's Pervis Ellison or Duke's Danny Ferry. Sean Elliott and Glen Rice were also projected to go high, and they did. It was during the middle of the draft, between the eighth and 14th picks, when the Sonics held their breath the most. Once the Celtics took Michael Smith at 13 and the Warriors selected Tim Hardaway at 15, Bickerstaff and his team felt confident they'd land their guy. After Denver selected Todd Lichti at 15, they were set. The Sonics selected Dana Barros as the 16th pick and Shawn Kemp at 17.

SuperSonics president Bob Whitsitt was pleased. "Shawn Kemp, had he stayed in school, would eventually have been a top-five draft pick," he said. "We think he has a great future in the NBA. We will bring him along slowly."

Chapter 10

The Glove

Gary Payton's left hand rested easily on his left knee as he sat in a folding chair wearing his black tear-away pants with white and red stripes down the sides. His baggy Skyline High School V-neck shooting top, with the word *SKYLINE* in big, bold red letters above a thick, black line, swallowed up his skinny frame. His legs were splayed open and the conference trophy sat on the ground next to him, rising up to just about his chin. His taller teammates stood in a row behind him and the other guards sat on the other side of the trophy. The photographer lined up the shot and Payton gave the camera an unmistakable, cocky look that for any other player would've been worth a thousand words. But with Payton's reputation for yapping, it was probably worth ten thousand. At the very moment Payton's mouth closed, the photographer snapped his picture and captured the only millisecond of Gary Payton's time in a basketball uniform when he wasn't talking.

Throughout his career, Payton's NBA teammates and opponents spoke frequently about the avalanche of words that poured out of his mouth on the court. When they ran into someone who played against Payton in college, they'd inevitably ask, "Did he talk this much in college?" And the response would always be, "yes." When Payton was in college his teammates and opponents did the same thing: They'd ask anyone they came across from Payton's hometown, "Did he talk this much in high school?" And the answer, again, was "yes."

While Payton was at Skyline High in Oakland, California, the team was nearly unbeatable because it had not one, but two, future NBA players in its lineup. Greg Foster, who would be a longtime NBA reserve and college star, played alongside Payton and they won back-to-back All-City titles in 1985 and 1986. Payton talked and dribbled and scored and threw the lobs; Foster dominated and intimidated and finished off the alley-oops. It was a partnership that started in elementary school and continued through junior high, AAU travel teams, all the way to the last game of their high school careers. By the end of their senior years, both players were named to the All-City, All-State and Best in the West teams. All of this speaks to the point that if anyone knew how long Payton had been yammering away on the court, it would be Foster. When asked if his trash talking was worse in the NBA or in high school, he didn't even hesitate.

"Worse," Foster said of their high school careers. "This [NBA trash talk] is nothing compared to what he did then. What he does now is mild. [Oakland] was a wild time. But it was fun."

Skyline was a member of the famous Oakland Athletic League, a league that was so rough that many games had armed guards on hand to keep the peace between fan bases. "You talk about rowdy," Payton once said. "In Oakland, the players were on you. The refs were on you. The stands were on you. You had to talk back or you were a sissy; you'd get run out of the league. Afterward? Yeah, it was kind of a, uh, struggle to get out of the gym. Cops had to be everywhere. Which was lucky."

Skyline head coach Fred Noel said that in the Oakland Athletic League, "verbal combat, the necessity to seem cool, was as important as the game itself."

Yet somehow, amidst the smack talking and the superlatives and the security guards, there was a genuine lack of interest from the nation's top basketball schools when it came to Payton.

"He was really underrated then," Foster said. "A lot of schools were kicking themselves after the fact."

While Foster went to UCLA (and eventually transferred to UTEP), there was a recruiting lull rather than a buzz for Payton. Some of it could be attributed to being underrated or overshadowed by his big man teammate, but a portion had to do with his attitude. He'd been suspended as a sophomore for poor grades and disciplinary reasons. "I messed up," Payton said. "Fighting, trashing teachers and coaches. Everybody."

His father Al, who took such pride in being a hard-ass coach that the vanity license plate on his Datsun 280Z read "Mr. Mean," refused to let young Gary go down that path. He was called to school to deal with his son numerous times and was so fed up that he once laid down the law in front of his peers in an actual classroom. And it worked. Payton got his grades up and his attitude down (off the court, of course).

But even with his act together, schools like Duke and North Carolina and Kentucky weren't calling. For a brief moment, Payton thought he was headed all the way across the country to slug it out in the old Big East for Lou Carnesecca's St. John's team, but at the last minute the Johnnies coach backed off the commitment. Carnesecca has since admitted it was a huge mistake, but his excuse at the time was that he didn't want to tick off any local New York City recruits by grabbing a west coast point guard. Once the St. John's offer disappeared, his mom and dad urged Payton to accept an offer from Oregon State, with his dad telling the coaches that if his son got out of line to "slap him upside the head" courtesy of his father.

Entering his freshman year, Oregon State Head Coach Ralph Miller told Payton that the only way he'd start was if he committed to playing hard defense. Payton, who had no plans to spend even a fraction of a second on the bench as a sub, accepted the challenge and became an elite stopper, earning the Pac-10 Defensive Player of the Year honor as a freshman (along with Conference Freshman of the Year). With his reputation for defensive prowess solidified, Payton spent the next four years shutting down opponents, improving his offense and racking up wins. He started every game and won nearly every award there was to win: Consensus First-Team All-American, three-time All-Pac-10 Team, three-time MVP of the Far West Classic Tournament, and nine-time Pac-10 Player of the Week.

And of course, there was some epic trash talk, like the time he caught fire from the floor and the Stanford University bench tried to get under his skin, to which he screamed, "Get someone out here who can guard me!"

"I started talking back and it was like thousands against just Gary—who's going to win?" Payton said. "It hyped me up. If somebody talks to me from the crowd, I can talk back because I can back it up. As soon as I do something good, they're going to shut up."

On the flip side, whenever he did "something good" at home, the fans at the Gil Coliseum went ballistic. But no night gave the Beaver faithful the chance to give their full-throated appreciation to Payton like his second-to-last game in Corvallis, when 9,878 fans witnessed one of the greatest college scoring performances of all-time. That night, Payton poured in 58 points, the second-most ever by a Pac-10 player behind Lew Alcindor's 61. And it wasn't against some scrub team. It was against USC and its own young scoring star,

Harold Miner, who had 27 points. "It was as good a one-man performance as I've ever seen in this league," USC Coach George Raveling said after the game. "Walton, Jabbar, anyone you want to name—especially when you consider Gary's size."

He finished his senior year averaging 25.7 points and 7.6 assists and earned the coveted unofficial title of "best point guard in the 1990 NBA Draft Class." And yet, concerns about his on-court antics lingered slightly. Teams wanted to meet him to find out if "the mouth" was a motivational act or a legitimate problem to control.

"There's a lot of speculation on their minds," Gary admitted at the time. "I've been going to teams interested in me to show them what kind of person I really am. I play cocky because that gets the job done. But when I go to the interviews, I show them that on the court it's just a business, that they don't know the real Gary Payton."

Going into draft night, it was widely suspected that the New Jersey Nets were going to take Derrick Coleman from Syracuse with the number one pick. After that, the Sonics had the second pick and were in dire need of a point guard. But so were Denver, Orlando and Charlotte, who had the third, fourth and fifth picks, respectively.

Payton didn't care where he went. "I just want to play in the NBA," he said. "It would be fortunate if I could stay on the west coast, but whatever happens I'll be happy."

As luck would have it, fortune smiled on Payton because the Sonics selected him with the number two pick, specifically to pair him with their selection the previous year, Shawn Kemp.

"He's a great point guard," Sonics President Bob Whitsitt said after the pick. "We agreed point guard was a need for us and we wanted to fill it."

Bernie Bickerstaff, the ex-coach and now vice president of basketball operations, was excited as well. "In terms of being a quarterback, Gary Payton has shown he can do it at this level over the last three years."

After going 41-41 under first-year Sonics coach K.C. Jones the previous season, the team believed that Payton would provide the direction and the spark to ignite the franchise past the .500 mark and back into contention.

Payton had faith that he was the perfect guy to do it. "I'm confident I can help Seattle out," he said. "They need a leader. And they think so, too. That's why they picked me."

Almost instantly after the pick, the talking started.

"The moment I drafted him, he's on the radio saying, 'Point guards like Magic Johnson and I don't come along very often.'" Bob Whitsitt recalled. "Gary didn't stop talking from the moment you drafted him until the day his career was over; probably hasn't stopped talking today."

Then-Sonics owner Bob Ackerley remembered a dinner with Payton shortly after he was drafted that would foreshadow the next half-decade of the franchise.

"I'm married to a woman still who was an All-American swimmer at Arizona State," he said. "But she knew nothing about basketball. When Gary was first drafted, we were at a preseason dinner and she asked me after the dinner, 'Who was that guy sitting across the table?' It happened to be Gary Payton. She looked at me and she said, 'That guy's going to be a winner. You can just see it in his eyes. He has the eye of the tiger. He's never going to let himself fail.' She's very rarely ever made comments about players—except at that time—and it was a pretty bold statement."

Bold and true.

Chapter 11

Furious George

"I did not know George. I knew of George. Let's say the number was thirty people I talked to regarding George. Twenty-nine of them said, 'Don't touch him with a 10-foot pole. You will lose your job in no time flat.' They all had the same horror stories. Temper, egomaniac, drinks too much. One guy was neutral on him and he said, 'Look, I can't recommend him, but I won't kill him because he is a smart basketball coach.'"

The above was Bob Whitsitt's response when he was asked what his research on George Karl revealed before he hired him. The interview was for an oral history of the '90s Sonics by Bleacher Report, and Whitsitt was, let's say, extremely candid about how far out on a limb he was going to bring in Karl. In fact, you'd be forgiven for thinking these quotes were about someone he *didn't hire.*

"I do my homework," he continued in the interview. "What I'm liking about George is a combination of things. He had a tiny bit of success as a very young NBA coach in Cleveland, and unfortunately that tiny bit of success he had was the wrong thing for a young George Karl, because his ego was so massive. This was like putting gas on the fire and it was like George creating more problems for George, and George became his own worst enemy. Then he got a run in Golden State, and all hell broke loose and everybody in the NBA hated him, and he ended up self-destructing… he deserved to self-destruct, but this is a guy who went from thinking he was the biggest hotshot in the NBA to he couldn't get another job in the NBA, but he loved the game so much, he went and coached in the CBA. ... Then, he tried to go up to a higher level of play, because he still couldn't get into the NBA and he was coaching over in Spain and this was a guy who would tell people he could speak Spanish. George could say *hola* and *adios* and that was about it."

According to Karl, he knew a few more words in Spanish than that, but not many. In his book *Furious George*, he explained his philosophy about coaching in Spain with a language barrier like this: "Basketball is an international language. Blocks, rolls, screens, defense—the fundamentals are universal. With the help of bilingual assistants, I could teach and coach. I proved very poor at picking up the new language. My Spanish was confined to *digame* ('talk to me,' an alternative to *hola* when answering the phone), *gracias*, and *otra cerveza*, *por favor…*). I caused some laughter among the waitstaff at a restaurant when I ordered *polla* (penis) when I really wanted *pollo* (chicken)."

If you want to give Karl the benefit of the doubt, maybe he knew eight words in Spanish. But more importantly, you may have noticed a theme here. Beginning in the late seventies, he held a large amount of coaching jobs in a relatively short period of time. Karl's coaching career began as an assistant for the San Antonio Spurs from 1978 to 1980. Then he coached the Montana Golden Nuggets of the Continental Basketball Association (CBA) for three years, taking his team to the finals in '81 and '83 and winning Coach of the Year both years. After that, he coached the Cavs for two years and the Warriors for two years. When the Warriors gig imploded, he got a job as the head coach of the Albany Patroons of the CBA, the same team with which Phil Jackson won his first championship as a coach in 1984. Karl didn't win a title like Jackson, but he did lead them to a 50-6 regular season record and an undefeated mark of 28-0 at home. He spent two years with the Patroons but supplemented his time by coaching Real Madrid in Spain during the CBA's off-season. Real Madrid is considered a version of the Celtics or the Lakers in European Basketball. Players like Drazen Petrovic and Arvydas Sabonis played for the team and they won dozens of tournaments. It was with this team, in Spain, that Whitsitt believed he'd found his man to replace K.C. Jones after Jones was fired thirty-six games into the 1992 season.

"I went to my owner when I told them who I was thinking of hiring. I'll never forget it," Whitsitt says of his meeting with Ackerley. "I went out to his house and all I had was a CBA media guide to show them, and my owner says, basically, 'Are you kidding?' And his wife looks at me and she goes, 'He does nothing for me.' I'm like, *Great, now I've got to sell the wife too. …* I'll give him credit, he looked at his wife and he said to her, 'Honey, we don't want George Karl. We've made that clear to Bob, but I hired the last coach in K.C. If he's really insistent on this guy, let's let him do it and this is on him and he knows his job is on the line.' And she looked at me too, she goes, 'You know you won't have a job if he doesn't pan out?'"

Whitsitt knew the level of risk he was taking, but he was banking on the fact that Karl had spent four years in exile, taking his medicine in central

Spain and upstate New York. He had a hunch that Karl was so desperate to return to the NBA limelight that he'd been humbled and was ready to make good. His hunch was right.

A few days after New Year's Eve in 1991, Chicago Bulls General Manager Jerry Krause asked to meet with Karl to get his thoughts on two European players he was thinking of drafting: Toni Kukoc and Arvydas Sabonis. Deep down, Karl had been hoping for some signal from Krause that his name had been brought up in NBA circles to return to coaching. He got nothing.

"[That meeting] was about the only contact I had had with the NBA," he explained. "Why hadn't I heard from the friends I'd thought I'd made in the league? Why wasn't I at least rumored to be someone's new head coach? What else did they need to see to let me back in? My combined record in Spain at that moment was 47-20. My combined record for my four years in exile: 134-44. Pretty good, but the phone didn't ring. Then it did."

In the weeks following Krause's meeting with Karl, Whitsitt was doing his above-mentioned "homework" on the man he wanted on the sidelines in Seattle. At first, however, he thought he might want to bring in Karl to help K.C. Jones as an assistant. "Two weeks after that dinner…Bob Whitsitt called. I'm pretty sure Krause *had* endorsed me. The Seattle GM asked if I'd be interested in being an assistant to their coach, K.C. Jones, for $100,000. I might be interested, I said, but first I'd like to know if K.C. wants *me.* Whitsitt called back a day later with K.C's answer: no. The Sonics were a good, young team whose record defined mediocrity: They'd won exactly as many games as they'd lost in a year and a half under K.C. Whitsitt probably wanted me to bring a little spark. End of story, I thought."

Around the time this first conversation took place, the Sonics were 18-15. They were above .500 but were very much having another "meh" season. There seemed to be no rhyme or reason to their wins and losses. There was no momentum swing one way or the other; no sign that the team was about to put things together and make a run. They'd win two and then lose three. Then they'd win three and lose four. Up and down they went, and in the stretch after Whitsitt's first phone call with Karl the team dropped another three in a row. All the games were close and the kind of losses that GMs and front office types examine to see if a team is responding to a coach. *Are they digging deep? Are they snatching victory from the jaws of defeat?* Or, *do they just continue to feel flat?* Exhibit A, B, and C that it was the latter were losses to Houston (119-115), the LA Clippers (98-94) and then the Charlotte Hornets (117-116) at home. The game against Charlotte was the last straw. K.C. Jones was out.

"Ten days [after our last call] Whitsitt was on the phone asking if I'd like to talk about a much bigger, better job. I'd be very interested, I said. I flew from Madrid to New York to Dallas, where I paused for a few hours for barbecue and beer with Dan Strimple, the golf pro. 'George, this is your last chance at the NBA,' Strimple said as he dropped me off for the flight to Seattle. 'Don't fuck this up.'" Karl wrote. "I didn't. I nailed the interview… Whitsitt wanted my fire after K.C.'s low-key approach, and I wanted the job so badly that I took a pay cut and a laughably short deal, only a year and a half. I also agreed not to drink in public. I never drank to the point of being impaired, especially not in public, but I wasn't insulted. If this was what Whitsitt wanted, fine. I told Madrid, *adios*. I told Seattle, 'We're gonna win by being the hardest-working, most intense team possible.' Suddenly I had the most talented players I'd ever coached. Eddie Johnson and Ricky Pierce were great offensive players who really understood the game. Nate McMillan and Derrick McKey defended like crazy. Gary Payton and Shawn Kemp were potential all-stars and I knew I could coach them up."

In short, Karl believed it was time to put the "super" back into the SuperSonics.

Chapter 12

Seeds of the Boom

George Karl was making $340,000 per year coaching professional basketball before signing with Seattle. He earned $250,000 a season for Real Madrid and another $90,000 for Albany. When he agreed to coach the Sonics for $300,000, he was actually taking a yearly pay cut. No matter. He knew the juice would be worth the squeeze in the long run, so he got to work the second his plane wheels touched the tarmac at Sea-Tac. In short order he went 9-2 in his first full month, won the NBA Coach of the Month award for February, presided over the franchise's 1,000th victory on March 3, and installed a frenetic, stifling defense that played to his team's strengths and created chaos for their opponents. The milquetoast days of K.C. Jones were, well, toast—with George Karl came intensity and with intensity came winning.

On several occasions when Gary Payton reflects on those early days with Karl, he uses words like arrogant, cocky, hard-nosed and rough to describe him. In one retrospective he said at first he couldn't stand him because, "he came in from overseas and was one of those cats where he wanted to come in and try to establish that he was arrogant and all that, and we were the same way and that's why we clashed heads at the beginning. … Then when you start thinking about it, we had the same personality and wanted the same thing. We just wanted to win and wanted to get better, and he had the opportunity to get back in the NBA after he had been out of the NBA for a while."

For those first few months, with his new tenure in the NBA hanging by a thread, Karl leaned on what got him to the league in the first place: his basketball IQ. One of his first moves when he took over the Sonics was to retain assistant coach Bob Kloppenburg, a defensive specialist. Kloppenburg, a former Los Angeles City Player of the Year in high school and a college starter at Fresno State, was the mind behind the innovative SOS defensive pressure system. The system reflected Kloppenburg's philosophy of "contact switching" on every single screen, along with suffocating ball pressure. Karl and Kloppenburg recognized quickly that with Kemp's wingspan and speed, Payton's tenacity and the overall athleticism of the team, they should be running a high-octane transition game founded on a stifling defense to force turnovers and poor shots. The strategy paid off quicker than anyone anticipated and vindicated Bob Whitsitt by the time the playoffs rolled around. The Sonics finished the '92 season fourth in the Pacific Division with a record of 47-35 (27-15 under Karl).

"I didn't necessarily want an ass-kicker, an up-tempo man or a motivator," Whitsitt said when asked about the turnaround. "I wanted someone who understood coaching." And when it came to Karl, who understood that he needed to change his attitude a little bit after his flameouts with the Cavs and Warriors, he said, "I've matured and I've learned from my mistakes. An NBA coach cannot overshadow the players. They don't want to be embarrassed or confronted publicly in certain situations. I've learned that you have to have compatibility with your players. I kept telling myself that if I got another chance to coach in the NBA, I was going to do things differently."

The self-talk and the heaping serving of humble pie were certainly factors in Karl's NBA renaissance, but the catalyst for his comeback had to be the talent he inherited on the roster and the timing of his arrival. A few years earlier and the team would have been stocked with mediocrity; a few years later and another coach would likely be enjoying the prime years of Kemp and Payton and the upcoming additions to the roster. Karl was truly entering the Sonics organization in the goldilocks zone. They had no all-stars—yet—but you didn't have to be Nostradamus to know that the selections were coming. In fact, the 1992 NBA All-Star game would be the last game of the decade to not feature a Sonics player (usually Kemp or Payton or both). But the roster at that point wasn't built around the two young studs.

The Sonics' two leading scorers for the 1991-92 season were Ricky Pierce, aka Big Paper Daddy, aka Deuces, the 6'4" former all-star out of Rice; and Eddie Johnson, a 6'7" dead-eye shooter who played college ball at Illinois. The two men played for over a dozen combined teams during their careers and tallied more than 33,000 career points. They were better than journeymen, but not quite stars. They were exceptional scorers, but not quite franchise guys. When their paths crossed as members of the Sonics, they had more in common than most. They were both 32 years old, although Johnson, who turned thirty-three at the end of that season, famously claimed, "I can't be getting older, I'm still getting better." They'd both recently won the NBA's Sixth Man of the Year award and they were both still capable of dropping in twenty-five a night easy. Pierce and Johnson together averaged about 38 points per game. Throw in Kemp's 15 per game, Derrick McKey putting in 14.9, big man Benoit Benjamin averaging 14 per game, and Payton putting in about ten per game, and you've got a very late '70s-esque Sonics squad. They also had excellent on-court leadership with Payton and his early mentor, team captain and Mr. Sonic himself, Nate McMillan. McMillan was the starting point guard before the Sonics drafted Payton, and despite other athletes looking at the situation as a threat, McMillan saw it as an opportunity.

"They announced the day that Gary was drafted that he was going to be the starting point guard," McMillan recalled. "Gary really came in feeling that there was going to be a problem with he and I. It was totally the opposite. I introduced myself and I told him we were going to make this work and he was going to be the starting guard and I was going to come off the bench. I think from that day forward, he and I became almost like brothers, very, very close. And I was able to talk to Gary and kind of be that big brother to him throughout his career."

But let's get back to how Karl was going to do things differently for a second.

Yes, he could bottle up his in-game tirades. And yes, he could tone down his demeanor during practice. That's all fine and good and mostly for show, because his players knew if he had the goods and they would ultimately decide whether to buy in or not. Having truly learned from his past mistakes (for the time being), Karl went to great lengths to get his guys on board, all the way to the point of bringing the players in as de facto partners in the strategy sessions. A few writers dubbed it "basketball by committee."

"It's something I've never heard of, bringing the players into the total game process," Kloppenburg said. "I think it's easier to execute everything if they go through it step-by-step. I guess what's more important is that they seem to like it." Not only did they like it, they appreciated it. Karl and his staff broke meetings down by position and encouraged discussion as the film work took place and the coaches laid out the game plan. "Everybody is much more alert to what's going on in the game," guard Nate McMillan said. "We've always talked with the coaches before, but this is the first time we can feel our input.

We're the ones out there playing, and the coaches are smart to let us call plays on both ends of the floor. We just have so much communication now, we all understand the game better."

This transparency was a big reason why the team gelled so quickly once Karl arrived. The players knew there were no ulterior motives; no political jockeying; no bullshit. It gave the players a sense of security—especially the greener players. If there was a match-up that favored the Sonics by going with extended minutes for a veteran instead of a younger guy, both guys knew why the move was made. "If there's something we see on the floor, we react, then talk about it later," Derrick McKey said. "It makes us a smarter team, so we're able to do more things well offensively."

In the first round of the 1992 playoffs, the offensive versatility that McKey spoke about was on full display. Playing against Golden State and George Karl's on-again-off-again friend, NBA Coach of the Year Don Nelson, the Sonics unleashed their full suite of weapons. They took the first game in the series 117-109, lost game two, and then in game three they matched the Warriors' two elite scorers, Tim Hardaway and Chris Mullin, shot-for-shot and won 129-128. The Sonics then closed out the five-game series in Seattle behind a 21-point and 20-rebound effort from Shawn Kemp and some clutch play from Payton down the stretch, who sank a few key baskets and three pressure foul shots with the game on the line.

"Gary Payton was huge," Eddie Johnson said. "The Warriors were denying me and Ricky the ball, so they were saying, 'Gary, you beat us.' And Gary did. I'm just so proud of this team. I came here last year and there was a group of guys who just didn't know where they were going. Tonight, every time we needed a big bucket, somebody else stepped up."

The series win was quick and dominant and somewhat surprising. All season the Utah Jazz, Portland Trail Blazers and Phoenix Suns seemed destined to duke it out for the right to face (what everyone assumed would be) Michael Jordan and the defending champion Chicago Bulls in the NBA Finals. It was the upstart Sonics who were crashing the party in the semifinals against Karl Malone, John Stockton and the rest of the Jazz. The series, despite one win in game three, wasn't close. Malone averaged 29 points and 10 rebounds a game while Stockton averaged 14 points and 14 assists. The Sonics were on the right trajectory, but they hadn't arrived just yet. Kemp, who had the unenviable task of banging with the muscle-bound Mailman every night, took the series in stride. "It was definitely a good challenge for me," he said. "His strength was a huge factor in this series. That's what I'm here for. To learn."

Also, he was there to dunk.

While that year's playoff run itself was not memorable, one moment has lived on in highlight reels and YouTube dunk mixes for all eternity. Of course, we're talking about one of the best, if not *the best*, in-game dunk in NBA playoff history: Shawn Kemp's Lister Blister.

The dunk took place midway through the second quarter of game four against Golden State in the first round. Alton Lister (ironically, a former Sonic) had been spot-guarding Kemp for a few games and was getting praise for somewhat stifling the Reign Man, which led to his frustration and the two trading punches in game three. By the time we get to this play in game four, Kemp was done messing around. After receiving a pass from Nate McMillan out by the three-point line, Kemp took a single dribble toward the basket, coiled his body, cocked the ball back and launched toward the hoop. Lister, seeing Kemp soar to the hoop, tried to take a charge, which ended up being one of the worst split-second decisions in NBA posterization history. Kemp thundered toward the hoop and wiped out Lister, knocking him to the ground as he slammed the ball. When Kemp landed, he crouched down, gave Lister a vintage double point and then ran down the court.

The dunk.

The taunt.

All of it.

It's breathtaking.

"I think it's the number one dunk of all-time," Payton said.

Lister Blister aside, the team had shown remarkable improvement under Karl in just over four months. So much so that opposing coaches had taken notice. "I'd like to say this about Seattle," Jazz Coach Jerry Sloan said. "Give them credit for where they are, for what they were able to accomplish in a short period of time under Karl." Members of the team believed that they'd have gone further in the playoffs if they'd had a whole season under him. "I think if we had a training camp with George we'd still be playing," Eddie Johnson said. "We have to learn from this, as Utah has in the past. This [loss] should not linger. We had a great second half of the year, and we beat a great Golden State team. We have some flaws to correct, but we're going to be tough next year."

To sum up the half year in modern NBA parlance, the Seattle SuperSonics were about to become a problem.

Chapter 13

Slam Jam

The megawatt stars of the planetarium background on the poster draw your eyes for a millisecond before your pupils dart quickly to the bright neon box on the clear basketball hoop. Your gaze then skips down to the forest green foam barrier at the bottom of the backboard and then, finally, you focus on the two figures suspended in outer space, mid-jump, coming in hot about to slam the hell out of a basketball. The man on the left, with his legs spread like the wings of an F-14, his arm cocked back and his mouth wide open is Shawn Kemp, who has fast become the most popular athlete in Seattle. The man on the right, wearing a wool hat, with the ball locked and loaded as far behind him as he can stretch is Jeff Ament, the bassist for Pearl Jam. They both hover over an oddly placed cut out electric guitar with various highlighter scribbles on it. The word *slam* is under Kemp in a bright green, slim serif font and the word *jam* is "spray-painted" in purple under Ament.

This poster was handed out to roughly 15,000 Sonics fans at their first home game of the 1993-94 season, and if ever there was a graphic that was both quintessentially '90s and quintessentially Seattle at the same time, this was it. We've got the bassist for the most successful Grunge band of the '90s at the height of its popularity next to the city's most popular basketball player since the days of Slick Watts, "Downtown" Freddie Brown and Jack Sikma.

"They're going to have to keep Shawn here," guard Dana Barros said when asked at the time about the hype surrounding his draft mate and teammate. "Because if anything ever happens to him they're going to have some riots. If he is ever traded, I think the city is going to lose its mind."

Kemp had only been a Sonic for a few years, but he'd already earned two all-star nods before the age of 24 and competed in three dunk contests, coming in second in 1991. More importantly, he'd entered the cultural zeitgeist of not only the city but the wider sports world as well. As his play continued to improve on through 1992 and '93, Reebok put the wheels in motion to give Kemp his own signature shoe, the electrifying and highly aggressive 'Kamikaze I', with its jagged black and white color way. The "Reign Man" persona had gone from a local thing to a bona fide '90s phenomenon, with the Costacos Brothers immortalizing Kemp and his nickname on an instantly famous poster in which it looks like he's doing a reverse one-handed slam on the Space Needle itself.

Pearl Jam, for its part, was at the forefront of Seattle's '90s music explosion, and the entire band considered themselves huge SuperSonics and NBA fans. As music trivia aficionados know, the band's original name before Pearl Jam was "Mookie Blaylock," in a nod to their favorite NBA player (although Mookie never played for the Sonics). "You gotta understand Seattle," Duff McKagan, Seattle-native and bassist for Guns 'N Roses, told *Rolling Stone*. "It's *grungy*. People are into rock & roll and into noise, and they're building airplanes all the time, and there's a lot of noise, and there's rain and musty garages. Musty garages create a certain noise."

That "certain noise," especially of the ilk that Pearl Jam produced, seemed tailor-made to weave into the fabric of a live NBA game. Kevin Jackson, an executive at ESPN from Seattle, wrote this as part of a column on Pearl Jam and the Sonics. "Pearl Jam songs became the soundtrack for the Sonics' playoff runs in those years, and any Seattle fan worth his salt could close his eyes and tell you what was happening on the floor at the Seattle Center Coliseum by the tune being played during timeouts. 'Even Flow' meant our boys had blown the game open, 'Alive' meant they were waging a comeback, 'Go' meant they had a big lead in the fourth quarter but the house was urging us to 'not go on them now' and bolt for the exits."

In 1992, Pearl Jam front man Eddie Vedder had a small role in Cameron Crowe's movie *Singles*, which took place in Seattle and became a critical and cultural hit, putting the city at the epicenter of Generation X. The movie featured a greatest hits list of Seattle landmarks, with scenes shot at Jimi Hendrix's original grave at Greenwood Memorial Park, the Pike Place Market, Capitol Hill and Gas Works Park below Northlake.

The following year, Tom Hanks and Meg Ryan starred in the mega hit *Sleepless in Seattle*, which grossed over $225 million in the United States alone. Hanks' character lived on a floating houseboat in Westlake, and some of the more famous scenes took place along First Avenue, the Inn at the Market, the Athenian Inn (now the Athenian Restaurant Seafood and Bar) as well as the Fremont Bridge. The two movies were veritable advertisements for the city to the rest of the country. Couple the above with (deep breath) Nirvana's national influence and Soundgarden's success and the fact that the Mariners had the biggest star in baseball in Ken Griffey Jr. and a budding star in Alex Rodriguez, and the University of Washington football team was in the midst of three straight Rose Bowl appearances and a split National Championship in 1991… and what you're left with is a city in full (it had come a long way from the *Let's skidaddle to Seattle* days). All that remained to tie everything together was a new world championship from one of its sports teams. The betting money heading into the 1992-93 NBA season was on the Sonics.

***

Right up until June 5 of 1993, if the Seattle SuperSonics '92-'93 season was an episode of the A-Team, then George Karl as Hannibal would have confidently said, "I love it when a plan comes together." Beginning with a sweep of the Houston Rockets in the Yokohama Arena in Tokyo, Japan to start the season as part of the NBA's international outreach (Kemp had 29 and 20), the Sonics were a locomotive, chugging through the season and gaining momentum with few stops. They posted an 8-4 record in November, a 10-4 record in December, a 10-5 record in January and on it went, punctuated with a ten-game win streak that spread across February and March. Kemp made his first NBA All-Star team (but played the least minutes of anyone on either squad with nine) and the rest of the starting five—Michael Cage, Derrick McKey, Ricky Pierce and Gary Payton—continued to play well together and, equally as important, were getting to know each other.

"When I first got there, Kemp and I were hanging out and then we started practicing together. Once you hang out with somebody off the court, I think it's a little bit easier because you get to know them and then you get to looking for each other on the court," Payton said. "I don't know if people realized that, but once you get close to somebody, you start knowing what he's going to do or where he's going to be, and then it makes the game a lot easier."

Karl also brought in assistant coach Tim Grgurich, another defensive-minded basketball vet who was a pioneer of the amoeba defense from his tutelage as an assistant under Bob Timmons at the University of Pittsburgh. In addition to being a basketball guru, the taciturn Grgurich was an important counter to Karl's intensity. He was tireless in his work with the players and it endeared him to them often giving him the role of good cop to Karl's bad cop. *Seattle Times* columnist Steve Kelley described him this way in a piece: "It doesn't matter who you are. Dream Teamer or 12th man, all-star or CBA refugee, Grgurich will give you his time. Jump shot, jump hook, pregame, postgame, before practice, after practice, Grgurich is available. With Grg, you get the feeling if equipment manager Marc St. Yves wanted help with his post-up moves, Grgurich would be there for him. Grgurich turned 50 in June, but he has the energy and enthusiasm of a rookie. He gets results. When he came to the Sonics in March 1992, he made the improvement of Gary Payton's jump shot his first priority. He played Angelo Dundee to Payton's Muhammad Ali."

Payton agreed completely with Grgurich's importance to the team's success. "When Coach Grg came in, he knew how to deal with us, and he would be the buffer. We'd get it, we'd cuss each other out in closed doors and then when we get out there, we'd play hard-nosed basketball. It was a great thing for us to get that." Payton also had slowly but surely earned Karl's trust, and that freed up the two hot heads to work under what Karl called a "commitment to compromise." The head coach gave a little. The point guard gave a little. Everybody won.

"He proved himself to me when he started letting me be the guy I wanted to be," Payton said. "When I stopped making mistakes and he started believing in me and pulling me over to the side and saying, 'Look, this is your show. Run what you gotta run. Do what you gotta do.' And I think that was the starting point of me knowing that this guy had a lot of trust in me, and once he had a lot of trust in me like that, I knew I had to be that guy to always come through for him and win basketball games without me looking over at the bench."

The only friction on the roster that needed to be addressed was that Karl loathed the lackadaisical approach that Benoit Benjamin had toward playing basketball. Couple that with his team-high $3.175 million salary (a full million more per year than the next closest guy) and his poor body language, and he was essentially the opposite of everything Karl wanted in his players.

Fortunately, Bob Whitsitt knew this and had Karl's back, vowing to trade Benjamin at the deadline.

"By the middle of the season I'd parked Benoit's ass on the bench, so I was ecstatic when Whitsitt traded him to the Lakers for Sam Perkins, a fellow UNC alum whose game I loved," Karl wrote. "And in what you might assume was the most minor of roster moves, we got a player you've never heard of from the Quad City Thunder of the CBA, Steve Scheffler. Scheffler didn't play much, but it was all-out war when he did… A lot of NBA coaching is keeping negative energy away from your team. I want winners who act like winners, not moaners and groaners. That's why a really positive bench and practice player like Schef is worth more than a talented guy who bitches all the time that he's not getting enough minutes… If they hurt your chemistry and camaraderie, they're not worth the effort."

The final tally on the 1992-93 season was 55-27, good enough for second in the Pacific Division and a first-round playoff rematch against the Utah Jazz. This time, with the addition of Sam Perkins, who Karl moved into the starting line-up after game one, the Sonics won the first-round match-up 3-2. Six guys averaged double digits. Eight guys played in all five games. It was a thing of beauty. In game five, the team rallied back from a franchise worst 30 points in the first half to win, thanks to Perkins hitting four-of-eight three pointers. "He's the ultimate team player," McMillan said of Perkins. "He kept our confidence up at halftime and then came out and hit some big shots."

The pre-championship Houston Rockets were up next, featuring First-Team All-NBA Center Hakeem Olajuwon, Vernon Maxwell, Kenny Smith, Otis Thorpe and a young Robert Horry. The series started easily enough for the fighting Karls, as they won the first two games at home before dropping the next two on the road. With the series tied 2-2, the Sonics promptly blew out Houston by 25 points at home in game five, then lost at Houston in game six (with Olajuwon suffocating Kemp) to force a seventh game back in Seattle. Game seven was an overtime classic that is mostly remembered now as the Perkins and Pierce show. The scoring savvy veterans combined for 48 points as an answer to Olajuwon shutting down the paint and keeping Kemp, who only scored a single free throw in game six, at bay.

"It's hard to finish with Hakeem there," Kemp said in one of the all-time NBA understatements. "I decided if I went aggressively at him [in game seven], I might get some free throws." The strategy worked and Kemp bounced back to add 18 points to his 11 boards. The deciding game was tight the entire fourth quarter and regulation ended in a 93-93 tie. In overtime, the teams were stuck at 95 points apiece until Pierce hit two free throws and Kemp knocked down a much-needed jumper. The Rockets then pulled within one point twice, first on a free throw by Olajuwon and then on a soft twelve-foot hook he hit in the lane with 15.9 seconds left to make it 101-100. Kenny Smith then intentionally fouled Derrick McKey, who missed both of his free throws, giving the Rockets a chance to win game seven, on the road, with the final shot. Rockets coach Rudy Tomjanovich drew up a perfect play for Vernon Maxwell, who got off a clean 18-footer at the baseline with .08 left… but it missed, sending the Sonics to their first Western Conference Finals of the George Karl era.

The team was elated but physically pummeled, particularly Kemp, who immediately sought refuge in the locker room by collapsing on a chair and wrapping his throbbing knees in bulging ice packs (it was not a dream to face Hakeem). Before his legs could go numb and he could catch his breath, reporters were already asking him about his highly anticipated next round match-up against the Phoenix Suns and Charles Barkley. "To be honest with you, I'm not going to worry about Charles until tomorrow," Kemp said, his eyes staring off into the distance. "I played against Karl Malone and now I've played against Hakeem. Even though Charles is a terrific player, I don't feel like it gets any better than against Hakeem. I don't care what anyone says, Hakeem is the best big man in the game today." Seattle beat the Suns in two out of their three match-ups during the regular season, but Kemp and his squad knew the ante had been upped. "We challenged them during the season and we were able to beat them in our series, but this is the playoffs and it's a little different now. It's going to take a lot of work."

***

For a generation of NBA fans who have grown up on Charles Barkley the playful, puffy, suit-wearing co-host of TNT's legendary basketball show *Inside the NBA*, it's a little jarring to learn that Barkley, along with his parade of nicknames (Sir Charles, the Round Mound of Rebound, the Chuck Wagon, the Incredible Bulk, Boy Gorge, Bread Truck), was a fighting, cussing, controversial, hard-court hard-ass who was a top-ten player in the league for a decade. Listed at 6'6" (but really closer to 6'4") and 250 pounds (more like 270) Barkley, whose playing weight was close to 300 pounds in college at Auburn, was an absolute menace on the court and made first- or second-team All-NBA for a decade straight. By the time the '93 Western Conference Finals rolled around, he was at the tail end of one of the most fascinating 10-month spans in the history of pro sports.

On April 18, 1992, Barkley wrapped up his eighth regular season in Philadelphia with a forgettable 13 points against the Washington Bullets to finish with a terrible 35-47 record. He'd been vocal all season about desperately wanting out of Philly. He was miserable. The team was losing. He hated it there and he wanted a fresh start so badly that he started day drinking one afternoon in February celebrating what *he thought* was a trade to the Lakers. "It was going crazy for two weeks so I knew it would come down to Portland, the Lakers or Phoenix. So I get a call from my agent one morning and he said, 'Philly has traded you to the Lakers'. So I went to lunch and started drinking. I'm fucking excited that I am going to the Lakers. Three hours later I get a fucking phone call from my agent saying that the Sixers backed out of the deal. I said, 'Oh, shit, I'm feeling pretty good right now.' So I went out and played that night. I don't remember anything about that game. I have no idea what happened in that game."

The trade was rumored to be Barkley for James Worthy and a few other players, but it was never revisited. After the season ended, he played on the famous Dream Team in the Olympics and became the team's second-most popular player internationally behind Michael Jordan. A few weeks after he returned to the states, he was finally and officially traded to the Phoenix Suns on June 17. Over the course of the next nine months, Barkley embraced Arizona, connected with his new co-stars Kevin Johnson and "Thunder" Dan Majerle, and led the team to sixty-two wins and first place in the Pacific Division of the Western Conference. Along the way he earned 859 votes to pick up his first MVP award over Olajuwon, Jordan, Patrick Ewing and Dominique Wilkins. This made him the third player to win the MVP award in his first year with a new team, following Kareem Abdul-Jabbar with the Lakers and Moses Malone with the 76ers. For those who paid attention to such matters and who were also a touch spiritual, there was a sense that the basketball gods were smiling on Barkley and were nudging him toward one destination: the NBA Finals. That put the Sonics in a match-up not only against a reinvigorated Sir Charles and a revived Suns team, but also against what many felt was destiny: a Barkley vs. Jordan title fight.

***

"Phoenix, Arizona. High noon. The America West Arena the scene for game seven of the NBA Western Conference Finals. The Chicago Bulls await the winner. Fans of the Suns have celebrated the best ever Phoenix season. The most wins in their twenty-five-year history but they are still one precious victory away from an NBA Championship round. Ohhh myyyy!!!"

This was Dick Enberg's famous call leading into game seven of the Western Conference Finals. The opening "high noon" bookended with his classic "oh my" had millions of viewers primed for an all-time playoff match-up. Outside America West Arena the atmosphere was a bit like Mardi Gras. Fans rolled in with the Suns logo painted on their car windows and entered the arena to trumpets and live music, waving purple and orange pom-poms at each other. To enter, they crossed under electronic billboards that flashed *You Gotta Believe!* Once inside, all 18,000 people were handed purple signs with the words *Beat the Sonics* on one side and *Go Suns* on the other. During pre-game, when the fans screamed and waved their banners in unison, the audience looked like a pulsating orange that was bleeding purple.

The series up to the deciding game had gone back and forth every contest. Phoenix won game one, Seattle won game two, Phoenix won game three, and on it went to game seven. Ricky Pierce was a steady offensive hand in almost every game, but Shawn Kemp, still only 23 years old, was nothing short of brilliant. He led the team in minutes, points, rebounds, blocks and free throws. By game four, the storyline of the series was clearly Kemp "the budding star" versus Barkley the "established superstar." In game five, Kemp put up 33 points, 6 rebounds, 4 assists and 3 blocks—big numbers, to be sure, but Barkley was out for blood. All night he countered Kemp's buckets with scores of his own, feeding off the home crowd and gaining strength as the game wore on. Like the Incredible Hulk (a far cry from his Incredible Bulk college days), he seemed to get angrier and stronger each quarter on his way to a monster 43-15-10 triple-double and a Suns win. The effort was one for the ages, but it wiped him out. In game six he appeared lethargic and worn down.

At a pivotal moment, Barkley brought the ball down to the wing and surveyed the court by the Sonics sideline. Kemp sprinted to match up with him, splayed his legs wide, grabbed the bottom of his shorts and dropped into a deep defensive crouch. Barkley took his eye off Kemp for a split second and all 6'11" of the Reign Man dove at the ball, knocked it loose and passed it into transition as Barkley dove on top of him. This was a microcosm of the game and Barkley admitted afterward that he was tired. Kemp, who effectively shut down Sir Charles (13 points), would have none of it. He said it was his defensive effort that thwarted the MVP and that's why the Sonics won game six. It was into this heated atmosphere that the Sonics and Suns collided in Phoenix for a game seven that, in Ricky Pierce's words, was "going to be a dogfight."

"Home court or no home court," Kemp said. "This is what dreams are all about. And it's our dream to win a championship. If you can't get yourself up for that, you just can't get yourself up. We've played in a lot of big games, but I, myself, have never played in a game at this level."

Barkley had played in games at this level and he made it abundantly clear what he expected the outcome to be. "I don't believe I'm going to let us lose. I'm looking forward to it. I'll be ready. The whole season I've been a dominant player. This is game seven. Everybody is going to have antsy feet and be jumping around, and I'm certainly going to be leading the way. As a kid, you grow up hoping to be in this situation. This is a monumental game."

Kemp concurred. Forget about who played well up to that point. Forget about trends or game plans. The two best teams in the conference had clashed for seven games and all they could do now was put it all on the line in sudden death. "I don't think momentum really matters right now," Kemp said. "It's the seventh game and we have a chance to go to the Finals. It comes down to pretty much who wants the game the most."

The answer to this question, based on Kemp's criteria, was one Charles Wade Barkley, who played, by his own estimation, the best game of his life. From the moment Suns center Mark West pushed the opening tip to Barkley, he was a one-man wrecking ball. Yes, Suns point guard Kevin Johnson had 22 points and yes, Tom Chambers helped off the bench with 17, but Barkley was the relentless tip of the spear, punishing the Sonics with 44 points and 24 rebounds to earn his first trip to the NBA Finals. Neither Kemp, Perkins, McKey or Payton really got going in the game, and the only Sonics player who rose to the occasion was old man Eddie Johnson, who reached back to the fountain of youth to pour in 34 points on 17 shots.

Afterward, George Karl was furious about the number of "home" foul calls Barkley and the Suns were getting. Phoenix shot a then-playoff record sixty-four free throws and Barkley took twenty-two of them all by himself. To be fair, Barkley was the aggressor all night, but the constant fouls ruined the Sonics' rhythm.

"It took away our aggression," Payton said. "Because every time we played the way we've been playing this whole series, we heard a whistle.... No, we don't feel cheated. We just feel like we played another team on their home court." But that was just lip service. The Sonics fans, the front office, even many reporters thought the foul calls were complete BS. Surprisingly, it was a columnist for the *Tacoma News Tribune* who summed up the way the Sonics felt the best. "This game was a travesty, an embarrassment to the NBA," he wrote. "The whistles made for a bad game and bad TV, but the result brought the match-up the nation wants..."

See, the basketball gods *were* smiling down on Barkley. All the Sonics could hope for was that soon it would be their turn.

Chapter 14

"It Was Sort of Like a Death in the Family"

Tim Grgurich was like a kid stuck between two warring parents, except he was in his fifties and the two "parents" were Gary Payton and George Karl. They had always fought (bickered, if you want to put it politely), but now, in the midst of the 1993-94 season, with the Barkley beatdown in their rear-view mirror, they incessantly ripped on each other and used Grg as a go-between. "Tell Gary if he's going to be that careless with the ball, I'm going to sit his ass on the bench," Karl would tell Grg. "Tell George to quit yelling shit at me and sit *his* ass on the bench," Payton might respond.

Grg, feeling like a kid whose mom says, "Tell your father next time he makes a sandwich to put away the mayo" with his father in the same room, did his best to keep the peace. Like any tight family, the Sonics, who had now endured two disappointing playoff runs in a row, cared for each other but knew how to push each other's buttons.

Payton, ever rebellious, ever talking, hated to be told what to do and how to prepare. As tenacious and aggressive as he was in games, he could be equally laid back and chill at shootarounds—especially game day shootarounds. Some days he'd take off his sweat suit, some days he wouldn't. Some days he'd listen to what Karl was saying, other days he'd half-ass it. This would, as you can expect, drive his coach mad. And when Karl would yell at him to pick up the pace, Payton would casually reply, "You want me in the shootaround or at 7 o'clock tonight?" Translation: "I'm saving myself for the game. Screw off."

With Kemp, effort was never an issue. He had one speed on the court, and he played with an all-out, forty-inch vertical, swat-your-shot-into-the-tenth-row swagger that his coach and his teammates loved. He was also a gym rat who would shoot the lights out until the lights went out. Getting to the gym *on time*, however, was a different issue entirely. Local team appearance? Kemp was late. Practice? Kemp was late. Bus leaving for the airport? Kemp was late. It was like the team was in the Pacific time zone and Kemp was in a different section of the country. The players and coaches jokingly called it "Shawn Time," but Kemp was so overwhelmingly popular with his teammates and with the entire city that everyone let it slide. And even though this was smack dab in the middle of the era when hip-hop started dominating the NBA music scene,

Kemp connected with the local Grunge musicians in Seattle and miraculously became one of their own. He was all things to all people in the Emerald City, as iconic as the Space Needle itself.

One pronounced difference to the team in 1993-94 was the absence of Derrick McKey, who was traded to the Indiana Pacers for 6'10" all-star Detlef Schrempf. For Schrempf, it was a bit like coming home, but not all the way home. He was born in Germany, but actually played his senior year of high school basketball in Centralia, Washington and then attended the University of Washington, where he helped the Huskies win two regular season titles and reach the Sweet Sixteen in 1984. The Mavericks took him as the eighth overall pick in the '85 draft, but he played only two years in Dallas before being traded to the Pacers, where he won back-to-back Sixth Man of the Year awards in 1991 and 1992. The move was a gigantic pick-up for the Sonics, giving them three all-stars and no excuses for not winning a title.

"He's a versatile athlete who does it all," Karl said at the time. "We think this improves our shooting and gives us another player who can help us get to where we want to be. This puts us in a situation where we've got to produce. We've opened up a two- to three-year window to contend for the championship. If we don't win a championship in two to three years, we should be scrutinized very closely."

We'll put this last quote in the "beware what you wish for" category for now. Although the team was chaotic in the locker room, they coasted in the standings. They opened up with a blistering 26-3 record and were 35-10 at the all-star break. Kemp was selected as an all-star again and Payton made his first squad. To top it off, since the Sonics had the best record in the west, George Karl coached the game, putting the three Sonics stars in the national spotlight and firmly making their national imprint on the rest of the league. The team stayed hot after the break and won a league-best sixty-three games. They ranked fifth in defense, sixth in offense and were the odds-on favorite to come out of the west and win the title, especially considering the fact that Michael Jordan was off playing baseball and the league throne was effectively empty.

As the number one seed, they drew the 42-40, eighth-seed Denver Nuggets for their first-round playoff match-up. The series was supposed to be a cakewalk.

Sure, Denver had a few good players like Dikembe Mutombo and Mahmoud Abdul-Rauf, but they weren't in the same class as the Sonics, who jumped out to an easy 2-0 lead in the series. All they had to do was win one of the next three games against a barely .500 team and they were on to the next round.

No sweat.

At halftime of game two, the Sonics headed to the locker room up 50-38. On the outside, they were cruising. On the inside, they were fuming. Particularly Gary Payton and Ricky Pierce, who were arguing the entire second quarter about the offense and ball distribution. From that point on, there are two versions of the story and how their feud escalated. This is the first one, from Glenn Nelson in the *Seattle Times* after the game:

"The most publicized development of the series, a tiff between Payton and Ricky Pierce, had occurred before and during halftime of the Sonics' 97-87 victory in game two. Pierce has publicly blamed the squabble on a disagreement over Payton's ball distribution, but Payton's account, largely substantiated by teammates and other witnesses, paints a more convoluted picture.

"With the Sonics on their way to a 50-37 halftime lead, Pierce broke off a play, tried to make a one-on-one move, but was stripped of the ball. Soon after, Payton told the team, 'Let's run the offense.' Taking umbrage, Pierce told Payton that since he dominated the ball, it was his responsibility to get Pierce more shots.

"During a timeout shortly after, the argument escalated. Pierce was pulled from the game during the break and, believing Payton had influenced the substitution, became incensed. Heated words were exchanged during the walk back to the Sonic locker room, where teammates told the two to stop bickering.

"Payton and Pierce did not come close to blows and were not forcibly separated, as has been reported in other accounts, Payton and other Sonics say."

The second version of the story comes from quotes by George Karl and a couple other team and media members after they'd all had some space from the incident.

"[Payton] and Ricky Pierce got into some kind of a discussion at halftime of the first Denver game, and they were threatening to get guns," Karl said. "The players told me they had guns in their bags. It was, 'I'll kill your family.' It was crazy."

Hmmmm. A gun threat versus a "tiff." That's a pretty big gap. Steve Kelley, a sports columnist for the *Seattle Times*, heard a similar version of the more serious variety that Karl had heard. "Something happened at halftime of game two in Seattle. One of the cops came up to me and said, 'You'll never believe what happened at halftime and you'll never hear it from me.' Years later, we found out that Ricky [Pierce] and Gary got in a fight at halftime of game two, and the whole series changed on that night."

Payton and Pierce have both publicly acknowledged that there was a disagreement that night, but neither have confirmed that there was an actual fight, or that guns were threatened, or that Payton actually said he'd kill Pierce's family. Regardless of whether you believe it was an all-out brawl or just a regular team shouting match, the incident completely threw the Sonics off and they never recovered the chemistry or their courage, losing the next two games to force a game five that they never should have been in.

"Before the series, the Sonics had so much confidence we could have sold it in jars," Karl wrote. "Now [in game five] we looked shaky against a team that barely qualified for the playoffs. Our arena was humid and overheated, filled to the brim with seriously edgy people, including me. Someone wrote that I looked like the defendant in a murder trial just before the jury foreman reads the verdict."

In this case, the verdict was a stunning loss.

In fact, the loss was so shocking, nothing like it had ever happened in the league before. The 1994 Sonics were the first number one seed to lose a first-round series to an eighth seed. It was devastating.

"It hurt me very deeply. It was sort of like a death in the family," owner Barry Ackerley said afterward. "As with any severe trauma, you sort of, like, walk away from it for a while."

In two and a half seasons the Sonics went from scrappy overachievers to, historically, the biggest choke artists in the NBA. Only a title in the near future could erase the embarrassment. Unfortunately, the potential for that relief was a few years off.

***

The twelve months following the upset loss to Denver were marked by franchise-altering trade rumors, the weight of expectations, a crushing defeat, and the reality that the Sonics were squandering one of the most talented basketball teams of the entire decade. On the trade front, it was an open secret in the off-season of 1994 that the Chicago Bulls were searching for a trade partner to get rid of Scottie Pippen. On the eve of the NBA Draft, reports surfaced that the Bulls and Sonics were finalizing a deal that would send Pippen to the Sonics and Kemp to the Bulls.

Basketball-wise, a pairing of Pippen and Payton was intriguing and would have been downright scary on defense, giving Seattle arguably two of the top five on-the-ball and open-floor defenders in basketball. Offensively, there would have been a slight drop off, but Schrempf (now a two-time all-star) and newcomer Kendall Gill could have picked up the slack. On paper and from an Xs and Os perspective, it could have worked…and it could have worked really well. Even assembling the team on *NBA2K* gives you an idea of how much of a mismatch that team could have been. Furthermore, the basketball guys in the Sonics organization liked it.

"I was a huge Pippen fan and I was a huge Shawn fan. We, at that stage, were seeing Shawn wear out a little bit," Karl said. "…at that time, [it was] a very difficult choice, but I would have made the trade. I would have gone with the speed and athleticism and great defense. Shawn was a good defender, but not a great defender. Pippen, I think, is an elite, top, maybe, 10 defender of all time."

Steve Kelley, who covered the team at the time, said, "George and Tim Grgurich wanted to do it. And then Wally Walker had his finger in the air and felt the breeze and decided that it wasn't a good thing to do. So Wally kiboshed the trade."

Wally Walker was hired to replace Whitsitt, who lost his job after the Denver loss. He was really just a consultant at the time of the draft, and it was very much like, "Hey, how are you, here's your parking space and your key to your office, and oh, by the way, should we trade Shawn Kemp?" As is usually the case with franchise-altering trades, owners have to be involved, despite the basketball guys in the front office wanting to make the move.

"It was an odd circumstance," Walker said. "There was no general manager in place when the discussions were going on. You had a coach who wanted to make the trade, but the owner needed to make the final call because it was a potential landmark moment for the organization. There was active discussion. I wouldn't say there was ever a signoff internally to make the deal."

As the discussions hovered in neutral, behind the scenes Michael Jordan talked with his fellow UNC alum George Karl about how great Pippen was. He told Karl that he thought the Sonics could win a title with Pippen. But Karl had already made his opinion heard, and all he could do was wait to see what his owner wanted to do. Ackerley, for his part, agonized over the decision. He adored Kemp. He knew how much the city adored him. *Did he really want to be the owner who traded away possibly the most popular Sonics player of all time? In his prime?* In the end, Ackerley took the temperature of the city, trusted his gut, and killed the deal."

"Ackerley called me and told me they weren't going to make the trade," Kemp said. "He was telling me people were calling the local radio stations saying they were going to burn down the stadium if I was traded."

So Kemp stayed. And the team played well. Kemp, Payton and Schrempf all made the '95 NBA All-Star team. Kendall Gill and Sam Perkins were solid. Vincent Askew was a strong contributor. They won fifty-seven games and finished fourth in the Western Conference, leading to a first-round series against the Lakers. Once again, they didn't get out of the first round. And these weren't yet the Shaq and Kobe Lakers; these were the Nick Van Exel, Vlade Divac, Cedric Ceballos Lakers. The Sonics were a more talented, deeper and far more experienced team. There was no excuse.

"When you average sixty wins the last two seasons, we all feel we should go beyond this stage of the playoffs," Wally Walker, then the Sonics President, commented after the game.

Detlef Schrempf, who now had two seasons under his belt to witness some of what went on behind the scenes with the organization, was crushed and gave a supremely candid evaluation of why they were once again going home early. "We're a very relaxed group. We don't have any discipline," he said. "We don't practice hard when we need to—those are things that add up. If you keep winning, you have a tendency to overlook things. We said the same thing last year."

George Karl knew that if he even had a job after the off-season, his seat might as well be made of molten lava it was going to be so hot. And he was ready.

"It's a time to face our embarrassment, be humbled, feel the humility of the sport and go on and try to figure out some things," he said. "We are a better team than we've played in the last two years of the playoffs. Everybody in that [Sonics locker room] knows that."

Karl wasn't fired, but it was clear he had one more season to keep his job.

Chapter 15

Biting the Mailman

One of the curses of having regular-season success is that winning more than fifty-five games eventually becomes, well, regular—ordinary, even. Starting with the '93 season, the Sonics won fifty-five, then sixty-three, then fifty-seven games. They then won sixty-four games in 1996. Every single move they made (or didn't make) paid off. Shawn Kemp and Gary Payton both earned Second Team All-NBA honors. Payton also won the league's Defensive Player of the Year award. Detlef Schrempf averaged 17-5-5 a night and former all-star Hersey Hawkins, who the Sonics picked up from Charlotte, could score fifteen points a game. They had bruisers like Vincent Askew and Frank Brickowski, glue guys like the ever-reliable Nate McMillan, and savvy veterans like Sam Perkins and David Wingate. They were a top-to-bottom force and they closed out the season on a 14-3 run and earned the number one seed in the West. But they all knew that absolutely none of it mattered unless they finally cashed in their playoff chips and won a title. Another first-round flameout was unthinkable.

If the definition of insanity is truly doing the same thing over and over again and expecting a different result, then Karl decided he'd jump off the train to the loony bin and shake things up a bit heading into the 1995-96 season. Prior to training camp, he set up a coaches retreat on Lake Chelan in the hopes that the azure-blue glacier lake and the fresh mountain air and the vineyards would inspire his staff to revamp their approach to avoid another tragic ending to the season. The first issue they addressed was a near total lack of discipline and accountability when it came to practice. To right the ship, they pulled a page directly out of pre-schools across the world and developed a set of three simple rules for everyone to follow: no sitting in practice, no rehab during practice and no talking while a coach is talking (see, straight out of pre-K). Then they tackled "Shawn Time" and the near team-wide refusal to be punctual by mandating that every player had to be at their locker thirty minutes before practice. For this, the coaches channeled the *Mission: Impossible* playbook.

"To remove any excuse for lateness on practice days we synced the digital clocks in the gym, the training room, the locker room and the weight room," Karl wrote. "When it was 2 pm it was 2 pm everywhere a player might be."

They also dropped the hammer when it came to the physical fitness of their players with common-sense but necessary edicts like no more beer after games and no soda or potato chips or junk food on the plane. The idea wasn't that these changes would show up in the box score overnight, but rather when the team reached the playoffs, they could fall back on good habits when times got tough rather than letting bad habits sink them. In addition, Karl's top relationship priority was to make sure that he and his court general, Payton, were on the same page in good times, in bad times and especially in crunch times. No more senseless arguing. No more using Grg as a middleman. No more alpha dog bullshit that they'd both sweep under the rug from October to April only to have it rear its ugly head and catch up with them in the playoffs.

Prior to the season, Karl asked Payton to meet him at the Pro Sports Club in Bellevue for an airing of grievances. Karl told him he was through with all the nonsense and that it didn't matter who won an argument or who came off looking stronger or who didn't lose face after a shouting match, if at the end of the day they failed to reach their team goals. He wanted to end the confrontations once and for all and start tackling problems from the same perspective. It worked. Payton bought in and the rest of the team could feel it. *This year was going to be different.*

***

Unlike the 1995 playoffs, there was very little drama in Seattle's first-round series against the eighth-seeded Sacramento Kings. The Sonics won game one, lost game two, overcame a tight stretch in game three with back-to-back-to-back three-pointers from Brickowski, Perkins and Hawkins to win, and then they led for almost all of game four to close out the series. *Whew.* The first-round monkey was off their back. Whatever happened, at least they didn't pull a reverse three-peat. They then swept their old nemesis Hakeem Olajuwon and his Rockets in the semifinals, setting up a Western Conference Finals showdown with Karl Malone, John Stockton and the annoyingly excellent Utah Jazz.

Through four games against Utah things seemed to be working in their favor. They smoked Malone and crew in the opening match-up by thirty and handled a low-scoring game two with a 91-87 win. The Jazz got the usual lift by returning home for game three and won by twenty. In game four, the Sonics won an 88-86 slugfest that finished with John Stockton's potentially game-tying, wide-open 24-foot jump shot clanging off the rim. It was a shot that in previous years might have fallen. It felt symbolic and the Sonics were allowing themselves to believe that this was the year things were going to break their way. "We feel good," Payton said about taking a 3-1 series lead. "We know they're going to come back strong. We've just got to go home and take care of business [in game five]."

All you need to know about whether business was, in fact, taken care of in game five is this post-game quote by Payton:

"We messed up."

Neither his 31 points nor Kemp's 24 were enough to close out a Utah team that wasn't quite ready to go home yet. Or, as Sam Smith of the *Chicago Tribune* wrote, "Utah forgot to pack its U-Haul trailers for the summer."

Specifically, John Stockton, who was in the midst of one of the worst playoff series of his life and who only scored two points in the first four quarters, simply wouldn't go down. The game was 90-90 at the end of regulation, and in the final five minutes Stockton grabbed a crucial offensive board, hit two free throws and had a pivotal steal to rip the victory from the Sonics on their home floor. Karl Malone reveled in the idea that the Sonics and their fans had left his team for dead.

"At our shootaround Tuesday at the KeyArena, there was a line outside selling Bulls tickets," Malone said. "They said the Jazz were done, stick a fork in them. We knew they were trying to blow us away. Those are things you keep in the back of your mind. Well, we ain't done yet. We're still cookin' a little bit."

There was a sense in the locker room after the game that the Sonics may have had their heads in Chicago while their bodies were on the floor in Seattle. "If anybody on our team was thinking about the Bulls, they got a lesson tonight," Payton said. While he likely wasn't talking about anyone in particular, aside from him and Kemp, the rest of the team was a no-show. Schrempf scored only seven. Perkins missed all of his threes. They weren't aggressive, taking only half as many foul shots as the Jazz on their home floor. The lackluster performances meant that instead of flying to Chicago (their destination of choice) they were flying back to Utah for game six (the last place on earth they wanted to be).

On the morning of the game, Karl Malone, who, like the Sonics, had knocked on the door of the Finals for several years but never made it, sat in the kitchen with his wife and they talked about the upcoming game. Well, he talked. And talked. His wife listened. *There was just something different about this year.* "I'm so close this time I can taste being there," he told her. Across town, in the visiting team's hotel, the Sonics vacillated between confidence and concern. If ever there was a time to see if Coach Karl's new approach to discipline and structure was going to pay off, this was it. "This team has fought hard all year. It has character," he said. Shawn Kemp agreed. "It's no time to hang your head and pout. There's no reason to get upset and get tense now."

As the rest of the team weighed in during their various media responsibilities, a glimmer of optimism seemed to envelop them. "I don't think anybody should panic here," Perkins said. "There's no need to." "We're still in the lead," said Detlef Schrempf. "We're still in the driver's seat," Frank Brickowski added. "We still feel good."

Cue the proverbial record scratch. The Sonics might as well have done all the things they said they shouldn't do: hung their heads, panicked, hopped out of the driver's seat—all of it. Game six was a blood bath. Utah jumped out to a thirteen-point lead in the first quarter and mopped the floor with them for the full forty-eight minutes, winning 118-83. If it were a boxing match, the trainer would have thrown in the towel. It was a complete embarrassment. "We got blown out, period," Payton said. "It's over now and we've got one more game. But we're in our building and hopefully it'll work out to our advantage. It's what we worked for all season."

But that was just lip service. The cloud of the past playoff failures hung in the locker room like steam in a hot shower. *Had they come this far, just to choke in another game seven?* Their hometown paper had a headline that read, "Sonics Leave Guts Home as Gut-Check Time Looms." There was so much to mull over on the two-hour flight back to Seattle, and no matter how hard they collectively tried to push the thought out of their minds, the prospect of losing a game seven at home lingered throughout the cabin. Also, the team was physically beat up. Shawn Kemp, in particular, felt like he'd been wrestling a grizzly bear for a week.

As the plane descended through the clouds early Friday morning and the players stepped off the runway into the lonely cool before dawn, they were greeted by 2,000 fans who made their way to Sea-Tac to show their support. And just then, the players didn't feel so lonely anymore. An entire city had their back. Seattle's faithful crawled out of bed before the sun came up just so the Sonics knew they weren't in this alone. Later in the day, nearly 15,000 people showed up at a pep rally downtown in support of the team. The city put the words *Go Sonics* around the ring of the space needle. If Karl and company were going to get past the Jazz, they were going to do it with the help of the entire city.

On game night, the sold-out KeyArena waved banners saying *Sonics '96: In to Win*. The Sonics wore their bright white shooting warm-ups in pregame and there was no doubt they looked focused—dare we say it, relaxed—before the game. "I think you're going to see a damn good basketball team play a damn good basketball game," Karl predicted. Shawn Kemp personally went out on a limb and said he was ready to have the game of his life. As the lights went out and the Sonics hype video began to play, there was a palpable shift in the air. On the JumboTron above center court, the video showed the Seattle skyline and then a shock of electricity blasted off of the space needle, leading to the Sonics logo rising from the ground as the speakers blared, "Your Seattle Suuuuuuuuuuuuuuuuupersonics." The fans were practically busting out of their seats by the time Shawn Kemp was introduced last, but just to make sure the arena was in an all-out frenzy, famed boxing ring announcer Michael Buffer took the microphone and led everyone in a "Let's get ready to ruuuuuumble!" cheer. And then, finally, with the official decibel level topping 105, the game/wrestling match began.

For four quarters the crowd and the Sonics never let up. Every time the Jazz scored the Sonics answered. It was 21-21 after the first quarter and 44-41 at the half. Neither team could get a clear edge on the other and the stars barely came off the court. Kemp, as he'd confidently spoken into existence, had one of his best games of the year. He led all scorers with 26 points, grabbed 14 rebounds, hit 10 of 11 foul shots and overall dominated the game.

"We rode on Shawn's back today," Hersey Hawkins said afterward. "He doesn't get enough credit for his toughness. He's emotional and sometimes he gets into foul trouble and sometimes he has tough games, and that's all anyone talks about. But what about the seventy other times when he's winning games for this team?"

For Hawkins it was a rhetorical question, but with about five minutes left in the fourth quarter, and the Sonics barely hanging on to an 85-80 lead, the notion of Kemp winning games for his team became a full-on reality because the entire team went arctic-level ice cold. They went four minutes and eleven seconds without a bucket, whiffing on four shots and turning the ball over. With 1:49 left, Stockton hit a short jumper and the game was suddenly 85-84 and looked to be slipping away. Karl drew up the next possession for Kemp, who was fouled by Antoine Carr and then calmly hit two free throws to put his guys back up three. Then Malone hit a lay-up to cut the lead back to one with about thirty seconds left. Again, Karl put the ball in Kemp's hands and again he was fouled by Carr. With the weight of what felt like the entire Pacific Northwest on his shoulders, Kemp sank both foul shots to effectively put the game away (Malone missed some free throws that could have made it closer).

The arena. The players. The city. They all went bonkers. After all the struggles they'd endured and the playoff embarrassments and the pressure and being called "gutless," it was as if they'd won the championship.

"Every player who plays basketball dreams of stepping up to the line at the end of a game and knocking the big free throws down," Kemp said. George Karl felt like the win finally slammed the door on all the naysayers and negativity that had been heaped on him and the team for the past performances. "We've been through two years of whatever you want to call it, but now people should realize we're a legit team—and we're going to Chicago because we deserve to. It was a win by a bunch of guys that fought a perception of negativity, but they persevered and fought as much as any team I've had. It's an unbelievable opportunity to play a team that won seventy-two games, but I guess the team that should play them is the team that won sixty-four."

Around town, Seattle celebrated like it was 1979. "Sometimes we get so caught up in winning the championship, but that night after they beat Utah, it kind of felt like that. The town went nuts," Mike Gastineau, a local radio personality, said. "It's quite a payoff for the torture they put us through," Patrick O'Connor, an employee at the Sonics Team Shop down the street from the arena said. As KeyArena emptied, about a thousand fans started an ad-hoc parade around the city that quickly got out of hand. Policemen on horseback were called in to keep the peace, and even the official Associated Press piece couldn't resist reporting that "a blonde woman on a red Porsche bared her breasts to the crowd, and another woman in a BMW followed suit a little later." There was no reporting on the breasts bared by women not driving luxury vehicles. "This win means a lot to the city. Seattle has a reputation of being a laid-back town," Keith Perry, a bicycle cab driver, said. "But this win rocks and will show Chicago that Seattle can rock too."

"It's hard to describe what a buzz is," Kemp said. "But there was a definite buzz around town unlike anything I can remember."

The players hugged and screamed and shouted and brought their families on the court after the final buzzer. The ultimate '90s stadium anthem Jock Jams blared. Fans held up *Bring On Da Bulls* signs as the players put on their fresh new Western Conference Championships T-shirts. They'd finally done it. They were going to the Finals.

After the game, when Jim Gray asked Gary Payton about the Bulls and mentioned that the Sonics don't have too much time to enjoy the win, Payton wouldn't have any of it.

"Well, we can enjoy it for a day or so," he smiled. "But then we're going to go out there and give it all we've got."

Chapter 16

Finally, the Finals

They carried a deep exhaustion.

This was the thought running through George Karl's head during the Sonics' practice the morning after winning the Western Conference. He let them go out and celebrate the night before. They'd certainly earned it. Hell, *he'd* earned it. After four years of falling short of the Finals, the team deserved at least one champagne-induced all-nighter with Outkast and Nas and Tupac lyrics pulsing in the background.

But damn, Jim Gray was right: There was no time to relax. In seventy-two hours they'd be facing the league's first 72-win team in the Chicago Bulls. It had taken the Sonics ninety-nine games to get there—eighty-two in the regular season and seventeen in the playoffs, the last half-dozen of which could have taken place in Mad Max's Thunderdome. Karl could see all ninety-nine of those games on his players' faces. Their eyes were heavy; their brows furrowed with sweat much earlier than when the season started. He could hear it on the floor. His troops' legs were heavy sandbags. There wasn't as much squeaking as normal. The lightning-fast stops and sharp cuts were slower, rounded. The wars against the Jazz had left his team physically battered and mentally drained. They were going into the fight of their lives, immediately after surviving the fight of their lives. And worse, the Bulls, having swept the Orlando Magic in the Eastern Conference Finals, had been relaxing, resting up and recuperating for a week; they'd basically been on vacation.

As practice ended, Karl had his players gather around him in a circle, as he always did. He'd been preparing this pep talk all night (maybe subconsciously all season). He looked his men in the eyes and got to work:

> We're not just happy to be here. We're here to win. This needs to be a physical, boring series. If they're able to pressure you and make you passive on offense, their pressure will only grow and kill you. But if you attack their pressure, it will shrink and wilt and they'll go away from it. They got the ball out of Penny Hardaway's hands [in the Orlando series] and he just stopped playing. They'll do the same thing to Gary, and try to make

> Hawk and Det handle the ball. Gary, you've got to keep working to beat them, get the ball back, hurt them. Gary, Nate, get up on Pippen. He doesn't like it physical. He really likes the walk-up three—most of his threes come in transition. Hard fouls. Don't give him any easy baskets or lay-ins. Kukoc is soft. Hit him. Hit all of them. Schef, you're gonna knock someone on his ass and set solid screens. You're gonna frustrate Rodman. They give Steve Kerr the second most offensive opportunities on their team. He shot fifty-one percent on threes this year. Respect him, be aware of him. Gary, Hawk, Nate, David, Det, Vince—we're gonna mix it up on Michael. Give him different looks all night long. When he gets the ball, make him see a crowd, and double him from the top. When he doesn't have the ball, push him out. The farther away from the basket he catches it, the better for us. He's mostly a jump shooter now. He doesn't want the rim like he used to. We can't give him lay-ups. We can't foul him. I don't want him to shoot more than five free throws in any game. We've got to make him take as many hard shots as possible. While we're on Michael…he's a trickster. He's competing against you all the time, even off the court. Even if your kids are asking you to get his autograph. I don't want anyone hanging with him, buying him a cup of coffee or going out to dinner. You'll think he's your friend but he's softening you up.

If this had been a sports movie, and maybe the late Philip Seymour Hoffman was playing George Karl, the music would have risen to a crescendo, Hoffman would have given a final motivational scream, and we'd smash-cut to a mini-montage leading to the tip-off of the NBA Finals, where David (the Sonics) would take on Goliath (the Bulls). Make no mistake about it, the Bulls *were* Goliath, maybe the biggest, baddest goliath the NBA had ever seen. Nearly every single media personality, broadcaster and sports book picked the Bulls to win. As a joke (sort of), one sports book in Vegas put up a sign that said: *Wanted: Sonics Bettors.* The Bulls were favored nine-to-one and sat at the all-time apex of the NBA. Historically, the only team that came close from a statistical perspective to what the Bulls had accomplished in 1996 were Wilt Chamberlain's 1972 Los Angeles Lakers, who went 69-13 in the regular season and 12-3 in the playoffs.

Heading into the 1996 Finals, the Bulls were 72-10 in the regular season and 11-1 in the playoffs. And they owned the season's awards and statistics like no team in history. Jordan won MVP. Rodman won the rebounding title. Phil Jackson won Coach of the Year. Jerry Krause won Executive of the Year. Jordan, Rodman and Pippen all made the NBA's All-Defensive team. Tony Kukoc won the NBA's Sixth Man of the Year award. The Bulls were basketball's Avengers, and to many, the Sonics were just the next foil in their quest for world domination. And we can skip the trite comments and motivational clichés about how nobody outside of the Sonics locker room or the greater Seattle area believed in them because, in this case, that was absolutely true.

"We really thought we could beat them," Nate McMillan said.

"We had a very confident, borderline overconfident group," assistant coach Dwane Casey said.

Belief. Confidence. Every team in the Finals is chock full of both. They could easily close their eyes and envision a path to victory:

Maybe Payton has the defensive series of his life and locks up Jordan, and maybe Kemp outplays Pippen and Schrempf matches Kukoc shot for shot, and maybe Brickowski and Hawkins and a slew of others rattle Rodman, and Perkins hits more threes than Kerr, and if the ball bounces their way a few times, well, that's how they beat the Bulls. Done. Now that the Xs and Os are out of the way in this scenario, there was another concern many of the Sonics didn't want to acknowledge that had nothing to do with the match-ups but had everything to do with the moment.

Were they ready to handle the pressure and the press and the scrutiny that comes along with the Finals?

Nate McMillan remembers a moment right after the team plane landed in Chicago and was met on the tarmac by a police escort to take them to their hotel. Sirens wailed. Pedestrians looked on. They were treated with all the pomp and circumstance of a foreign dignitary visiting an embassy. A few players took out their camcorders to record how surreal the moment was. This was the very opposite of the old, play-it-cool adage, "act like you've been there before." McMillan took in the whole scene: his teammates with their wide eyes, the caravan through the city, the media hype... all of it. And he had one overriding thought: *I don't know if we are ready for this.*

***

The defensive plan for game one was to throw Schrempf and Hawkins and a bunch of bodies at Jordan for three quarters and then let Payton take him in the fourth. Why? Because Payton was secretly nursing a calf injury and Karl didn't want to burn him out early and lose him on the offensive end of the floor. It was a reasonable plan based on common sense and logic, except the problem was, the person it was supposed to stop was Michael Jordan, and he couldn't be stopped.

Early in the first quarter he blocked Hersey Hawkins on one end of the floor and then hit a long jumper over Schrempf on the other end. Moments later he purposely found Payton on the floor, backed him down, bodied him and then hit a patented fadeaway right over the top of him. After three quick buckets he had the Bulls up by nine in the first quarter. Schrempf couldn't stay with him. Hawkins couldn't handle him. They were like two kids trying to stop a Labrador from jumping into a pool. A couple fakes here and there and then...splash. Making matters worse, the Sonics seemed to have no answer for (checks notes) Luc Longley. Yes, the unheralded center came out hot and was three-for-six to start the game.

On the offensive side of the ball the team was out of sync at best and tired at worst. At one point in the middle of the quarter they missed five straight shots. Perkins and Askew hit a few threes, but the lone bright spot was Shawn Kemp, whose graceful jumper and athleticism around the basket were the only things keeping the Sonics in the game. He finished with 32 points on 9-of-14 shooting. For most of the game the Sonics hung tough, trying five different defenders on Jordan and staying within two points headed into the fourth.

"I anticipated them throwing a lot of different players at me on defense. That was their way of making other players step up and hurt them," Jordan said. "I think we proved that other players can step up."

Sam Perkins, Jordan's former teammate at UNC, knew that, in the end, stopping Jordan was only one part of the game plan. "The thing is, Michael is such an extraordinary player, he'll get his points by hook or by crook. He can get shots whenever he wants. We have to contain the other players."

Newsflash: The "other players" were not contained. Pippen had 21, Ron Harper had 15, Longley had 14, Kukoc had 18, and the Sonics were outscored by fifteen in the fourth quarter and lost 107-90. Just like that, they were down 0-1 in the series.

"There's nothing wrong with us," Payton said. Then, as if answering critics as much as the doubts in his own head, he continued. "We didn't get worn out. We were right there in the fourth quarter. We just turned the ball over and didn't rebound."

Right. As *Philadelphia Daily News* writer Jon Smallwood put it in his column, "Last time I checked [turning the ball over and not rebounding] are pretty good signs that you're getting tired."

***

You'd be forgiven for thinking that the beginning of game two wasn't a Finals match-up, but instead a YouTube video assembled to show off every single weapon in the post- "Air Jordan" arsenal.

"Can I still take off? I don't know," Jordan mused before the Finals. "I haven't been able to try it because defenses don't guard me one-on-one anymore. But honestly, I probably can't do it." Whether he could take off from the foul line or not was beside the point anyway. What mattered was that MJ, the 33-year-old gunslinger, still had a million and one other ways to make you look foolish on the basketball court besides ripping a dunk on your head with his tongue hanging out and chain dangling. While getting faked on a shoulder shimmy and then reaching out in vain as Jordan sinks a fadeaway right over the top of you wasn't a posterizing moment, it was still worth two points and was equally demoralizing. And so, for about ten minutes early in Game 2, Jordan put on a clinic of craftiness and creativity and crisply honed post moves.

There's Jordan with a backdoor bucket over Ervin Johnson. There he is again, taking it straight at Kemp for a lay-up. Then Jordan bodies up Perkins for an easy finger roll. Now watch as he hits a beautiful fadeaway over Hersey Hawkins and then another one over Vincent Askew. The Sonics had barely broken a sweat in game two and Jordan was five-for-five and had damn near scored on everyone on the roster. It was like a game of basketball whack-a-mole—whichever Sonics defender he saw, he hit 'em with a bucket. Someone had to step up and stop this nonsense or the Sonics were going to get blown out. Again. Once more into the breach steps Gary Payton.

Payton was tired of hearing about how tired his team was supposed to be. He didn't want to hear any excuses about how they'd lost the heart of their team, Nate McMillan, to an ill-timed back injury. He was sick of the United Center's crowd oohing and ahhing at every basket their basketball god Jordan made. It was time to make a stand.

Midway through the second quarter, he had his chance when he suddenly found himself out on the wing one-on-one with Jordan. As MJ had done all game, his eyes lit up when he saw he was in single coverage and he tried to move to a preferred spot on the floor. He lowered his head, leaned his shoulder, took a few hard power dribbles toward the foul line, planted and rose up for what looked like a clean jump shot. Just as it appeared that Jordan had Payton beat The Glove slid over, extended his arm and knocked the ball loose in the middle of Jordan's motion. He then pushed the ball forward to himself, starting a two-man foot race/fast break between him and Jordan. The younger Payton had position the whole sprint, and with one step in the paint he cuffed the ball, threw down the dunk of his life and quickly turned to talk a mouthful of shit to His Airness. It was like the moment in *Rocky IV* when Balboa finally lands a haymaker on Ivan Drago and draws blood. *You cut him! You hurt him! You see. You see. He's not a machine. He's a man!*

For a brief period the role reversal worked. The Sonics were up three after the first quarter and down only two at the half. But they were turning the ball over and over and over on their way to twenty giveaways. In an especially excruciating 180-second stretch of the third quarter, they went from being down two points to down eleven points. They never recovered. In game two Kemp was the best player on the floor with 29 points, 13 boards and 4 monstrous blocks. Once again, it wasn't enough. The team was 3-15 from three and no other scorers topped sixteen points. And that idea about bodying up Rodman to keep him off the glass? Didn't work. He grabbed 20 rebounds and a then-Finals record 11 offensive boards. Bulls win, 92-88.

Game three for Sonics fans was like a horror movie that you only need to see once in the theater to remember forever, and you swear to yourself you'll never watch it again. Instead of getting a bounce by returning home to the KeyArena, they somehow got bonked, as in the mountain climbing term when your body and mind no longer perform and you become lethargic and listless. The game was over inside of twelve minutes. The Bulls were up 34-16 after the first quarter, 62-38 at the half, and won 108-86. The Sonics were left shaking their heads in disbelief.

How could they not show up?

At home?

Phil Jackson believed they were the victim of a self-inflicted, boneheaded scheduling move. "… the Sonics made a tactical error after game two, flying back to Seattle Friday night after the game rather than waiting, as we did, until Saturday morning to take a more leisurely flight," Jackson wrote in his book, *Eleven Rings*. "The Sonics looked bleary-eyed on Sunday afternoon."

On the other side of the floor, George Karl had his own theories and emotions. "It didn't take a genius to see that what we were doing with Michael wasn't working," he wrote. "We didn't get loose balls or long rebounds and we didn't play hard for the entire forty-eight minutes…. I was one pissed off motherfucker afterward. The shit luck of losing Nate meant a huge part of our puzzle was missing…"

As Karl fumed in his office late into the night, Payton came by and said, "Nothin' to lose now. Let me take him."

"Him" being Jordan.

Chapter 17

Gary Payton vs. Michael Jordan

George Karl was kicking himself. *Why the hell didn't they just do this from the beginning?* After the first possession, when Payton's attempt to front Jordan failed and ended with MJ draining yet another fadeaway, his squad started rolling. With the Jordan gauntlet laid down and Payton accepting the challenge, the team was coming back from the dead. In fact, they were downright Frankensteinian (not a word, but you get it).

Gone were late switches and lack of effort on the boards. In their place was a frenetic pace and a renewed vigor. And as Payton's jaw, which seemed to have been jacking at half-speed in the first three games, came back full bore, firing off words and cusses at a frenetic pace, so too did the Sonics. When Payton connected with Kemp on a half-court lob, then knocked down a quick three, the Seattle crowd exploded and finally—*finally*—the Sonics had that regular-season electricity back. With five minutes left in the first quarter, Karl put in the team's most beloved player, Nate McMillan, who was still hurt, and it was like a popular band bringing a local legend on stage in the middle of a song. *Ladies and gentlemen... Nate McMillaaaannnn!!!!* The crowd ate it up.

As the decibels soared over 100 and stayed there, Payton played hip-to-hip on Jordan like Deion Sanders on Jerry Rice. He was in his face and in his feet, even taking away his patented jab step. Jordan, for the first time all series, was stymied. To this day he says it had no effect on him, but the stats say otherwise. In game four he scored just 23 points on 6-of-19 shooting, and it knocked the rest of the team off kilter. Kerr scored 5, Pippen had 9 (but also 11 boards and 8 assists) and Kukoc managed only 14 points. The second quarter was the Sonics' signature twelve minutes of the series, as they scored 28 points while strangling the Bulls for only 11. The teams played perfectly even the rest of the way (31-31 in the third, 23-23 in the fourth) and the Sonics got their first Finals win in seventeen years. They were still down in the series 3-1, but the team now had something they didn't have when they woke up that morning: hope. And as Andy Dufresne wrote to Red in *The Shawshank Redemption*, "Hope is a good thing. Maybe the best of things, and no good thing ever dies."

At least in the Sonics' case, hope didn't die in game five. Karl kept Payton on Jordan and they swarmed the perimeter to keep Chicago's shooters at bay. The plan worked. The Bulls team as a whole was frigid from the three-point line and shot 3 of 26. Jordan scraped together 26 points (only five foul shots), but Pippen had only 14 and nobody else on the team had more than 11. Steve Kerr and Kukoc combined for 18 points. On the flip side, the Sonics had three players score more than 20 (Payton, Kemp and Hawkins) and they outrebounded the Bulls as a team by one (41-40). It appeared for the moment that they had the Bulls busted, and the media noticed. "Kemp Rains on Bulls Parade" was a popular headline among writers. Ray Ratto of the *San Francisco Examiner* went with "Bulls Lose Some Wind in Their Snort." However it was cleverly framed, the Sonics won the game 89-78 and had successfully clawed their way back into the series.

"We just didn't hit shots, it's as simple as that," Rodman said of the Bulls' frustrations. "They hit shots and we should have capitalized on the things they did wrong, but you know, that's the way it goes."

Heading off the court, Payton commented to Karl, "We should have come with this a little earlier." Karl couldn't help but wonder if he was right.

Later that night, James Edwards, the Bulls' back-up center, arrived for his usual post-game cigar in Jordan's hotel room. This was a new playoff ritual that he shared with Jordan and Ahmad Rashad, win or lose, and it was something he looked forward to. Things were a little different on this night, as described in Roland Lazenby's outstanding Michael Jordan biography, *Michael Jordan: The Life*. "When he [Edwards] stopped in after game five, he was startled at Jordan's fury. 'I had never seen him that upset before. He kept saying, "We should have won today. It should be over." I told him we would get it when we got home. He didn't want to hear that at all. He kept saying it should be over...' He [Jordan] was ending the year just as he had opened it, with his harshest emotions on display. He had wanted to end this series as soon as possible, to unburden himself of the immense pressure he had shouldered since deciding to return."

***

A little before nine o'clock on the morning after game five, the Sonics team gathered at Boeing Field for their flight to Chicago. The best-of-seven format was 2-3-2 at the time, which meant the Sonics were either coming home as the first team ever to battle back from being down 0-3 to win the NBA championship... or they were coming home losers. There was no in-between.

The Bulls were still favored, but there was a slight frailty in them that wasn't there during the first three games. Jordan looked tired in the fourth quarters. Pippen was shrinking from the spotlight. Kukoc was erratic. Kerr wasn't in a long-range rhythm. And Phil Jackson, the Zen master himself, hadn't been able conjure up the right Native American spirits or tribal chants to counter what the Sonics had done for eight quarters straight.

"They used to be a lot more confident," Payton said heading into game six. "They thought they were on a roll and that we couldn't hang with them. We've switched the momentum a little bit, and we know we're a team that can beat them."

***

June 16, 1996. Sunday. Father's Day. This was to be the setting of game six of the 1996 NBA Finals. It was a day loaded with emotion for Michael Jordan, who had recently lost his father in a tragic shooting. Secretly, the reason Jordan was so upset about not ending the series in Seattle was that he did not want to play on Father's Day. For the game's greatest player, the atmosphere for game six was a torrent of emotions that only heightened as the United Center's crowd hung on every dribble.

George Karl's mantra for the last few games had been simple: Forty-eight minutes. Meaning, don't let the Bulls breathe for one second. Take no plays off. Stay in their face and in their space all game, specifically Gary Payton on Jordan. This was to be the defensive effort Karl had dreamed of all series. To paraphrase Christopher Walken in *Man on Fire*, a man can be an artist in anything... food, whatever. It depends on how good he is at it. Karl and Payton's art for three games was stopping the Bulls' offense. They were about to paint their masterpiece.

This was the Jordan Rules 2.0, and for the third game in a row it appeared it was working. Jordan shot a measly 26% on 5-of-19 shooting, with one three-pointer.

Kukoc shot 36% from the floor. Pippen was under 50%. Kerr shot only two threes and made one. They held the Bulls to 24 points in the first quarter and only 21 in the second quarter. This was a pace that favored them—a winnable pace—but their shots would not fall.

Early in the game Kemp missed a jumper. Then Schrempf. Then Frank Brickowski clanged an easy dunk off the back of the rim. Ron Harper was back in the Bulls lineup and it showed. Every offensive possession for the Sonics either ended with a miss, a foul or a mess of bodies on the floor. Nobody was open. Nothing was easy. The Bulls seemed to be cutting off every passing lane, clogging up every shooting lane, and getting to the spots on the floor that the Sonics wanted to get to a flash earlier.

Man, it's like they know every play, Karl thought to himself.

Despite the Sonics having the Bulls' offense in a headlock, the Bulls had the Sonics' offense in a chokehold. They were limited to 18 points in the first quarter and 20 points in the second. In the third, a mix of turnovers and bricks added up to a 19-9 streak for the Bulls, punctuated with a Rodman reverse and some classic WWE showmanship to get the crowd roaring. After sinking a foul shot, the Bulls went up 62-47.

Kemp and Payton would not go gently into that good night.

Payton hit one of his three three-pointers and Kemp stayed tough around the basket to pour in a few. But with just under seven minutes left, Pippen missed a three, gathered his own rebound, and sank a quick two to make the game 77-63. The Sonics at that point were in the midst of an ill-timed 1-for-6 slump and went almost four game minutes without scoring before Schrempf hit a jumper. The Bulls' second-chance buckets (Rodman had 11 offensive rebounds again) and their own scoring droughts were killing them. It was like trying to win a running race with your shoes untied and a pebble in your sneaker.

At one point the scoring futility reached one made basket in eight attempts and one basket in 6:50 of game time. With two minutes left, the game was 84-68 and the Bulls effectively milked the clock the rest of the way. As the last few seconds ticked away, Schrempf finally drained a three, but it didn't matter—it was whipped cream on shit.

The Sonics lost, 87-75.

"I can't thank my team enough for the spirit," Karl said. "They have rejuvenated my spirit for basketball, and my team is pretty special in my mind. And even though we did not play well here in Chicago, I think we showed the nation that we had a big heart and played with a lot of pride."

Schrempf was crushed.

"We were so close," he said. "I've been waiting for this moment for eleven years, and this is very disappointing to have it end this way. If we could have won this one, anything could have happened in game seven."

"We thought we could beat this team," Payton added. "But when you turn the ball over this many times, something we didn't do in Seattle, you're not going to do it."

For Bulls fans and for NBA fans at large, the lasting image of this game is of Michael Jordan hugging the game ball, splayed out on the floor of the locker room, sobbing and overcome with emotion. This was his first championship without his father and his first title since returning from baseball. If you were alive in the '90s the image is burned into your head. It's raw and it's real and it's unforgettable.

If you're a Sonics fan, the image that's likely frozen in your mind is of Shawn Kemp, sweat-soaked, worn out and fouled out, slumped over on the bench, tears also streaming down his face. He gave it everything he had, averaging 23 points, 10 rebounds, 2 assists and 2 blocks per game.

"Shawn Kemp was the best player on the court," Karl said.

As with all big losses in big games, this one hurt. A lot. But the Sonics, despite their seemingly long window of success, were still relatively young. Kemp was only 26. Payton was 27. Hersey Hawkins was 29. Detlef Schrempf was 33. They'd be back, right?

"Our goal is to win the championship next season," Wally Walker said. "Our team has had a great year. I think it's a team that deserves to stay together. We're going to try to keep it together."

Chapter 18

The Dynasty that Never Was

For all intents and purposes, the glory days of the '90s Seattle SuperSonics ended after game six of the 1996 Finals. If you close your eyes and picture the key members of the team and the highlights they created and you hold them in your mind, the images you conjure all occured either during '96 or before '96. There are no post-'96 Sonics memories to hang on to for that bunch. The supernova stars in Shawn Kemp and Gary Payton would never shine as bright. The collective coolness of the team and its spot in pop culture and basketball influence was never higher. Kids on playgrounds across the country wore Kemp and Payton jerseys. Anyone who played tight defense in pick-up games was called "the glove." Hell, anyone who talked a ton of shit on the court was bound to get a "you think you're Gary Payton or somebody?" comment.

If you knew someone who dunked ferociously on a ten-foot hoop—or an eight-foot hoop in middle school—you likely called them Air Jordan or Dominique or Reign Man. Kemp never won a slam dunk contest, but he was easily the third most popular dunker in the league—maybe tied with 'Nique for second for a few years. When friends got together to play *NBA Jam*, they'd fight over being the Sonics, who were perfectly built for that game, with Kemp able to dunk and block and Payton getting steals and passing, and Schrempf and Perkins the perfect three-point threats. The '90s Sonics were more than a great team; they were an iconic team in an iconic era in a town going through an iconic moment.

"For those seven years, from 1990 to 1997, I thought we were a pretty good team," Payton says, thinking back. "We could beat anybody. Even the Bulls in '96 we'd beaten during the season. I thought once we got over the hump with the Jazz, we'd have a few more years to take our shot. But the window just closed."

In life it's hard enough to get two moons to align properly, let alone three. And as it is with such phenomena, all it takes is the slightest nudge to knock the whole thing out of whack. In this case that nudge was named Jim McIlvaine.

McIlvaine was a 7'1" back-up center for the Washington Bullets. He barely averaged twelve minutes a night, rarely scored, and at most was a playoff team's eighth or ninth best player. But like a guy who sits down at a blackjack table and gets a string of picture cards for an hour, McIlvaine hit the free agent market at the absolute most opportune time for himself, and he wound up signing a contract with the Sonics before the 1997 season for $33.6 million. Good for him, right? Who in the world is going to turn down that kind of money if it's offered? And if that's what the Sonics think he's worth, it's not your money, so who cares? Well, one person cared, and he cared a lot: Shawn Kemp. Kemp cared because this bum from the Bullets was now making more money than he was…and he still had several years left on his deal. And he couldn't handle it.

Wally Walker has said several times that, due to NBA rules, the team was unable to revisit Kemp's contract because he had just signed a renegotiated deal in 1994 and the league prohibited a renegotiated deal from being altered again for three years. Nevertheless, it didn't sit right with Kemp and he went to war with management during the 1996-97 season.

"It ruined the team. It shouldn't have. Shawn should have been a bigger person, but Shawn went into the tank and George benched him at several points during that year, and George being George was very public about the fact that Shawn wasn't playing hard," Steve Kelley said. "And then McIlvaine was horrible and the rest of the players kind of looked at McIlvaine like he was an interloper. You had Shawn and McIlvaine. You had George and Wally. You had Whitsitt and Ackerley. You had all these little fires that grew into one raging inferno."

Behind the scenes, Gary Payton says that he tried to talk to Kemp and convince him that the Ackerleys were good owners, but it didn't work.

"I told Shawn to let them work it out and he'd eventually get paid," Payton says. "But he feuded with ownership and everything went downhill."

The situation devolved to the point where Kemp wouldn't speak to anyone on the team. Not even Nate McMillan, who felt personally hurt by the situation. "When he didn't speak with any member of the team all summer, that made a statement," McMillan said. "Me, him and Gary [Payton] had been together eight years. I didn't think we had anything to do with his negotiating problems. For him not to return calls all summer, I knew things would be different. He couldn't just come up to me when training camp started and explain why he didn't return my calls. I think he pushed it to a point of no return."

By September of 1997, Kemp declared that he'd never put on a Sonics jersey again, telling ESPN, "I will never, ever wear that uniform again. It's been so negative there in the city over the last couple of years, it would be impossible for me to be in that situation again. I would never let myself go back there to play another 82-game season in Seattle." This was the "point of no return" that McMillan spoke about. On the 27th of September, the Sonics traded Kemp to the Cleveland Cavaliers for Vin Baker. Baker was a three-time all-star and a solid player, and when the trade was finalized the Karl and Kemp and Payton triad was officially done.

"I can't deny that when the trade happened I was a little sad," Karl said. "I remember my first year with Shawn and where we've come. I don't think I'll coach many players better or as talented as Shawn Kemp. Even though we had some bumps in the road, we have a very respectful relationship."

In Kemp's last year in Seattle, the 1996-97 season, the team finished 57-25 but was wracked by the inner turmoil swirling around Kemp and management, and was knocked out of the playoffs in the Western Conference Semifinals by their old rivals, the Houston Rockets. The following year Vin Baker, who nearly mirrored Kemp's numbers on the court, slid in seamlessly and averaged 19 points and 8 rebounds per game, and helped the team to a 61-win season and first place in the Pacific Division. For the second straight year they'd go on to lose in the Western Conference Semifinals, this time to the Lakers.

Following that season, George Karl left to coach the Milwaukee Bucks and Paul Westphal arrived. The team finished with a .500 record, failed to make the playoffs, and was clearly in transition. By the start of the 1999 season, barely three years after the Finals in 1996, Gary Payton was the sole member of that team still on the roster. He was still an all-star. He was still a top-ten defender. And years later he was still bitter about the titles the team left on the table by breaking up after their magical '96 run.

"I think we could have come away with at least two championships," he said. "I think we had a window and should have gone back to the Finals like Chicago. We didn't get a chance because we got a new general manager who didn't know what he was doing. He took over and tried to work off of numbers and didn't have any idea about what to do."

The prior Sonics philosophy of building a team around a stable of core leaders was thrown out the window, and instead of a championship window the team became a revolving door for players. There was no longer a "Sonics Way." There was just a parade of new people in Sonics uniforms.

"That period from 1998 to 2003, we had too many players," Payton says. "We had two coaches. We had people coming and going. We had no chemistry."

In 2003, Payton was traded to the Milwaukee Bucks to briefly reunite with George Karl, and with that, the final piece of the 1996 Sonics team was gone. Payton competed for titles by playing for the Lakers in 2004 (with Shaquille O'Neal, Kobe Bryant and Karl Malone), the Celtics in 2005, and then finally won his NBA Championship at the age of 37 with the 2006 Miami Heat. He averaged 7.7 points, 3 assists and a steal per game. In 2013, Payton was inducted into the Naismith Basketball Hall of Fame.

Shawn Kemp made one all-star team as a member of the Cleveland Cavaliers, played five more seasons with the Cavs, Trail Blazers and the Orlando Magic, and retired after the 2003 season at the age of 33.

"I think if we would have stayed together, like I'm in the Hall of Fame now, I think Shawn would have been in the Hall of Fame too," Payton said. "We would have made a huge dynasty, but it didn't happen."

Twenty-five years later, George Karl has similar thoughts.

"We won fifty games every year," Karl says. "We won sixty a couple of times. We got to the Finals once and probably should have at least twice. We blew some opportunities, but it was a seven-year journey that was the best part of my career."

In the end, the legacy of the '90s Seattle SuperSonics isn't their lack of titles; it's the generation of basketball talent they inspired in the Pacific Northwest, and the swagger and culture they left in their wake.

Chapter 19

Ray Allen's Short-Lived Resurgence

In 2003, Milwaukee Bucks head coach George Karl was bickering so much with his current superstar, Ray Allen, that he decided to trade him for the former superstar he bickered with all the time, Gary Payton.

The specifics of the deal were Allen, Flip Murray, Kevin Ollie and a first-round pick in the '03 draft for Gary Payton and Desmond Mason. But the headline of the trade was Allen for Payton. On its face, the deal looked like Karl was divorcing his new wife to re-marry his ex-wife. Since leaving the Emerald City for Cream City in 1998, Karl had been above .500 every season, made the playoffs in all but one year, and had a run to the Eastern Conference Finals in 2001 after winning fifty-two regular season games. That team was a high-scoring, high-octane juggernaut built around one of the best pure shooters the game had ever seen, Ray Allen, and several other talented scorers like Glenn "Big Dog" Robinson, Sam Cassell and Tim Thomas. They finished second in the league in offense, and both Allen and Robinson drained twenty-two per game. As had been the case with Karl over the years, he took over a team with a losing record, turned them around, got them to the cusp of greatness, and then things fizzled out—which is a polite way of saying he pissed off a few people, usually an owner or executive or a star or two. In the case of Milwaukee, he pissed off three.

"For what was at stake, and for what they were being paid…I wanted a lot more focus and passion. I wanted losses to hurt," Karl wrote about his relationship with Robinson, Cassell and Allen. "I laid it out for Ray, Sam and Glenn in training camp. You three are selfish, individualistic, and obsessed with your own numbers. You're always thinking about your next contract. You don't work hard enough, and I don't see enough professionalism or accountability."

Damn, George. But how do you really feel?

Keep in mind Ray Allen was only 25 years old and Glenn Robinson was 28. Sam Cassell was the veteran of the trio at age 31. At first, the players didn't respond, starting the year 3-9. But when Karl started questioning their manhood publicly (something he has since said is not a good strategy), they responded and the team raced all the way to the conference finals, where they lost to that year's NBA MVP, Allen Iverson and his 76ers.

The following year they dropped down to a 41-41 record, and in 2002-03 the team was headed for more of the same when Karl told ownership it was time to make a move. He'd had enough of Allen.

"Ray's a perfectionist," Karl told Jackie MacMullan. "He's also a very confident person, and, in a way, that can be somewhat detrimental when he's trying to fit into a team. His attention to detail, at times, was antagonistic to his teammates. He had to work to find a comfort level with them. We were managing a lot of egos."

Allen didn't disagree that there were, let's just say, *issues*, between the two men. "There always seemed to be some angst between George and me," he said. "No animosity, just angst. It was almost like I was the one guy in his way. I was close with Senator Kohl [the Bucks' owner] and it was like I was the one guy over [Karl's] head, maybe more powerful than he was."

By the end of the day on February 20, 2003, whatever power Allen thought he had over Karl was gone, because that night Karl slept soundly in his bed in Milwaukee while Allen had to start packing for Seattle. It was a decision that Kohl and the franchise regretted almost immediately. "Well, [Ray] and George Karl got into it and it just didn't work so we traded him," Kohl told Gary D'Amato of the *Milwaukee Journal*. "I didn't make the trade, but I let it happen. It became very much of a personality thing and so we traded Ray. In terms of unfortunate moments, that was our most unfortunate moment, letting Ray go."

Looking back on the trade now, Allen says he was initially disappointed. "It seemed as though we had done some good things in Milwaukee," he said. "But we were headed in the wrong direction. Then I was excited because I was on to a new place and I could put the negative stuff behind me."

On the flip side, Seattle had maxed out between forty and forty-five wins per year since George Karl's departure and the front office felt it was time to shake things up. The fans, however, disagreed. "They traded away the whole team," super Seattle fan Larry Roth said on his way into the first game post-Payton. "When you think of the Sonics, you think of Gary Payton. That's gone now." A twenty-year-old named Matt Schmitz believed that the trade was another idiotic move by Wally Walker. "I know Wally Walker had something to do with it. He's made so many terrible decisions going back to Jim McIlvaine. They should have traded Wally instead of Gary."

Payton, in his twelve and a half years with the Sonics, had become an institution in the city. He was as much a part of Seattle's day-to-day life as the I-5 or the aquarium. Like a billboard or familiar building you passed every day on your way to work, Payton was just there. And then he wasn't. To insiders, it was no secret that Howard Schultz, the CEO of Starbucks who had bought the team from Barry Ackerley in 2001, wasn't pleased with the way the team had been playing for much of the last few years. In particular, when Payton chose to hold out for a new contract prior to the 2002 season, Schultz was incensed. *How dare you disrespect us!* But Payton and several other players had already tuned him out.

"He [Schultz] just talks, that's all he does," Payton said during his first press conference with the Bucks. "He just took over that team a year ago and now he knows everything about basketball. I really don't think he knows anything about basketball."

Worse yet, the organization botched the entire handling of the trade, choosing to let Payton find out about it via the media rather than giving him the news face-to-face or at least with a phone call. This is rule violation number one when you're letting go of a franchise player: If you want to save face with fans at all, you have to handle your ex-franchise player's exit like it's a Faberge egg. Gently. Carefully. Gracefully. You definitely don't let him discover that he's been traded on television.

"That's just the way that organization works," Payton said. "I wasn't putting anything past the Sonics people. I knew they weren't going to come to me and tell me. They made it personal, so we just had to make it back personal." But Payton wanted to make it clear that any issues he had were with the organization and owner, not the people of Seattle. "I appreciate the support of the Seattle fans. The fans of Seattle are great."

Ten years later, when Payton was asked about the trade by the *Boston Globe*, he maintained the same position. "It went from being a family team to a business," he said. "The people who took over the team ran their team like a business, like how they made their money, and you can't do that."

For Ray Allen, the timing couldn't have been better. He and his fiancée had been having conversations privately about moving on from Milwaukee. When the trade was announced it was one of the moments couples have when they feel like, for that moment, the universe is working in their favor, giving them a little nudge toward where they want to go. "My fiancée is really happy because over the past three or four months, we've grown a little frustrated," Allen said after his first game in a Seattle uniform. "We always talked about the fact that it may be time for a change."

A personal change. A change of atmosphere. All of it.

"It was exciting because it was sixty degrees in Seattle and in Milwaukee it was twenty," Allen said. "People were out and moving around and it was a much more social environment. But Gary had done a lot of great things for the city so the reaction was mixed. People were very pessimistic at first and they didn't know me. They were upset at trading a hall of famer and they were upset at Howard and Wally. When I first got to the arena, there were signs that said 'Trade Wally.'"

Allen's first game with Seattle was the equivalent of a friendly new neighbor introducing himself and then inviting you over to move a couch. Yes, the Sonics franchise was looking forward to having him in the lineup... but also, you know, we're playing Shaq and Kobe and the Lakers tonight, and Kobe's in the middle of a historic run of nine straight 40-point games, so here you go, can you guard him please? Although the Sonics lost 106-101, Allen hung with Bryant the whole game, scoring 26 points, grabbing 13 boards and dishing out 9 assists.

"I'm like a rookie all over again," Allen said afterward. "I'm excited about this team. We didn't win the game, but we put some good basketball out there on the floor. I have to gain my teammates' respect and trust. Now it's about me trying to fit in and kind of creating my niche and helping them win."

Over time, Allen's appreciate for Seattle, the fans and the environment grew.

"Seattle is really a great fan base and KeyArena was a perfect environment for basketball," he said. "You walk right in and walk right out into the city. After a game the crowd spilled right out into the streets and engaged in downtown Seattle."

He also got to see first-hand the team's unparalleled involvement with the city.

"We did a lot of community engagement in Milwaukee," Allen said. "But this was just more. We did community outreach everywhere. There was such an open engagement with the players. There was a public relations guy who knew everybody and he just plugged us into different locations around the city to be with fans. We were able to touch the people of the city and the children and it was very positive."

***

Ironically, even with Gary Payton gone, there was still one member of those classic '90s teams on the roster, and that was head coach Nate McMillan. McMillan took over the team from Paul Westphal during the 2000-01 season and kept the job when the year was done. In his first full season as coach, the Sonics won forty-five games and lost in the first round of the playoffs to the San Antonio Spurs. There would be no immediate run to glory like George Karl had. Following the 45-win year, the Sonics dropped to forty wins in 2002-03 and then thirty-seven wins in 2003-04, Ray Allen's first full year with the team. The lone bright spot of the McMillan/Allen era was in the 2004-05 season, when the team managed fifty-two wins and advanced to the second round in the Western Conference Playoffs.

During Allen's time in Seattle his scoring attributes improved almost too fast for *NBA 2K* to make the updates. He'd gone from taking fifteen or sixteen shots per game in Milwaukee to twenty-one by the '06-'07 season. His three-point attempts, which were usually around six per game in the early part of his career, were up to over eight, while the percentage of his long-range "makes" held steady near 40%. His scoring average climbed every year: 23 points per game in '04, 23.9 in '05, 25.1 in '06, and then 26.4 in '07. During that time he made four all-star appearances, earned an All-NBA Second Team nod in 2005 and got to experience the uniqueness of the basketball brotherhood in Seattle.

"I stayed in Seattle year-round and starting in August we'd workout with all the local guys who would come back to the area," he said. "I'd work out with Jamal Crawford and Nate Robinson at the University of Washington. Or we'd go to Garfield High School and play with high school kids. In any given game there could be six or seven guys from the NBA, college guys, local high school kids. Those kids couldn't come to our facility to play, so we went to theirs. Basketball was basketball."

During Allen's run he was the Sonics' main star and for that one year in '05, while paired with fellow all-star Rashard Lewis, the team had a glimmer of hope for a bright future. It wasn't to be (as you'll read about in the next chapter). After '05 McMillan was gone, and then after '07 the team traded Ray Allen to the Boston Celtics, where he'd make three all-star teams and win a title. He won another title a few years after that with the Miami Heat.

The Sonics would never have an all-star or win more than thirty-five games ever again.

Chapter 20

The Robbery

Howard Schultz's press conference on July 18, 2006, announcing his sale of the Seattle SuperSonics to Clay Bennett's group from Oklahoma City, was a psychological case study in defensiveness and duplicity. Against the black backdrop of a media banner featuring the new "40th Anniversary Season" Sonics logo, Schultz sat in a gray suit, white shirt and golden tie and forced his way through his statement. While the words coming out of his mouth were meant to assure Sonics fans that Bennett was the best possible new owner and that the team was safe in Seattle, every single one of Schultz's gestures suggested otherwise.

His words:

> The ultimate goal has been, and continues to be, to preserve the future of professional basketball here in the Northwest region and to do it in a way that reaffirms our commitment to the fans... Although this is extremely difficult and, for me, personally disappointing, I'm really proud to be able to announce, that after careful analysis of all the possible scenarios, the Basketball Club of Seattle has entered into an agreement with the Professional Basketball Club LLC, to purchase the Seattle SuperSonics and the Seattle Storm… Five years ago when I sat here and…was in a position to buy the team, I remember saying that I viewed this as my responsibility as part of the public trust… I took that responsibility to heart and very, very seriously. Culminating today, that responsibility is now passed on to this group and to Clay Bennett. I believe in my heart that he understands the public trust of Seattle and the northwest and is going to try to do everything he can to keep the team here. We arrived at a place with a buyer who really wants to stay here. We would not have sold it to a new owner who we felt was going to take the team way.

And even more words:

> This is not how we wanted to go out... I told my children and the children of those I know, that I did this obviously with concern and trepidation. But I believe strongly this new group has a commitment to staying, provided elected officials meet them halfway. I do not believe this team is moving. I honestly believe that this group led by Clay wants to stay in Seattle.

His mannerisms:

Where to begin? You don't have to be an FBI profiler or CIA interrogator to pick up on the laundry list of "tells" Schultz displayed during his time on the dais. It was like a top-ten list of what not to do if you want people to believe you. Rather than sitting up straight and speaking in even, commanding tones, Schultz was slouched with hunched shoulders in his seat. When reading his statement, his words were slow and deliberate with odd pauses and emphasis on certain bizarre syllables. It seemed rehearsed, rather than heartfelt. When taking questions, his speech was shallow, he shifted in his seat and he clenched his jaw and sucked in his cheeks while preparing to answer. Sitting with his hands clasped in front of him and his forehead furrowed, Schultz methodically made his way through the conference, saying one thing while his body language said another.

Second only to Schultz's barely believable performance was Clay Bennett's laughably insincere statements about wanting to keep the team in Seattle. In addition to sharing a majority of Schultz's tells, Bennett added sweating around his mouth, even more shifting in his chair, eyes that darted downward, and a generally untrustworthy demeanor. Even saying the word "committed" caused his body to naturally recoil back in his seat when asked by a reporter about his intentions to stay in Seattle. He was lying as blatantly as a kid who had ice cream all over his shirt but denied sneaking a sundae. And if his tone and tenor and tics didn't scream that he was being untruthful, essentially every single thing about his past, including his own statements, would have any reasonable person 100% believing he was moving the team as soon as he could.

Here's what you need to know on this account:

Bennett was basically Mr. Oklahoma. He was born in Oklahoma City.

He met his wife in high school in Oklahoma City. He attended college at the University of Oklahoma. His family and his wife's family lived in Oklahoma City. His businesses are in Oklahoma City. His father-in-law's business is in Oklahoma City. When Hurricane Katrina ruined the Hornets' arena in New Orleans, he led the effort to have the Hornets play in Oklahoma City. He ran the Oklahoma State Fair, organized an Olympic festival and operated the AAA baseball team. The ownership group that he led to buy the Sonics included a group of businessmen who were *all from Oklahoma City.*

The very idea that Bennett was buying the Sonics to *not move them to Oklahoma City* was completely and entirely laughable to anyone who was paying attention. And here's what was worse.

Everyone was paying attention!

It was like Bennett was stealing the Space Needle itself in broad daylight in front of a crowd of people while Schultz stood in front of it shouting into a megaphone, "Clay Bennett is not stealing the Space Needle!" As if in response to this very absurd hypothetical, the *Seattle Post Intelligencer* had a front-page column titled, "Hey, Howard, We're Not Morons."

Ironically, the best round-up of pissed off quotes about the sale from Seattle media members was in *The Daily Oklahoman:*

> "[They] actually asked local fans to buy the notion this whole move was designed to keep the team in town. If you believe that, I have some swampland you can purchase in order to build your own arena so you can steal some other city's NBA team." — Greg Johns, *King County Journal*

> "Five years ago, the Lord of Lattes pledged an NBA Championship for the city of Seattle. Five years later, he gave it the shaft instead." — Steve Kelley

> "Forget the faux-festive scene inside the Furtado Center at Tuesday afternoon's news conference. The green-and-gold balloons tied to sneakers. The 1979 NBA and 2004 WNBA title trophies

on opposite ends of the dais. This is one of the saddest days ever in Seattle sports." — Steve Kelley, again.

"It is said that Oklahoma is where the wind comes sweepin' down the plain. Tuesday, it also deposited big chunks of manure." — Art Thiel, *The Seattle Post Intelligencer*

"You think the Sonics' virtual elimination from playoff contention by the winter holidays found KeyArena nursing a case of the old ennui last season? Stay tuned for the Lame Duck Supes, the reverse-migration Supes, the first pioneers in U.S. history to flee the Pacific Northwest for shelter and sustenance in the Dust Belt." — John McGrath, *the News Tribune*

"[Schultz and his group] concocted a spin that implied they were doing a great and noble thing for Seattle—selling to out-of-staters who in less than a year from now will have a 20,000-seat arena empty of big-time pro sports in a region desperate for them. The Sonics even festooned their practice facility with green-and-gold balloons to make it seem like a party…" — Thiel, again.

See, absolutely everybody who cared about the Sonics, which was everyone in Seattle, knew exactly what was going on, but they were powerless to stop it. That's why Schultz's press conference announcing the sale was so infuriating to the media members and Seattle citizens who were forced to endure it. The entire thing was one giant charade in which everyone who spoke lied, and the liars knew everyone in the room listening knew they were lying, but they lied anyway because, well, because they could. And because they believed the ends justified the means. In Bennett's case, the end was simple: Get a team to Oklahoma City any which way possible. Five months before he actually bought the Sonics, he said this in an interview: "We are acutely interested and very focused on bringing a team to Oklahoma City. The Sonics, yes, are a possibility, and a team that would do well not just here, but I'm sure anywhere that they played."

So, when he said the below statement during the press conference when asked about his intentions to remain in Seattle…

"Uhh, ultimately we hope for basketball in Oklahoma City, but it's unrelated, to, uh, this transaction."

… you could practically hear the entire media gaggle groan "bulllllllshiiiiiiiit."

While reading this you might think that Bennett is the bad guy here because he clearly bought the team in one city with the intention of taking it to another. But that would excuse Schultz, who expected Sonics fans to believe that he honestly thought the king of OKC, whose dream was to have a basketball team in OKC, had no intention of moving the Sonics to OKC.

Um. Right.

Yes, there was an entirely unenforceable and face-saving clause in the contract that said that Bennett would put forth "a good faith effort to keep the team in Seattle," but what did that mean anyway? Nothing. He just had to say the right things to cover his ass and then move the team regardless.

One of the members of his group that purchased the Sonics, Aubrey McLendon, told *The Journal Record* in Oklahoma in August 2007 that the team wasn't really bought to keep it in Seattle, and that the real intention was to move it to Oklahoma City.

Duh.

"McClendon was not speaking on behalf of the ownership group," Bennett said to the media, knowing full well he was actually speaking on behalf of the group. In fact, McLendon was probably the only guy in this whole episode who was telling the truth. And in the upside-down world of this transaction, the NBA fined McClendon $250,000.

During the fifteen months between Schultz announcing the sale and Bennett announcing that he was moving the team to Oklahoma City in November 2007, Sonics fans held endless rallies, founded the Save Our Sonics organization, and pleaded with state and city officials to keep the team in their city. Bennett, meanwhile, went through the motions of his "good faith effort."

One of the major sticking points concerning the solvency of the team was the KeyArena itself, which had been renovated in 1995 and only ten years later was deemed too small and not "up to date" enough to be a modern NBA arena. What did Bennett do to placate people who might scrutinize the "good faith" clause by checking to see if he tried to get a new arena deal done? He presented a proposal for the most expensive, ill-located arena in the NBA that he knew had no shot of getting approved by the city. No matter. The box could be checked that he made the effort to find a new home for the Sonics in Seattle. Wally Walker claimed that without the new arena they could sell every ticket in the building and still lose money...*it was that bad.*

Maybe that was true. Maybe it wasn't. It certainly didn't help the way the team unceremoniously dumped Gary Payton and the way Schultz knowingly and unknowingly irritated certain players. And then there were rumors as early as 2004 that Schultz was thinking of selling the team, which was a dealbreaker. Fans weren't about to invest in a franchise that was not invested in them.

When we began this story in the 1960s, Seattle was a one-company, fairly obscure city without a single major professional sports team. Entering the mid-2000s, it had become a business powerhouse, hosting the headquarters of Amazon, Starbucks, Nordstrom, Weyerhaeuser, Expeditors International and Alaska Airlines. Costco, Microsoft and Expedia Group also called the larger Seattle metropolitan area home. The city of Seattle's population grew from roughly 550,000 in the Sonics' first year to roughly 753,000 as of 2020. The greater Seattle metropolitan area's population had grown to over three million. During the past sixty years, the city had become an epicenter of expansion, entrepreneurialism and entertainment.

While Howard Schultz was attending board meetings about a new arena and sending e-mails to Clay Bennett about buying the team, the rest of the Seattle sports scene was on fire. Starting in 2003, Seattle Seahawks head coach Mike Holmgren turned the team into perennial playoff contenders, winning fifty-one games over five years and taking the team to the Super Bowl in 2005 on the legs of stud running back Shaun Alexander. To add insult to injury, the Seahawks were playing in their spanking new stadium (finished in 2002) that was financed when voters approved construction in a statewide election.

The Seattle Mariners won a Major League Baseball record 116 games in 2001, followed by back-to-back 93-win seasons. Ken Griffey Jr. was gone, but

Ichiro Suzuki was the new face of the franchise and one of the most popular players in all of baseball. They, too, had a new publicly financed stadium. The soon-to-be wildly popular Seattle Sounders FC of Major League Soccer would debut in 2007. And the Sonics' counterpart, the WNBA's Seattle Storm, was a budding dynasty, winning its first championship in 2004 (then three more over the next fifteen years). The original vision shared by Dick Vertlieb and Don Richman and Sam Schulman of Seattle being a first-class sports city had come to fruition with not just one team, but with competitive teams in every major sport. And yet, in a cruel twist of fate, the team that started it all was being stolen right before the city's very eyes. For many Sonics fans it was like being forced to donate an organ while being kept wide awake to watch the procedure: They were numb. They could see what was happening. They were losing something extremely valuable. And they were powerless to do anything about it.

Chapter 21

The One-Year Kevin Durant Era

While Howard Schultz lied and Clay Bennett connived and the Seattle fans petitioned throughout the fall of 2006 and spring of 2007 the actual SuperSonics basketball team was on the verge of acquiring a once-in-a-generation talent, the 6'10", slick-handling, smooth-shooting future Hall of Famer, Kevin Durant.

Durant owned the 2006 high school basketball season (first-team *Parade* All-American, McDonald's All-American Game MVP) and then was the best player in college basketball in 2007 (National Player of the Year, first-team All-American, Big 12 Player of the Year) and was a shoe-in selection for the Sonics with their second pick in the 2007 NBA Draft (after the Portland Trail Blazers selected Greg Oden).

That the Sonics were about to gain a franchise cornerstone now, at this moment, felt unnecessarily cruel—like breaking both hands and then getting a Fender Stratocaster for a present.

As the events leading up to that fateful draft unfolded, even longtime pro Ray Allen allowed himself a moment to dream about what could have been.

"As we got the number two pick that year for Kevin Durant, I knew we were going to be good because we have Durant, myself and Rashard Lewis," Allen says. "I'm thinking, *wow, we can do some great things here*. But Seattle had other intentions. So when draft day came and I saw all the Celtics players that were getting traded, I was thinking, *I'm out of here*!"

So that's potential title scenario number one: a Sonics championship window built on a potential Big Three of Durant, Allen and Lewis, which would have quickly become one of the more unstoppable trios in the league. The spacing, the range, the inside-outside game...how many teams would have been able to defend that squad? One? None?

On top of that, Durant had spent time in Seattle right after leaving the University of Texas and had already warmed to the city.

"My agents were based in Seattle, so I went there to work out right after I got out of school and I was in a very heavy basketball environment there," Durant says. "A lot of guys who played at Washington came to work out in Seattle. Jamal Crawford. Nate Robinson. I saw those guys throughout the summer before I got drafted. There was a real strong culture there that I didn't know about until I was able to workout there. It was a family-like atmosphere where everybody really hangs out with each other and really knows the game. It felt like such a deep clan of guys that were all from Seattle."

Through traveling teams and high school basketball and his time at Texas, even as a 19-year-old, Durant had been to plenty of different cities across the country and observed their hoop culture. But the atmosphere and the tightness of the local Seattle crew stood out. There was a unique closeness he hadn't experienced in other places.

"Each city has its own character and identity," Durant says. "Everybody competes against each other within those cities, but it feels like it's a way healthier competition in Seattle, you know, than in other cities. It was cool to see. It was like, 'We're going to compete hard between these lines, but we're brothers,' and I felt that energy from day one. Just being in Seattle for that year I really enjoyed that culture and I really felt like I was a part of it."

In addition to Crawford and Robinson, Durant got to know and play with other local legends like Brandon Roy and Will Conroy and Terrence Williams and Spencer Hawes. Every pick-up game and gym session gave him a deeper understanding of the connection the city had with its players. It was a unique, symbiotic relationship, with basketball feeding off the culture, which fed off the community.

"Those guys from Seattle stuck together and it was amazing to see how many of them made it to the NBA," Durant says.

Once Durant was drafted, he was thrown into one of the most unique scenarios a prized rookie could be in. First, he had to adapt to the schedule, the lifestyle and the professional responsibilities of being an NBA player after only one year of college. Second, he had to build relationships with his new teammates and coaches and the Sonics staff. Third, he had to be the new face of the team at events throughout the city. And fourth, he had to do this under the bizarre set of circumstances where the fans despised the ownership and knew the team had one, if not both, feet out the door.

"At the time I really had no clue what was going on behind the scenes," Durant says. "I really didn't. They did a good job of shielding the players from that and keeping us focused on basketball. As I get older now I realize there was a lot going on back then and a lot of emotions floating around in the city. We felt that in a few games here and there, but for the most part, I locked in on the basketball season. But it was a lot. You definitely felt the tension. It wasn't for the guys on the floor—there was a disdain for the ownership. When we were in the community or went to the airport, we had fans cheering for us and we still felt that love in and around the city. As players, we understood."

Despite the strain and the souring relationship between the fans and the front office, Durant averaged 20 points per game and won the 2008 NBA Rookie of the Year award. The team itself wasn't very good (which is what happens when you trade away all your all-stars and assets), winning only twenty games. As a show of confidence for the young team, the past players who still lived in the city made an effort to be around the team and share their stories about the history of Sonics basketball.

"I got to meet Spencer Haywood and Slick Watts and Lenny Wilkens," Durant says. "Guys like that came and supported us as much as they could."

Still, there were no big win streaks or mad dashes to the playoffs. There was, however, the last game in Sonics franchise history, which Durant and his teammates used to send a message.

On April 16, 2008, the 19-62 Sonics hosted the 48-33 Golden State Warriors, who were led by Baron Davis and Monta Ellis. It could have been a rollover game, a mail-it-in, goodbye-to-this-season deal in which the Sonics players mentally checked out, eager to put the pressure-filled season behind them.

Durant would have none of it.

"The last game of that season, it felt like the Finals," Durant says. "It was a statement from the players to the front office and the ownership group. It was like, 'You want to take this team away from us, but this is what we were really all about'. Reflecting on it now, as I get older, that's what it felt like."

At the time, it was a good old-fashioned put-the-team-on-my-back kind of night for KD, who scored 42 points, grabbed 13 rebounds and had 6 assists to give the Sonics a victory in their last home game. It wasn't just a win; it was a pure gesture of heart and effort to end an otherwise tumultuous several years in the team's history. It also left the fans, and Durant himself, wondering what could have been.

"You know, I think about it sometimes," Durant says. "With the energy the city shows for the Seahawks and how they play and what it was like when they won a championship. The energy for the Sonics would have been unmatched around professional sports. The enthusiasm for both teams would have been great. Especially, at that time, the fans would have had a young and up-and-coming team like ours would have been, with me and Russell Westbrook and Serge Ibaka and James Harden."

Durant also thinks the team would have had a trick up its sleeve when it came to rounding out the roster.

"You know, having all of us representing the city, it would have brought so much excitement to basketball around there," he says. "And in my opinion, we would have convinced guys who were from Seattle, who were free agents, like Jamal Crawford, to come play with us. It's something I let myself take a peek at here and there. You know, thinking about what could have been."

So, potential title scenario number two for the Sonics included a young core of Durant, Westbrook, Harden, Ibaka...and maybe Crawford and Jason Terry as the veterans to lead the way.

Damn.

That's a squad.

But like Durant says, we'll never know what could have been.

Chapter 22

The Fallout

Leave it to Gary Payton to openly say what everyone else in Seattle is thinking.

"That was the worst ownership I've ever seen in my life," Payton says. "They were shipping people in and out and they didn't care. We all knew the team was going to Oklahoma City no matter what they said. We went from a winning team with packed stands to a losing team with no fans under that owner."

By the spring of 2008, one by one, despite all of Clay Bennett's bluster about "staying in Seattle," any red tape that would hold up a move was ripped off as quickly as a Band-Aid on a kid's knee.

Here are a few dates that will go down in infamy in Seattle hoops lore:

- April 18, 2008, the NBA's Board of Governors—comprised of the owners of each NBA team—voted 28-2 in favor of the Bennett ownership group's motion to move the SuperSonics to Oklahoma City. The city of Seattle also filed a lawsuit against Bennett's ownership group to keep the SuperSonics in Seattle through the remainder of the lease at KeyArena, which expired in 2010.
- July 2, 2008, the Seattle City Council terminated the Seattle SuperSonics' lease with KeyArena in exchange for a $45 million payment to the city.
- October 8, 2008, the former Sonics team, now the Oklahoma City Thunder, played its first preseason game against the Minnesota Timberwolves, officially ending the franchise in Seattle.
- October 29, 2008, in the first game of the first regular NBA season without the Sonics in over forty years, future MVP and Hall of Famer Kevin Durant scored 12 points for the Thunder and rookie Russell Westbrook, also a future MVP and Hall of Famer who was "drafted" by the Sonics but never played for them, scored 13 points.

The loss of the team hit fans hard, and many of them spent 2006 and 2007 voicing their frustrations to no avail through rallies and petitions and campaigns. It was a city in pre-grief mode, doing whatever they could to head off the oncoming pain they knew was coming.

"The fans in Seattle are so, so loyal," Payton says. "They are so dedicated.

We had mothers who would come and give us cookies when we drove up to the arena. We had moms and kids bringing us gifts if we didn't have family in town for the holidays. You could feel the vibe with them. They were so dedicated and never gave up on you. Now the team was giving up on them."

When all was said and done, and Durant and Westbrook were playing in blue and orange instead of green and gold, the three groups that were hurting the most were the standard bearers of the team's legacy, meaning ex-Sonics players; NBA players who grew up in Seattle and loved the team; and the crop of high school players and younger in Seattle who were having their team ripped from them in the prime of their falling-in-love-with-basketball lives.

"I really felt for those great players who built that franchise," Durant says. "That's where my mind was. The players who made a legacy there and then the team left."

"I still don't believe the team is gone," George Karl echoes, thinking back on his time there. "I don't think it's right. I know business is business, but there's no reason it had to happen. That's the way I feel right now. Why the hell did it happen?"

As the years have passed without a team, the ripple effect of the basketball camps Payton and Karl helped build, and of their appearances and willingness to spend time in the community, has become a foundational piece of the Sonics legacy that lives on to this day.

"When I was there in the '90s, I don't think high school basketball was nearly as big as it is now," Karl says. "Seattle is one of the hotspots now. Back then we put on the MLK Hoopfest, and the Friends of Hoop program was just starting. What I enjoyed most about being there as a pro coach was the connection I had with the high schools and the colleges. We had some great players come from the inner city of Seattle and it was interesting to see a high school guy who went to our camp become a college player or even a pro. We saw Jamal Crawford and Nate Robinson come through. We saw Isaiah Thomas. Those guys have done a great job of representing their city. I'm proud of being a part of that."

Dozens of those '90s and 2000s campers have gone on to play in college, and an elite group, as Karl mentioned, made it all the way to the NBA, something that gives Payton a tremendous sense of satisfaction.

"I played in Seattle for thirteen years and I saw first-hand how important basketball is to the city," Payton says. "We saw how important Gus Williams and Freddie Brown and Lenny Wilkens are to people there. When I played I wanted to run camps where I'd directly be a part of the kids' growth. If kids went to a Michael Jordan camp or something, he wasn't there every day. He'd likely come in at the end and give a talk or a shootaround or something. I was at my camps every day. If you came to the Gary Payton Camp, you were working directly with me."

This one-on-one instruction proved pivotal for the next generation of hoopers from Seattle, because nearly all of them attended Payton's camps. Jason Terry. Jamal Crawford. Nate Robinson. Isaiah Thomas. That's where they got to work with their idol Gary Payton up close, but also where he got to know them and instill in them the work ethic and basketball culture he respected.

"My camps were very intense," he says. "I remember when I first worked with Jamal and Nate and IT and Jason. I picked out all of these guys and worked with them individually. We had a lot of fun. We'd give out awards and have campers versus coaches and things like that, and these kids got to play with me and other NBA guys. They were really intrigued by it."

If that was the end of the interaction, the camps may have been only a fun memory for the budding Emerald City basketball brotherhood. But Payton made a point of taking it a step further. His goal wasn't just to have a fun week with the kids and be done with it. He wanted to actually, you know, *make a difference.*

The kids looked up to him and he took that responsibility seriously; same with George Karl. They both felt it was their duty to give back.

"My foundation in life and a lot of my basketball life was my coach in college, Dean Smith at North Carolina," Karl says. "Coach Smith always said that you have to give back to the game that gives to you. It's a gift to get a college scholarship. It's a gift to get paid to play in the NBA. It's a gift to be able to coach in the NBA. When the game is good to you, it's your job to turn around and be good to someone else."

Payton took that ethos to heart and made it a point to get involved in individual kids' lives if they were truly passionate about reaching their goals.

"When I saw all these guys at camp, I used to tell them if they keep working hard and doing the right things that I'd come watch them play," Payton says. "I'd go see guys like Nate and IT play at UW. I'd go to high school games to show my support for them. I wanted them to know that they could make it to the next level. When I see guys get scholarships and then get to the NBA, I take great pride in that. They took advantage of the opportunity and then they represented their city and the Sonics in the NBA, even after the team was gone."

And now, it's their individual efforts that keep the spirit of the Sonics alive.

From Doug Christie to Jason Terry, to Jamal Crawford, Brandon Roy, Nate Robinson and Isaiah Thomas, the heart and soul of the Sonics franchise is carried on in their lives, their passion, their philanthropy and their careers.

Part II:
The Legacy

Chapter 23

The Rainier Beach Boys

The stout rear admiral in the Royal Navy had a round face, round glasses and a belly round enough to stress the buttons on his tight shirt. His white hair was parted and curled to the side of his rosy face. While fighting for the British in the Revolutionary War he was wounded, and upon recovery, he was promoted to captain of the HMS Astraea. He manned the Astraea for four years and then was promoted to captain of the HMS Monarch. He'd won some battles. He'd lost some wars. He'd been a part of his country losing an entire other country. He'd lived life on the high seas fighting for Her Majesty, and that was his legacy. It was a local legacy, and his name would likely not be much remembered long after his passing… That is, until one fateful day on May 8, 1792, when this rear admiral's pal, Captain George Vancouver, who was on what he called a "voyage of discovery" in the north Pacific Ocean, came upon a glorious site that he described like this: "The weather was serene and pleasant, and the country continued to exhibit between us and the eastern snowy range the same luxuriant appearance. At its northern extremity, Mount Baker bore by compass N. 22E, the round snowy mountain, now forming its southern extremity, and which, after my friend, Rear Admiral Rainier, I distinguish by the name of Mount Rainier."

That's right, the rear admiral in the above story was Peter Rainier, the namesake of Mount Rainier, even though Peter Rainier himself never laid eyes on the mountain and actually fought against the independence of the United States, where the mountain would one day reside. *Pete! It's George! Guess what? I named a mountain after you, buddy!* Of course, Vancouver ignored the fact that the Native Americans who'd been living there for centuries already had several names for the mountain, like Tahoma, Tacoma and others.

Over the years Mount Rainier begat the Rainier Valley, which ultimately begat the group of neighborhoods known as Rainier Beach. The point of this story is not to illustrate how easy it was in the late 18th century to have a fourteen-thousand-foot mound of earth named after you. The point is to show how the man whose name is all over the region in modern times actually has an obscure legacy, while the man whose name *isn't* on anything in the Pacific Northwest might have the most lasting legacy of them all. We're talking about

Rainier Beach High School's boys basketball coach Mike Bethea, who has certainly affected more lives and given more pride to the Seattle area than Pete Rainier, who had never been within 3,000 miles of the place.

***

The first thing you notice about Mike Bethea (or Coach Mike to anyone who has lived in Rainier Beach over the last two decades) is the rock-breaking, jaw-clenching focus he has on the sideline of a basketball game. His eyes are narrow. His cheeks appear sucked in. There's a slight tilt of concentration to his chin. His arms are either crossed or clasped behind his back like in some of the team's photos. At least that's when he's not up and shouting instructions to his kids. When asked many years ago to pick one word to describe his coaching style, he chose "intense."

"Intense. That's one thing I hope rubs off on my kids. I pray they understand how intense I am and how serious I take this game, and hopefully they'll emulate that kind of intensity," he said. "I suppose you could say I lead by example in that way. I'm pretty sure it works, because my kids can play with a lot of fire."

Bethea has been head coach at Rainer Beach since 1994 and has created one of the nation's true high school basketball juggernauts, with eight state titles (1998, 2002, 2003, 2008, 2012, 2013, 2014, 2016) and six additional championship game appearances (2001, 2004, 2015, 2017, 2018). He got his work ethic from his dad Robert Bethea, a man he describes as a country boy from North Carolina. Although Bethea grew up in Seattle, his father imbued in him a sense of downhome wisdom from his southern upbringing that included sayings like, "opportunities don't go away; they go to other people."

When Bethea was initially offered the job in 1994 after head coach Francis Williams stepped down, he said he didn't want it. Rainier Beach's athletic director called BS. He told Bethea that he was making him head coach, and if Bethea didn't like it, he'd have to resign and explain his decision to the players and community. This was at a time when the Emerald City was consumed by basketball. The Sonics had just come off their 55-win season and played against Charles Barkley in the Western Conference Finals, and they were in the midst of their league-dominating sixty-three wins the next year. Gary Payton was sniffing around about starting an AAU team in Seattle. There was a freshman on the horizon named Jamal Crawford who rolled out of bed with ten points in the first quarter.

Not interested? C'mon.

"I think not wanting to do it was more than likely a little bit of doubt," Bethea has since said. "I was so new to coaching and I didn't have full confidence in my ability. It was another big challenge for me. I sat back and thought, *What can we do with it?*"

The answer to his rhetorical question came quickly. *What can you do with it?* You can build the greatest high school hoops dynasty the state has ever seen. Even better, there was a straight line between the popularity of the Sonics and the success of Rainier Beach. The better the Sonics played in the mid-'90s, the more elite young athletes became interested in hoops and the better Bethea's talent pool became. Not to mention he had befriended Sonics coach George Karl. The rise of both the pro team and the high school team (as well as the talent and schools regionally) seemed to run in relation to one another. Maybe the '90s Sonics wouldn't ever get their championship, but Bethea certainly believed he'd get his. "I'm that shoot-for-the-stars-and-the-moon type of guy," he says.

***

You'll never hear an excuse or complaint leave Mike Bethea's lips. He's a man defined by his actions and deeds. His coaching and mentoring philosophy for the young men in his charge are like a sports and life version of Newton's Third Law of Motion: for every action there is an equal and opposite reaction. "Whatever they put into life, they'll get back," he has said of his players. "If they want to give a half-hearted effort, that's what they'll receive in return, and that goes with schoolwork, chores, basketball or whatever. It all carries over to their effort. I tell it to them on a daily basis, that they should just get used to giving 100 percent if they really expect that back in any way."

It's tough for a kid to say, "Yeah coach, sure, whatever," when that kid knows full well that Bethea rises at 4:30 AM for his day job at Boeing, and then may end his day at the gym around midnight working with a player who's trying to get shots up to maximize a college opportunity. It's damn hard to be lazy in the face of that kind of commitment. This is why Bethea considers himself more of a life coach than a basketball coach, and why he considers his players and former players to be extended family. Yes, some of those family members have reached the pinnacle of their sport. You know their names: Jamal Crawford, a three-time NBA Sixth Man of the Year award winner; Nate Robinson, a three-time NBA Slam Dunk Contest winner; Dejounte Murray, Terrance Williams and Kevin Porter Jr. And dozens more earned college scholarships, like Lodrick and Rodrick Stewart and Ryan Anderson. Bethea even coached seven-time Mr. Olympia bodybuilding champion Phil Heath. But no matter how high his Rainier Beach Vikings fly, they always return to pay homage, to give back, to show support. Crawford donated $100,000 in 2005 to refurbish and renovate Beach's home gym, including a floor upgrade, new logo, electronic scoreboard, new backboard and rims, and a new scorer's table.

"I talked about giving back when I was going here," Crawford said at the time. "To me, this is bigger than scoring 50 points in a game because it comes from the heart. "When I'm dead and gone, this place will still have my name on it. That's something I'll cherish forever. It's a surreal feeling." When fellow Vikings alum Nate Robinson saw the new court for the first time, it quickly brought him back to the old days of a court so beat up that it seemed it was never in playing condition. "It's like a real court now," he said then. "It can compete with anybody's. When I first came here, you had to mop the court five or six times, it was so slippery. It had dust all over. It was a mess. But it was home for us. We called it ours."

Inspired by Crawford's generosity, Robinson donated $10,000 to sponsor Rainier Beach's Washington Assessment of Student Learning math program several years ago. He and Crawford have since put their time and clout behind countless benefits for the program. "There are some things Crawford beat me to," Robinson said in 2005. "I don't want to forget where I came from. Jamal came from here. He's showing his love. He's giving back. If you keep giving back, you make the world a better place."

Case in point, the "giving" isn't just financial. Crawford famously hands out his personal phone number to any Vikings player who asks for it. *Call me if you need anything.* It's something he got from Coach Mike. Be there for your brothers. Be there for the next generation. Robinson still lives in Rainier Beach, his son plays for Coach Mike, and he's a regular at practices, offering pointers and constantly "consulting." It's a comfort to the kids to know that someone has their back outside of their own home. It's also motivation via osmosis: Robinson and Crawford's success can be their success too.

Of course, it's easy for Bethea to talk about the success stories he's had. Who wouldn't enjoy that? *Yeah, Nate's winning dunk contests by jumping over Dwight Howard and Jamal's dropping 50 and Kevin Porter Jr. was a first-round pick.* That's the fun stuff. But there's pain, too.

"Everybody looks at my success stories," Bethea once said. "I mean, I've had some heartbreakers, too. Kids that I love to death that I've lost."

Heartbreak can only come from truly caring about another person; in a basketball program, it comes from brotherhood. It comes from countless hours practicing, traveling, eating together, sweating together, winning together and, most importantly, losing together. It comes from sticking together no matter what. It comes from the path that most Rainier Beach players undergo from schoolmates to teammates to friends to family. And that's exactly how Bethea wants it.

"Ever since I've taken over, that's been one of the things I've had my guys say in the huddle," he says. "We say 'family on three'. Every huddle we break. And I don't want guys just saying the words. I tell them, 'You don't say it unless you mean it'. I'm serious about that. This team and this community are all about family. And you've got to always take care of family."

***

A cluster of satellite trucks for television stations across the country were jammed next to each other as if set up to be run over by Gravedigger. Their dishes faced the sky, beaming live footage of the unfolding frenzy from coast to coast of the United States. The camera crews and reporters who had emptied from the bellies of the trucks hours before were scattered throughout the Convocation Center in Cleveland, Ohio on this cold night in mid-December of 2002. Were they trying to get a glimpse of the president? Was Jay-Z performing a surprise concert, or Chris Rock doing a spot stand-up event? No, no and no. The media and the mayhem and the 11,000 fans, some paying $100 per seat, were on hand to watch 17-year-old LeBron James and his 22nd-ranked St. Vincent-St. Mary's Fighting Irish face the number one high school basketball team in the country, the Oak Hill Warriors. ESPN 2 televised the game and put their big dogs on the broadcast: Dick Vitale, Bill Walton and Jim Gray. "I came here with high expectations," said Hall of Famer Walton, who specifically asked ESPN 2 if he could cover the game to check out LeBron. "I'm leaving more impressed than I could have ever believed. This guy has the complete package."

James scored 31 points, grabbed 13 rebounds, had 6 assists, and threw down a windmill dunk that likely would have scored an 8 or a 9 in an NBA dunk contest on the way to a 65-45 rout of Oak Hill. It was a historic night for ESPN, for LeBron James and, most importantly, for the Rainier Beach boys basketball team, who monitored the game from 2,400 miles away. The Vikings started the 2002 season as the number two high school team in the nation behind Oak Hill, according to the *USA Today* rankings. After defeating West Aurora, Illinois in a 69-62 overtime thriller, Bethea and his boys knew that their best shot at taking the number one spot was if LeBron's Irish could pull off an epic upset. When King James delivered, the throne was theirs. It was the first time the Vikings had ever been the number one team nationally and only the second time since 1984 that a school from the state of Washington earned the top spot. "It's great for the state of Washington. It really shows that basketball here is at as high a level as it is anywhere in the country," Dan Jurdy, Rainier Beach's athletic director, said at the time. "Hopefully, we'll represent Washington well."

To be fair, the Vikings had some extremely talented teams before the 2002 squad. Former Sacramento Kings star Doug Christie's 1988 team was the first Beach team to win the Washington state title, but they didn't have a national presence. The 1998 team that starred Jamal Crawford and future Mr. Olympia Phil Heath had plenty of national recognition, competed in the major invitational tournaments, and won Bethea his first state title, but they never reached *USA Today*'s top spot. Nope, it was the '02 team with Nate Robinson and the Stewart twins that gave Beach its first taste of being number one nationally to go along with its state title.

On the local level, Rainier Beach had taken on all comers on the way to its nine state championships. In the title games they defeated Sequim High School in '88, Olympia High School in '98, Mercer Island High School in '02, Issaquah High School in '03, Lakes High School in '08, Seattle Preparatory in '12, Lakeside in '13, Eastside Catholic in '14, and O'Dea High School in '16. Though clearly considered among the top teams in Washington every year, a few schools have had the firepower to go toe-to-toe with the Vikings at the highest level. Garfield High School beat them in a gut-wrenching overtime game in the state championship in 2018 and defeated them handily in the 2015 championship. O'Dea, Garfield and Franklin, where NBA all-star and champion Jason Terry played, all served as proving grounds of sorts. Getting through that gauntlet undefeated every year often meant a shot at a championship. And for the individual players, performing well against those schools (or in those games if you were an opposing player) usually gave them a leg up among the recruiters who scoured the Metro and the surrounding leagues for college talent.

From Rainier Beach on down to Franklin High in Mt. Baker, and further on down to Tacoma, the basketball riches of the Emerald City have been a veritable feeder system for the Pac-12, major college programs across the country, and the NBA. And with so much talent teeming on the shores of places like Eliot Bay and Lake Washington and Commencement Bay and Poverty Bay, they've had a staggering number of local hoops legends achieve national hoops success.

"When I was in high school the basketball scene was very competitive," NBA Champion and Franklin High School alumni Jason Terry, says. "But nobody really knew about Washington. Every year the best players from the spring league would form two teams and we'd travel around the country and represent our state. It was competitive basketball at the highest level. I noticed they didn't have a lot of respect for Washington guys because the only one of us at the time who was a true legendary hooper from the area was Doug Christie. He had a Summer League and a camp that he'd speak at and we'd all attend. He was from Seattle and he made it. Then we all followed, and things changed."

After Christie came Terry, and then after Terry came Brandon Roy, and so on. Once the ceiling was shattered, the Pacific Northwest soon became a hotbed for college recruiters. They loved the grit and determination that ballers from the Seattle-Tacoma region had. When you talk to coaches and players, they'd often mention a Sea-Tac type, which was one of those descriptions that everyone understood but couldn't exactly describe.

"The type of players that came from our area has evolved over the years," Terry says. "The new terminology is that we're all 'a bucket'. If you came from Seattle, you knew how to get a bucket. Whether it was me or Martell Webster, or whether you had handles like Nate Robinson and Isaiah Thomas, or you were super athletic like Brandon Roy, or even a deadly jump shooter like Spencer Hawes, if you were from our area, you got buckets and that's what we were known for."

Chapter 24

Doug Christie

Roughly 125 miles south of Seattle down the I-5, where the Cowlitz River loops into the Columbia River, sits the old logging town of Longview. It is here, along the Washington and Oregon border, at his grandmother's house during the third week in June of 1992, that 22-year-old Doug Christie tries to fend off insomnia and get some sleep. Normally, he conks out shortly after his head hits the pillow.

But these aren't normal times.

After a stellar college basketball career at Pepperdine University, Christie is mere days away from the '92 NBA Draft at the Memorial Coliseum in Portland, Oregon, where he has been invited to sit in the green room as a projected early- to mid-first-round pick. With Shaquille O'Neal, Alonzo Mourning, Christian Laettner and Jimmy Jackson as headliners, experts predicted the class to be one of the deepest in the league's history.

That Christie was in Longview to get his head right before such a momentous event was poetic in a way. Though he was mostly raised in Seattle by his mom, his dad lived in Longview, and as a kid he spent the summers riding his bike all around town, usually with his fishing pole and usually headed to the old Long-Bell log pond. He'd watch fireworks at Lake Sacajawea on the Fourth of July with his grandmother and partake in what the local kids called "ice blocking," which involved wrapping towels on ice blocks and sliding down the grass hills on them like they were sleds.

"Being in Longview kind of brought me down and allowed me to reflect on what was happening," Christie says. "My dream was to make it to the NBA, and all of a sudden it's here. I dodged a lot of bullets to get there. I used to get into trouble. Some guys never got out of trouble. But I kind of just kept pushing through and had thankfulness to God that I made it."

From a basketball perspective, Longview also was the place were Christie merged his street hoop skills with much-needed basic drills. "When I was with my father, I had some step-brothers who were athletes as well, and they were a positive influence," he says. "When I went to Longview, I found the fundamentals. My coaches put us through pivots and passing and jumping to touch the rim for thirty seconds with both hands and all those kinds of things. I was from the inner city and, being a hood kid, we just hooped. In Longview, I put together the hood part of my game with those fundamentals and made a vast leap."

Prior to his junior year, he moved back to Seattle to be with his mother Norma. As had been the case since she gave birth to Doug as a 16-year-old, the two were inseparable; she was best friend and mom and motivation all rolled into one. As a kid, Christie watched her work two jobs and still find the time to take care of whatever he needed. "My mom did everything for me. I never make athletes my role models," he said. "I don't think you can have a role model that you can't touch and see every day. My mom is strong, and I know she's always there. I can relate to her."

With his best pal and personal inspiration back in his day-to-day life, Christie flourished in his return to Rainier Beach in both basketball and track and field, where he was a star high jumper and eventual state champion. On the court, he'd grown several inches and turned himself into a high school mash-up of Scottie Pippen and Magic Johnson.

"When I was growing up in Seattle, I was part of this pack," Christie says. "But when I came back after Longview I was better than the rest. People know me now for my defense, but back then I was a scorer."

His overall talent, knack for crisp passes, and sweet shooting stroke pegged him as the prototypical swingman before the era of swingmen. During his senior year at Rainier Beach, he averaged 18 points, 7 rebounds and 5 assists as he led the school to its first state championship while earning the Class AA Player of the Year award.

In addition to the accolades and the trophies, he also gained something more valuable: confidence. As his game improved, basketball evolved from a sport he loved to a potential ticket to college and beyond. Of course, every high school athlete who performs at an all-state level has hopes of playing for a big-time school and then maybe, *just maybe*, professionally, but to make that a reality, somebody has to plant the seed. For Christie, it was his head coach.

"My coach Mel Williams had an incredible impact on my life," Christie said. "I remember at one practice, we were all out of sync and coach Williams pulled us all in. 'Look,' he said. 'I don't know what you are all doing. Only one of you has a chance to make it to the NBA.' So, we all looked around. We were seventeen years old, like, who is he talking about? And he said it was me. He was the first person to speak that dream into existence and make me think it was really possible."

During his junior and senior years, Christie played in all the right showcase tournaments, and during a Las Vegas invitational he banged against the "best high school player he's ever seen" in Shawn Kemp. By the time recruiting season wrapped up, he'd whittled his recruiting offers down to two schools: Pepperdine University and Washington State. He ultimately chose the ocean and waves in Malibu over the woods of Pullman.

"I really liked Washington State, and I really liked Kelvin Sampson," he says. "He took me to the gym when I was about seventeen and he was like, 'dude, you're ready to play here.' But Pepperdine felt right to me. A new environment."

At the time, the NCAA's Proposition 48 stipulated that athletes' board scores must meet a certain level to compete, and Christie's were too low, meaning he moved all the way down to Southern California for basketball but couldn't play basketball. The news that he'd have to sit out his freshman year was devastating. Day after day he'd watch the Pepperdine team practice and wonder why the hell he was eleven hundred miles from home if he couldn't even step on the court.

"I was this inner-city kid who didn't have any money and Pepperdine had these really rich kids," he says. "I wasn't a good student and the academics there are high, and I was struggling."

He was frustrated, homesick and constantly thought about transferring to Washington State. He even went so far as to call WSU coach Kelvin Sampson, but he hung up before the coach answered. When he went home for Christmas, he saw all of his buddies doing the same things they'd always done, getting into trouble in the streets. Enter Norma, Christie's rock, who reminded him that he'd made a commitment to that school and that he was going to see it through. "Without basketball, I looked at the academics and said to myself, 'Oh God, I don't know how to study," Christie said. "But my mom told me to stick it out. She told me that I needed to get out of Seattle and find myself. So I went back."

Put an official assist in the box score for Norma Christie, because "sticking it out" turned out to be one of the best decisions her son ever made. First, he learned how to study. Second, he found his footing as a criminology and sociology major. Third, he finally got to play ball and he took the Pepperdine Wave to places the team had never been. He led Pepperdine to a 63-27 record in his three seasons as a starter and a 24-7 record in his final year, when he averaged 19.5 points, 5.9 rebounds and 4.8 assists. In addition to two NCAA tournament appearances, he guided the Wave to back-to-back Western Coast Conference championships and won back-to-back WCC player-of-the-year awards. So yes, sticking it out in Malibu was the right call, which takes us back to the fateful week in 1992 leading up to the draft when Christie couldn't sleep. In three years he'd gone from nearly quitting college to being invited to the NBA's green room with the nation's best players. Hence, the nerves.

"Going to Longview before the draft was good. It was exactly what I needed," Christie said. "I visited my grandma, and not a lot of people know me there, so I was able to hang out and get away from the press. But man, I couldn't be in a room by myself or I'd go crazy. I was up every night until 2 AM. I was really nervous, so I didn't sleep much."

On the night of the draft, Christie sat in the green room as all the big names went off the board.

Shaq. Mourning. Laettner. Jackson. LaPhonso Ellis. Tom Gugliotta.

Then the next tier went.

Walt Williams. Todd Day. Clarence Witherspoon. Adam Keefe. Robert Horry.

And the next tier.

Harold Miner. Bryant Stith. Malik Sealy. Anthony Peeler. Randy Woods.

By the time the 17th pick came up, the only two people left in the green room were Christie and Tracy Murray from UCLA.

"You always worry when you sit there and you're not being picked," Christie said at the time. "It's tough in the sense that you don't know when or where you're going, and this is like the beginning of your life. You don't know what lies ahead of you. It's like sitting there waiting to see if there's a bullet in the gun or a blank. For the first sixteen, they were all blanks."

In another twist of fate, his hometown Seattle SuperSonics owned the 17th pick, and after David Stern took what seemed like an entire NBA postseason to get to the podium, he announced that the Sonics had selected Doug Christie and he was going home.

"I love the city and the Northwest," he said after the pick. "I was planning to move to Seattle after my career was over anyway. Now I can start a little early."

If only it were that easy.

Despite the seemingly dream-like scenario of playing for his hometown Sonics, Christie's agent and Seattle general manager Bob Whitsitt could not come to terms on a contract. The two sides went back-and-forth the entire spring, summer and fall, and by November, Christie's camp had enough and demanded a trade without the Emerald City native having ever suited up.

"The Sonics have really left a bitter taste in my mouth," Christie said at the time. "It's kind of sad to say that they've come at me with ludicrous offers that I really can't accept. It's not that I've lost the value of the dollar, because I haven't."

Case in point: The player selected after Christie in the draft, Tracy Murray, signed a multi-year contract with the Portland Trail Blazers worth $725,000 in year one. According to Christie's agent, he'd only been offered $300,000 for one year by Whitsitt.

"I want to play basketball," Christie said. "If they don't want to sign me, then they should trade me. They should let me go and get along with my life."

Christie made that statement in November 1992, but it wasn't until February of '93 that Whitsitt actually let him go in a trade to the Lakers that netted the Sonics Sam Perkins. Finally, nearly a full year after Christie played his last game in college, he would begin his NBA career as a Los Angeles Laker.

Over the course of the next fourteen years, Christie played on seven teams, made four All-Defensive teams and led the league in steals in the 2000-01 season. He mentored a young Vince Carter and Tracy McGrady on the late '90s Toronto Raptors teams, and led the lockdown defense of the Sacramento Kings playoff teams for a half-decade in the 2000s. All the while, he let his gritty, hard-nosed Seattle basketball roots be his guide.

"Some people think I was the first guy to make it out of Seattle to the NBA, but that was James Edwards," Christie says.

Edwards won a high school state title with the Roosevelt Rough Riders in 1973, played at the University of Washington until 1977, and then was drafted by the Lakers as the 46th overall pick in the 1977 NBA Draft. He's best known for his role on the 1988-89 Bad Boy Detroit Pistons, when he won two NBA Championships.

From '73 to '92 there was a Seattle drought. Then, by the late 90s, the proverbial floodgates were about to open.

"When I was growing up the college coaches really didn't come to Washington to recruit," Christie says. "They'd go to California or maybe Oregon. But we always had the talent around the Metro area. You'd go to Rainier Beach and the gym was full. Garfield, the gym was full. These were intense rivalries with good players. They just weren't recruited deeply. And even when we had talented guys, they'd go to Cal or Stanford and not the University of Washington. We always knew if UW could keep players home, they'd be good. But we always had a great basketball community."

As the first player in over a decade to break out of the city and make it to the pros, Christie took it upon himself to give back and look out for the next generation of guys behind him. He launched leagues, hosted open gyms, started teams...and he made sure all of it was free so any kid could come. Most importantly, he wanted to be a visible member of the community, just as the Sonics were for him throughout his childhood. It sounds corny, but the level to which normal kids had access to their local NBA idols in Seattle simply wasn't found anywhere else. The Sonics players weren't just holding down a basketball job in the city, punching a clock and closing their driveways until the next game. They were part of the city. They embraced it.

"The Sonics were huge for me as a kid from the inner city," Christie says. "To have a professional team right here. I'd ride the seven Rainier downtown and get off at the arena, and we'd see Gus Williams driving in with a Rolls Royce with his *NBA 1* license plate. I loved those teams in '77 and '78, and then against the Bullets in '79. I remember when they didn't want to pay Gus Williams and fans had a going away event for him at the Seattle Aquarium. Thousands of people went to say goodbye and I went. There was a picture in the local paper of me, maybe ten years old, trying to get his autograph. He wore those classic Nike Blazers, and normally it said *Nike* on the back, but on Gus's it said *Wizard* and I just thought that was the coolest."

During the late '70s and early '80s, the Seattle police department had a challenging relationship with the inner-city areas. There was a lot of unrest and mistrust. One of the ways the police department thought to try to improve community relations, especially for the younger inner-city kids, was to give the cops Sonics cards, and if you were a kid you'd get the card if you approached a policeman and engaged in conversation. It was the perfect olive branch. The one thing everyone agreed upon in Seattle was their love for the Sonics, but their adoration didn't happen in a vacuum. The organization and the players took pride in getting involved. Even notoriously tough guys like Xavier McDaniel made sure to make time for the next generation of Sonics fans, including a scrappy kid who lived on Rainier Avenue.

> I was getting in a little trouble as a kid and my mom put me in this church group called Young Life. They had this thing where, if you were selected, Xavier McDaniel would come and pick up the kid and take him to the game, and that ended up being me. I'll never forget, he pulled up in a Range Rover and he had his wife with him. My friend Carlos and I got in the back seat and we talked sports and basketball and he asked us about school. Then we went to the game with him and we got to go into the players' entrance and do all the things you normally don't get to do. We went behind all the gates you couldn't get behind, and it was an incredible experience. Carlos and I kept elbowing each other, like, *are you serious right now?*

For a kid who used to sneak into games, having a backstage basketball pass with his favorite team's most popular player was hoop nirvana. And once he got to the league himself and played for several franchises, he realized how special his experience was. Very few NBA teams were as embedded in their community and with their fans as the Sonics were.

"The city of Seattle is just different," Christie says. "It's not Sacramento, but it's not New York either. The fans understood the game of basketball in many ways. If you ever went to the coliseum or KeyArena, it was rocking."

That intense passion is what led to the equally intense devastation when it looked like the team was on its way out of town. From Christie's perspective, the entire situation was unfathomable. There just was no Seattle without the Sonics. How could there be?

"When I first heard they were leaving, I always thought Howard Schultz should have just made a Starbucks Arena. That's what really turned fans off, was the fact that the city didn't want to build an arena," he says. "I was sad as hell. It was heart wrenching. As a kid, the Sonics grounded me. They put roots in me. And I knew there were going to be a lot of kids who weren't going to get that. Right now, Jamal Crawford could tweet out that he was going to have a summer league game at midnight, and three thousand people would show up. As big as hoops are in that area, to not have a pro team is a sin."

Chapter 25

Jamal Crawford

Jamal Crawford dropped 28 points in the delivery room about fifteen minutes after he was born. "It was a first for me," the doctor said. "He came out of the womb, nailed a jumper, drained a few threes... He started getting buckets and never stopped. He wasn't even a half-hour old. That's when I knew he was a special basketball player."

Do enough research on Crawford's childhood, about how he was dribbling a basketball at the age of two, or crossing up strangers with his ball at the airport at seven, or effortlessly sinking mid-range jumpers on a ten-foot hoop at only nine years old, and you might actually believe the delivery room story because... well, because everyone who talks about Jamal and basketball has a "that's when I knew" story.

"The first time he came to the gym, you could see he had a gift," Mike Bethea, his head coach at Rainier Beach High School, said. "He had no experience. His skills were there, you could see it, but he needed some fundamentals."

Crawford had no experience because he didn't play on a high school team until his senior year at Rainier Beach. This delayed start wasn't because he got cut his freshman or sophomore year; no, he didn't play ball before his senior year at Rainier because he actually attended Franklin High School as a sophomore and junior and wasn't academically eligible to play. Before that, he attended Dorsey High School near Watts in Los Angeles for a bit and didn't play there either. Oh, and he was at Morningside High in Inglewood for a spell as well. His childhood, like his eventual NBA career, was a long, winding road filled with different teams, different addresses, different cities and different people, but there was always one constant: basketball.

Whether he was with his dad Clyde, a former University of Oregon basketball player, in Los Angeles, or with his mom and his sisters in Seattle, Crawford's first love was hoops. His hobby was skipping school and hanging out with the wrong crowd, which almost sabotaged his athletic career. When he was thirteen, his mother, Venora Skinner, could sense that her son was headed down the wrong path in Seattle, so she sent him down to live with Clyde permanently in LA. Crawford loved his father and grandmother, but after a few run-ins with gangs, he didn't feel safe there. For a kid who was barely a teenager, the environment weighed on him, and except for playing in pick-up games with some friends, he rarely left the house.

"It was hard," he said. "I was doing counseling for a while."

Caught between the rock of his hostile LA neighborhood and the hard place of his mostly failing grades, Crawford realized that if he ever wanted to achieve his pipe dream of playing in the NBA (considering he'd never played even freshman basketball at that point), he'd need a plan that included both a renewed focus on his academics and, you know, actually playing organized basketball.

"What I didn't understand then I understood later on—that I would have to really buckle down and focus more on school and basketball than anything else," Crawford said. "Like, before I had a girlfriend or kids or friends, I had my basketball. My love for basketball was deeper than anything else, and I just had to figure out the best route."

After giving it plenty of thought, he realized what he had to do: move back to Seattle and get his grades up. When he told his dad and grandmother his plans, they flatly denied him, worrying that he'd go home and get back into his old bad habits. Undeterred, Crawford asked his sister to send him a plane ticket in the mail (back when that's how you got a plane ticket), and one day he up and left Los Angeles without a word, much like Good Will Hunting taking off from Boston. He did, like Hunting, leave a note for his grandmother and father, writing, "...I do still feel strongly about going back to Seattle, nothing against you, I just like it better there, so I am sorry." And with that, he was gone, ready to restart his academic and athletic lives and learn from his past mistakes.

"Before I went to high school, I didn't even know you had to have a certain grade-point average to play basketball," he once said. "You didn't have to in middle school, and that's where you're coming from. You're young, you're immature, you're in ninth grade. It's a whole new world. So it's, 'Oh, man, I'm in high school now. I'm going to have fun.' I wasn't really the most focused. I changed that focus and things really turned around for me."

After initially enrolling in Franklin High School to finish his junior year, Crawford transferred to Rainier Beach for his senior season, where he had arguably the greatest first year of high school hoops ever. He averaged a triple-double with 23 points, 10 rebounds and 11 assists; he won the city player of the year and the state player of the year awards; and led the Vikings to a state championship exactly ten years after Doug Christie's title. After having not appeared even in a high school starting lineup before the season, Crawford was suddenly a member of the *Parade* All-American team heading into his last year of high school basketball, aka his second senior year.

"Jamal was special to me. He was a bona fide star and you could see it in high school," Doug Christie said about his fellow Viking. "The types of things he was willing to try… you have to have guts to try them. He'd come in the summer league against grown men and they'd beat the hell out of you, but he wanted to play. There were always guys trying to work out with me, but with him I knew. He was really special."

Admittedly, trying to keep track of Crawford's hoop timeline can have you feeling like Deadpool navigating the X-Men film universe, so here's a quick primer: After playing his true senior year of high school basketball, which was his first actual season of high school basketball, Crawford received interest from several colleges and accepted an offer to play for Jerry Tarkanian at Fresno State. Following that, he learned that he would likely lose a year of college eligibility because he didn't meet the academic requirements. Not wanting to miss out on a year of basketball, Crawford appealed to the Washington Interscholastic Activities Association for a fifth year of eligibility so he could get his test scores up and play basketball at the same time.

Due to the fact that Crawford officially transferred twice in high school, had only played one year, suffered hardship, and wasn't up to speed with his class work, the WIAA approved the request, giving him a second senior year and a full suite of options for college. Once he was given another year, he rescinded his acceptance to Fresno State and re-evaluated his college opportunities, which included Minnesota, Washington, St. John's, Oregon and Michigan.

"Washington had just as much of a shot as everyone else. I just wanted to get away from home, learn some things," Crawford said about why he ultimately chose to attend the University of Michigan. But in order to step foot in Ann Arbor, he'd have to pass two core courses and raise his SAT score significantly.

This was his self-described "moment of truth," his sliding doors scenario.

Pass the courses, get a strong SAT score and star at Michigan, or become the subject of a local newspaper story ten years into the future titled, "What Ever Happened to Jamal Crawford?" Making matters more important, his high school girlfriend let him know that she was pregnant at about this time.

Crawford stuck to his plan. By day he was either in class or working with SAT tutors, and by night he shuttled popcorn from the bowels of the KeyArena to the vendors during Sonics games, at a job his older sister hooked him up with. This was at the tail end of the Gary Payton, Shawn Kemp and Detlef Schrempf years. As he walked around the court for work, he soaked in the entire atmosphere—the fans, the players, the arena sound system, the squeaking of shoes on the court, all of it. *This was home. He had to get there. Whatever it takes.*

"When I worked at the KeyArena, my job was to bring the food up from the basement," Crawford says. "It was supposed to be about a ten-minute trip. But I'd take forty-five minutes and look around and dream."

Wake up. Study for class. Study with a tutor. Work until 1 AM. Get up the next day and do it again. This was Crawford's life getting ready for college, and the intense focus paid off.

He passed his classes.

He raised his SAT scores.

He was finally eligible to be a Wolverine.

***

Seventeen games. That was the sum total of Crawford's entire career at the University of Michigan, when he led the team in scoring with 16.6 points per game. (The NCAA hit Crawford with two quick suspensions that he and the school fought, but they ultimately cost him a dozen games of his freshman season.) Early in the season on December 11, he was named CBS's Chevrolet Player of the Game against Duke when he dropped 27 points against the Blue Devils, which was the second time that week he scored 27 points. At the end of the year Crawford declared for the 2000 NBA Draft, despite several high-profile doubters, including his hometown hero Gary Payton. Crawford, who is now close with Payton, got no love from the Glove at the time, who didn't hold back when he said Jamal wasn't ready for the NBA, lacked weight and experience, and needed to stay at school.

For the NBA executives who saw potential where Payton saw red flags, they went about the pre-draft process full bore, combing through Crawford's past with a team of investigators.

"When I had Jamal Crawford, they didn't just reach out to me," Rainier Beach Coach Mike Bethea said. "They wanted to talk to some of the teachers he had dealings with. And that is not out of the ordinary. For them to invest in a player, they must make sure they are well-rounded, the total package."

Several teams liked what they saw, and the Cleveland Cavaliers selected Crawford eighth overall and then promptly traded him to the Chicago Bulls.

"We've always liked big guards," then-Chicago coach Tim Floyd said. "Jerry Krause fell in love with Jamal."

So did Krause's arch-nemesis, a retired-but-thinking-of-unretiring Michael Jordan, who still lived in Chicago and invited Crawford to train with him and run pick-up games at Hoops the Gym. Unofficially, Crawford and Jordan went undefeated at the famous gym over the two-year period they played. The professional team he was on, however, was terrible. The 2000-01 Bulls went 15-67. The next year, 21-61. Then 30-52, and in Crawford's final year in Chicago, the team dropped back down to 23-59. Meanwhile, Crawford led the team in scoring with 17.3 points per game. In 2004 he signed with the Knicks and reunited with fellow Rainier Beach star Nate Robinson, who the team selected as the 21st pick in the '04 NBA draft.

Once again, Crawford's team wasn't very good, but two patterns began to emerge as he made his way through his NBA career: One, regardless of the team Crawford signed with, he scored. He averaged more than 17 points per game nine times in his career, and over 20 points per game in his last year with the Knicks. And two, he signed with a lot of teams and had a lot of different head coaches, but he was always a positive for his squad. All told, Crawford has played twenty years in the NBA for nineteen different coaches and nine teams (but never the Sonics). Despite the bouncing around, Crawford has tied a record with three Sixth Man of the Year awards (one with the Hawks and two with the Clippers). He's the NBA's all-time leader in four-point plays, the oldest player to score 50 points in a game, and the only player to score 50 points with four different teams. He's also made the eighth most three-pointers of all-time, is considered a legendary ball-handler (hence, the J-Crossover nickname) and he's carved out one of the most uniquely exciting NBA careers we've ever seen.

But when it comes to his legacy, be it with basketball or his community or his family, it all comes back to Seattle and his early years as a Sonics fan.

***

"I was born in 1980 but the 1979 championship still resonated while I grew up," Crawford says. "The Sonics were everything to me. In elementary school I remember Dana Barros and Xavier McDaniel coming to our school to be involved in the community. I was lucky that I was able to see these guys growing up. They were like superheroes to me. I remember listening to Barros and he'd say, 'We have to leave now because we play Charles Barkley later,' and it was just amazing. They had an aura about them."

By the time Crawford was in middle school, the torch had been passed from Barros and the X-Man to Gary Payton and Shawn Kemp in the early '90s. This was the Sonics squad that made the deepest impression with Crawford. *These were his guys.* He watched endless highlights of Kemp posterizing fools on the court and Payton talking trash while picking someone's pocket. Like most kids in Seattle he dreamed of being on the floor and tossing lobs to the Reign Man or draining a three off a dime from the Glove. But unlike most kids in Seattle, by the time Crawford was old enough to get his driver's license, his basketball talent was able to turn most kids' fantasy into his reality.

"I was invited to the pro-am games as a high schooler and I'd be playing in the men's pro league," Crawford said. "That's when I think I first jumped on the bigger basketball radar. I played for George Karl's Friends of Hoops team. Then I played in tournaments that Nate McMillan sponsored. I played on Gary Payton's teams. I remember playing against guys like Detlef when I was only sixteen or seventeen years old."

In the 1990s, while the Sonics were emerging as an iconic NBA team, the Washington basketball scene was still under-appreciated nationally in terms of recruitment to big-time schools and in representation throughout the NBA. It was through the tournaments that Karl and Payton ran that Seattle basketball began to draw the spotlight and the attention it deserved. Crawford says that most people don't realize how instrumental George Karl was in getting Seattle high school basketball known nationally through his camps and teams. Same with Payton.

Bobby Jones, who grew up in Compton, California, but played basketball for the University of Washington and calls Seattle his second home, says that at that time among West Coast hoopers, Seattle was largely overlooked.

"Being a guy from LA, the biggest basketball scene out west, I had my typical thoughts that *our city is better than yours*, mainly because Seattle wasn't known as a basketball city," Jones says. "I mean, we knew about Grunge music and the space needle, but that was it. Seattle was nowhere near as big as Los Angeles, so I just knew LA was better. As the years added on and I met more guys and played with more guys, I got to see that the city has a good basketball culture. I mean, it looks like it might rain every day, so guys are always in the gym working.

> I started college in 2002, and for me, there was no big name that I heard of from Seattle until Jamal Crawford. When he went to Michigan and then the NBA right away, that put Seattle on the map. And when I saw how many camps Gary Payton and George Karl ran in the community, it had such a big impact. They helped jumpstart the basketball scene there.

The camps and teams sponsored by the Sonics and their players were long-term investments in the local basketball community. Each initiative was like planting a new hoops seed for the future, and as more and more kids fell in love with the game throughout the '90s and had access to NBA-level coaches and players willing to give instruction, and had sponsors donating high-quality gear, the talent began to improve and be nurtured at the grade school level. By the time these kids reached high school, there was a crescendo of All-Americans and Division I talent ready to roll across the country or stay home and attend the University of Washington.

"When I was younger, I remember thinking that more people were getting football scholarships than basketball scholarships," Crawford says. "If you played football you had a much better chance at going to a bigger school somewhere else. But George Karl took us to tournaments and helped us get seen. And I'd pick his brain. I remember we were at a Vegas tournament once and we were just talking about what made John Stockton great and what made Magic Johnson great, and I just filled up on knowledge from him."

Gaining access to tournaments and knowledge from Sonics icons was one huge part of why the Seattle basketball scene began to grow exponentially. Another major reason was due to the snowball effect of the individual athletes from the area taking their responsibilities as role models and mentors seriously. Case in point: the bond shared between Christie and Crawford.

"Doug Christie impacted my life so much. He showed me everything. He taught me how to prepare, how to eat right, how to train right, and even how to fix your shoes and socks so you were ready to go," Crawford says. "I remember one time we played one-on-one before practice, and I was so tired from that I could barely get through our workout afterward. I knew then, *man, there's another level I need to get to*. I knew that since he was taking the time to show me the ropes that I was going to do the same thing for the next generation."

A common theme when talking to Christie or Crawford or Jason Terry or any of the Seattle area ballers is how much they say they owe each other for their success. Yes, they're playing for their families and their community, but they're also playing for each other. It's a special camaraderie that brings to mind the three musketeers' slogan: all for one and one for all.

"I am so proud of what Jamal has done," Gary Payton says. "He has taken his Summer League and turned it into something really big. He gets everybody together and brings all these pros in and it's special for the community. It keeps the basketball tradition alive."

Crawford describes the scene in Chicago with the Bulls as one where guys would work out together but not necessarily hang out together. They were doing their own things in the community or in their own lives. He was determined to make sure his Seattle basketball brotherhood back home was different.

"When I am back home, I want everybody to be together," he says. "If Nate

Robinson has an event, or Isaiah Thomas has a backpack giveaway, or I have a charity game, or Spencer Hawes is doing something for an organization, we're all going to be there. We're all going to be there for each other. It's a brotherhood."

For much of this brotherhood's history, the athletes were linked by two things: basketball and their love for the Sonics. With the Sonics gone, a gaping hole exists in the city. Crawford says it still doesn't feel real.

"When I first heard rumors that Seattle might lose the team, I didn't believe it," Crawford says. "Knowing the city and the fans and how great they are for the Seahawks and the Storm and the Sounders and the Mariners… I just couldn't believe we wouldn't have the Sonics. Maybe I didn't want to believe it. And then when it happened it was so hard. That last year they were kind of like a lame duck team. You knew it was happening. You knew it was inevitable. You knew they were leaving. And it's still such a bitter feeling."

And yet, without any men's professional basketball team in the area, the collection of NBA stars who remain involved in the city have become a de facto professional team in their own right—they sponsor community events, hand out their numbers to high school players, speak to grade schools and middle schools and high schools, put on camps, and sponsor teams. The Sonics are gone, sure, but the men who grew up on their legacy make sure it lives on.

"In a weird way, we kind of fill that void of not having the Sonics anymore," Crawford says. "Without the Sonics, the closest kids can get to NBA players is through our group or a ride to Portland or the television. So, when we put on our pro-am, which I think is needed now more than ever, I ask young kids who they want to see. They might say Kevin Durant or Blake Griffin and I understand that's the bigger picture. I never ask people for anything, and to be honest, I'm uncomfortable doing it, but this is the only chance the kids in Seattle will get to see these guys. I remember what it meant to me growing up, so I want to do the same for them. So, I'll reach out and ask players to attend on their behalf. And I'm grateful when they can help out. It means so much. We're the pro basketball players in the community. It's on us now."

Chapter 26

Jason Terry

Fifteen years after Slick Watts led the NBA in steals and assists he was back in the gym, looking just as he did in his Sonics uniform: headband on and still cocked slightly off-center, a giant toothpaste-commercial smile slapped on his face, and the ball effortlessly bouncing from the floor to his hand with a light flick of his wrist. There was no home crowd or electric scoreboard or Western Conference rival to stare down; no, his only challenge that day was to handle the grade school kids in his charge at Dearborn Elementary. He'd become a physical education teacher and basketball coach in his post-playing career, and on this particular day, a third-grader walked in, saw him for the first time and his eyes lit up.

That's Slick Watts!

Watts acknowledged the boy and gave him a smile, completely unaware that he was about to become a major influence on the short, fishing pole-thin kid who would eventually play eighteen years in the NBA and win the league's Sixth Man of the Year award and an NBA Championship—all while wearing a headband in honor of Slick.

"I 100% wore the headband as a tribute to Slick," Jason Terry says now. "I remember I walked into elementary school and Slick Watts was right there, bald head, headband, dribbling a basketball. Growing up in the inner city of Seattle and being a fan of the Sonics, you become accustomed to seeing the great local legends. For me that was Gus Williams, "Downtown" Freddie Brown and Slick. To have him as my gym teacher every day was the ultimate pleasure."

From third grade until about seventh grade, Terry mostly played games at recess and during gym and after school and in rec centers with his friends. Like most middle school kids, his love for the game exceeded his skill. While many future NBA players show flashes of their later-life success—like the aforementioned Jamal Crawford dribbling a ball as a toddler—Terry, by his mom's questionably accurate assessment, was a mostly average early-teen hooper who didn't even play organized ball until he was in eighth grade.

"I thought it was just something to keep him busy," she once said. "He wasn't very good. He was all over the court. He was laughing and happy."

Moms.

Over the next few years, the laughter and happiness for the game remained as his skill level and physical gifts improved dramatically. First came the reflexes. He'd always been one of the speediest kids on the court, able to beat anyone on a fast break, but suddenly, as he moved through adolescence he discovered a level of quickness nobody else seemed to have. It was like his friends' cars went to third gear and his went to fifth.

He could jab step and juke at warp speed, and his first step seemed to be juiced with lightning. And though he'd always been on the skinny side, his legs were veritable pogo sticks. He stood only 6'1" for most of his high school career, but he had a near 40-inch vertical that allowed him to easily dunk and block shots and glide through the air.

"He was young for his age, a late bloomer, a small kid," Donald Watts, Slick's son, said. "But he had lightning-quick speed. A lot of other kids had speed, but Jason had a coach in high school who really taught him discipline and defense."

In the five years since his mom jokingly said he was "all over the court" as a knock, he'd blossomed into a kid whose coaches complimented him for being "all over the court," because he now instinctively knew exactly where he needed to be.

Speed. Quickness. Hops. These are all solid, helpful traits for succeeding in basketball. They're also not exceedingly rare. Parks and pick-up games and gyms across the country are filled with dudes who were the fastest or strongest or quickest in their high school or hometown. What separates those who make it and those who don't has nothing to do with genetics and everything to do with mindset and grit and determination. When it came to those three characteristics, Terry was a true prodigy.

As a grade-schooler he'd take on all comers (often losing) and try to goad older kids into playing him one-on-one. He even talked smack to Watts to get him on the court. "He just wanted to play basketball all the time, and he wanted to take me on," Watts said. "I'd say, 'Get out of my face, boy, you can't handle me'. And he'd say, 'Yes I can, Mr. Watts!'. He was always sure of himself."

Looking back on it now, Terry cherishes the relationship even more because he has the perspective of age. "Now that I'm an older guy and I see some of these younger guys always trying to challenge me and play me, I get it," Terry says. "They want to show me their stuff and I wanted to show Slick my stuff. He never did play me one-on-one, but he'd always have a new ball drill or shooting drill he'd challenge me with."

In sixth grade, a teacher asked him what he wanted to be when he grew up, and he answered, "a basketball player." Seems harmless, right? A lot of kids dream of playing pro ball. But when one of his counselors got wind of his response, they wrote his mom a scathing personal note telling her that her son needed to abandon his pipe dream to make it in life.

"A counselor wrote a letter telling me that he was never going to make it in life because a teacher asked him what he wanted to do, and he said one day he wanted to be a basketball player," his mom said. "'You're never going to make it if that's your dream,' the letter said. He was on the verge of flunking junior high. But after that letter, it just made him even more determined to prove them wrong. And that teacher is one of his staunchest supporters today."

When all of Terry's friends made an AAU team in eighth grade and he didn't, likely because he was not a great shooter at the time, he refused to sulk. Instead, he used the snub as motivation and convinced one of his friends to rebound for him while he shot upward of six hundred jump shots a day. He also studied his idol, Sonics superstar Gary Payton, realizing that his ticket to college and beyond could follow the Payton playbook: leadership, getting to the basket, facilitating, speed, and a commitment to deadbolt-like defense. The work ethic to spend hours a day mimicking Payton came from his mom.

"My mother was a single parent," he says. "I was the second oldest. So, I had a lot of personal responsibility to make sure the others had food, to make sure they got to school every day. And for me, basketball was a relief, because I was the leader of my team. Growing up I was never the best player or the one that they said, 'He's going to make it one day.' I had to work. And that work came from my mother."

The inspiration also came from Payton.

"Gary Payton has been a mentor of mine since my sophomore year in high school," Terry says. "So many times growing up, he'd be on the baseline of the game and then we'd hop in the car and get something to eat and just chop it up. We still talk once or twice a week. But on the court, at that time, defensively I really did try to emulate him. I remember thinking about who I could pattern my game after. Michael Jordan was an obvious answer, but I wanted someone who looked like me and liked to talk a little trash, and that was Gary. In my NBA career I became one of the best shooters, but my natural gift was defense because I worked so hard at it."

The old adage is that you can't teach speed. But you can't teach desire either. As a junior, Terry led the Franklin High School boys basketball team to a state title. As a senior, he led the team to a second title, going back-to-back by using an ever-increasing bag of basketball tricks, including his two staples: selflessness on offense and Spiderman-level defense. By the end of his final season, he'd grown to 6'2" and had what appeared to be a 6'8" wingspan, which gave other teams fits. During the state semi-final game in March 1995, Terry's Franklin High Quakers dominated the Mark Morris Monarchs 73-41, and Monarchs coach Bill Bakamus was left shaking his head at all that Terry could do on the court. Following his 16-point, 6-assist and five-steal effort, Bakamus said, "The thing that I really admire about Jason Terry is that he could go out and score 25 or 30 a game, but instead, he makes everyone else around him so much better. When we tried the box-and-one on him, he just went out to the sideline and they basically played us four-on-four. And if you have good offensive players like they do, you're gonna score doing that."

During a 17-3 run in the second quarter, Terry did everything on the court except levitate. In one sequence he had a fast break dunk, a steal and then a fast-break lay-up on which he got fouled and converted the three-point play, scoring 5 points in what felt like a fraction of a second.

Initially, Terry agreed to stay home and play his college ball at Washington and team up with Slick Watts' son Donald as a sort of local-boys-make-good dynamic duo. The decision made sense. Terry was from Seattle, his mom was a UW alumnus, and he'd spent his high school days working a part-time job selling popcorn at the Huskies home games.

"I had tremendous family ties to Washington," Terry says. "My cousin who is one of my true inspirations played football there. In fact, my cousin and Nate Robinson's dad played together on the 1981 Rose Bowl team. I mean, from my house in the central area you could walk down 23rd and end up at Husky stadium. That was what I dreamed about. I was in that locker room from middle school all the way up. I was die-hard purple and gold."

The trouble was that the Huskies, at that time, were down and out. From 1990 to 1993 they went 50-62, never finishing higher than eighth in their conference. In 1995 and 1996, the peak recruiting years for Jason Terry, the team was a standing-in-the-basement-with-no-lights-on 5-22 and 10-17, respectively. Terry's mom, who by this point truly believed her son had a chance at going pro, didn't feel that her beloved university was the best stepping stone.

"My mother just told me, 'Listen, I know you love Washington, but if you want to be a professional basketball player, the best place for you is the University of Arizona,'" Terry says. "'At least give them an opportunity to go for a trip. Let me call Lute Olson.'"

Terry agreed but didn't want to get his hopes up, because Lute Olson's Wildcats in the late '80s and early '90s were as good as it got in college basketball. In 1988 they won thirty-five games and made it to the Final Four. Over the next ten years, they never won fewer than twenty-four games and made the NCAA Tournament every season, with three Sweet Sixteen appearances and another Final Four showing. Considering the talent and success, there was no guarantee that Olson had room on his roster for Terry, even though he'd shown some interest during the recruiting process.

"Man, that was the best phone call I've ever experienced in my life," Terry continued. "Lute said, 'You know what, you're fortunate because we had two other point guards that we were recruiting. Mike Bibby's already committed; he's coming next year. But the two guys we recruited, they decided to go somewhere else. One kid, Brandon Lloyd, went to UCLA and another kid, Eddie Shannon, went to Florida. And that opened up a spot.' So there really wasn't a spot for me at the University of Arizona [previously], but you've got to believe in the higher power working. And my good friend Michael Dickerson was already there, so that was a plus for me. But going on my trip, on my recruiting visit and meeting guys like Kelvin [Eafon], meeting guys like Damon Stoudamire, Khalid Reeves, Joseph Blair, and seeing how close they were, it was something you wanted to be a part of. I didn't get that feeling for any other school that recruited me."

As the saying goes, mom is always right.

During Terry's sophomore year at Arizona, the team won a national championship. It was validation of his decision and also of his commitment to think of his teammates first. During the year, Terry could see that Miles Simon and Mike Bibby played better together when they started, so he proactively went to Coach Olson and asked if he could come off the bench to help his teammates' confidence.

"It was all about being selfless," he said. "Sometimes in life you gotta sacrifice to get to your ultimate goal, and it just worked out. Sacrificing for me right there in that instance led us to a national championship."

Jamal Crawford, who was peaking as a high school player at this time, felt the impact of the title back home in Seattle, saying, "I remember JT at Franklin winning back-to-back championships, and that was the ultimate thing in our area. But then he signs with a school like Arizona. I mean, that was a big-time program and we were from the same community. Then he wins a national championship. It made us believe. That was the first guy to do it for us. It was unbelievable for everybody and inspired all of us. And he was just getting going."

By the time Terry was a senior, he won Pac-10 Player of the Year and was first-team all-conference, which led to the Atlanta Hawks taking him as the tenth overall pick in the 1999 NBA Draft. He played five years in Atlanta as one of the team's leading scorers before spending eight years with the Dallas Mavericks, where he was a fan favorite, flying with his signature "JET" wings on the court of the American Airlines Arena and winning a championship with them in 2011—all while wearing Slick Watts' signature headband. Following the 2012 season, Terry spent one year with the Boston Celtics, one year with the Brooklyn Nets, two with the Houston Rockets, and two with the Milwaukee Bucks. His eighteen years in the league were a testament to his personal drive and the grit infused in him by growing up playing ball in Seattle.

"What I really liked about Seattle players is that they were coachable, and they were really interested in being part of a team," his college coach Olson once said. "The pros stick around there in the summer and work out all the time."

Terry believes that the reason for the camaraderie and the competition is two-fold: bragging rights, for one, and two, the water never stops falling from the sky, so there's not much else to do.

"It rains a lot, so we're always in the gym," he says. "You go to any gym in Seattle in the summertime, you'll see ten to fifteen NBA guys and ten to fifteen guys who were *this* close to making it, and they're still playing basketball in the city. And it's competitive. These are stories you're going to be telling your grandkids about, these summer games and summer workouts.

> All the guys are coming back from their pro teams and we'd go to [the Hec Edmundson Pavilion] on Washington's campus and we'd lace 'em up. It was like playing for the state championship. We'd have me and Brandon Roy on the same team playing against Jamal and Rosell Ellis, who was also from Rainier Beach. There'd be all different generations of hoopers. It really is a bond. We all wanted to see each other do well.

Fellow Emerald City legend Doug Christie agrees completely.

"When JT first got to the NBA and he was young, he hit a game winner against me and I just gave him a hug," Christie says. "It was important for all of us to be happy for each other."

As for the part about giving back, Terry says it's the natural evolution of how things are done in Seattle. The big names that broke through have a responsibility to look out for the big names that come after, and that included the Sonics organization.

"The Sonics throughout my lifetime would always put on clinics at Garfield or at inner-city gyms," Terry says. "The camps were free, and all different legends would come and speak. That's how you knew that our basketball was different—when the pro team is that involved in the community. It only bred a love for more basketball. You see it more in the modern NBA now, but back then, this was all we knew. There was no social media or YouTube to follow your favorite guys, so the Sonics and their star players were out in the community. They'd be outside on the courts with us with the chain-link nets. Not every team did that."

As Terry waxes poetic about his days on the playground courts with his childhood idols, the importance of the Sonics to his individual past and the community at large comes into clearer focus. Not only were they an omnipresent force in the community, giving back with their time and their equipment and dedicating courts, but the players and training staff were available to help the kids who had a future in basketball reach their potential.

"The Sonics had such a huge part in my individual growth and passion for me to take my game to the next level," Terry says. "Steve Gordon, a trainer, held workouts at the Seattle Pro Club in Bellevue. He'd have me and guys like Doug Christie or Michael Dickerson, and we'd play against guys like Xavier McDaniel and Detlef Schrempf—and those workouts were intense. They'd let you be like a punching bag for the pros, but when it was over they'd let you play five-on-five. So, you'd be playing with a bunch of Sonics or against them, and these were guys you idolized every day who were pumping you up telling you that you could make it like them. That's why, even when I played against the Sonics, I always rooted for them because I knew how important they were to the community."

From Terry's perspective, when the team was taken from the city it was more than just the loss of a basketball team to root for—it was a vital organ ripped out of Seattle's body.

"When we found out that the team was really going, the mood was just as cloudy as the skyline on any given day of the year," Terry says. "It was emptiness and it was like you're missing a part of your life. That feeling is still there even today. Every time I fly back home, I see the I-5 and the coliseum, but no Sonics. We have Russell Wilson doing amazing things with the Seahawks, and the Mariners' great stadium, and the Seattle Storm are great, and we even have a great soccer team. But no Sonics. Even NBA players on other teams loved coming here. They loved the food. Didn't mind the rain. They'd get out and go to Pike's Place and throw fish and take in our culture. It was one of our favorite trips. We need a team back in Seattle."

Chapter 27

The Husky Pipeline

At the corner of Snohomish Lane South and Montlake Boulevard on the southern peninsula of the University of Washington campus sits a pristine, Italian-brick building. The heavy moisture of Union Bay fills the surrounding air as Husky Stadium provides a looming backdrop. At the main entrance to the building, past the circular rotunda, the slashing white script of the Alaska Airlines Arena signage hangs above a row of arches. Up top and to the left, near the signature windows that frames the main venue inside, the logo appears again, at the apex of the structure. Walking in, it's easy to not notice the *other sign* written in copper, in a basic serif font, hung high off the back of the second level of the structure: *CLARENCE S. "HEC" EDMUNDSON PAVILION*.

It's one of those things you see all the time but actually never see, like a plaque near a park bench that you sit on every day but never bother to read. The complex has been called "Hec Ed" roughly since it was named for Edmundson in 1949 (it was built in 1927 and was previously called the Washington Pavilion). Hec Ed is so quick and short to say and think, that it rarely begs further thought or forces students or fans or alumni to ask, you know, who the hell is Hec Edmundson—and what kind of name is "Hec"?

We'll start with the latter. When Edmundson was a little boy, he'd become obsessed with mastering things (running, hobbies, whatever), and when he'd mess up he'd mutter "oh, heck." He did this so much that his mom started called him "hec" and the name stuck. Easy enough, right?

As for who he was, well, Edmundson was quite simply one of the most accomplished athletes and coaches in the United States in the early 20th century. He was a track star at the University of Idaho and represented the United States in the London Olympics of 1908 and the Stockholm Olympics of 1912 in the 400- and 800-meter sprints. In Stockholm he finished seventh in the 800 and sixth in the 400. After graduation and the Olympics, Edmundson coached at his alma mater for a few years before moving to Seattle to become the head track coach and then head basketball coach at Washington in 1920. His success in both sports was almost immediate, as he produced Olympians on the track and winners on the court. The basketball roster he inherited won seven games in 1919. In 1920 he more than doubled the win total and put together an 18-4 season. But like Al Pacino in *Scent of a Woman,* he was just gettin' warmed up.

From 1920 to 1947, Edmundson compiled a 488-195 record for a .714 winning percentage. He won twenty or more games eleven times, won twelve division titles and had only one losing season.

Most importantly, he invented the fast break, only it wasn't called the "fast break" back then because he hadn't invented it yet. Early in his tenure with the team, he'd often practice with his players, instilling in them the philosophy he borrowed from the track: speed wins. He called this strategy his "basket-a-minute" philosophy.

"The more you run, and the faster you run, the more you win," he said in the early 1920s. The man lived to coach, train, compete and promote sports. Every single high school basketball player in Washington owes him a debt of gratitude, in fact, because he both pitched the idea for and then organized Washington state's first high school basketball tournament. And whenever you see a basketball team gather before tip-off, put their hands together and say something like "win on three" or "family on three," that too was the brainchild of Edmundson. He called it the "five-man handshake." By the time Edmundson retired in 1954, nearly 400 former athletes showed up at the Olympic Hotel to pay their respects.

That's who Hec Edmundson of "Hec Ed" fame was: an Olympian, a legendary track and field coach, an absurdly good basketball coach, the inventor of the fast break and the pre-game huddle, and the man who created the first high school basketball tournament in Washington. To borrow a line from Ron Burgundy, he was kind of a big deal.

***

Art McLarney had one successful season as head coach at Washington after Edmundson left (with Hec's players and system intact) before flaming out in three years. His replacement, Tippy Dye, had three great years, taking his team to the Elite Eight in 1951 and the Final Four in 1953. But then the team tanked for six years straight before he was fired in 1959. For the next decade, the Huskies were as exciting as a plain bowl of cold oatmeal, playing .500 ball or less with nothing to show for it. Coach Marv Harshman brought the team back to respectability in the late '70s and early '80s, making a handful of NCAA tournaments behind his star, Detlef Schrempf.

Schrempf, aka "Det the Threat," won a state title in 1981, his one year at Centralia High School in Washington, after moving to the States from Germany. Standing at 6'10" and weighing 235 pounds, Schrempf was the prototypical combo forward—able to guard either front-court position while also being an offensive mismatch for smaller threes and bulky fours. He helped the Huskies win Pac-10 titles in 1984 and 1985, and was named to Washington's All-Century team before having a stellar NBA career that included two Sixth Man of the Year awards.

After Schrempf graduated, Harshman left and the next three coaches' records read like a heart rate monitor, filled with a couple blips (but mostly dips), until Lorenzo Romar, a former Washington player under Harshman, took over in 2002.

Romar is a potent mix of perfect-sunrise positivity and Tony Robbins-level persuasion, and his talent as a recruiter is unmatched. The man could recruit a salmon into a bear's mouth. During his fifteen years at the helm of the Huskies, he had fourteen players drafted to the NBA, including ten in the first round. All but one of Romar's teams featured a future NBA first-rounder (an odd, yet impressive stat), but he was never able to reach the Elite Eight in the NCAA tournament, though he did have three Sweet Sixteen appearances.

"I played for Marv Harshman and I looked at Marv Harshman as an icon when I played for him," Romar said. "And he coached at Washington for fourteen years. When I first took the job, I'm thinking about goals and all. And I thought, if I could be the coach here at Washington for fourteen years, that would somehow mean things went pretty well. Well, we were there fifteen years."

In terms of judging the totality of Romar's time at Washington, which spanned from 2002 to 2017, his ability to draw talent to the university and keep homegrown kids at home is his true legacy. When Romar was released from the school in 2017, *Seattle Weekly* writer Seth Kolloen wrote, "He was a tireless recruiter of local talent, no matter the consequences—I once saw him at a Garfield High School basketball game on Valentine's Day with his wife."

Brandon Roy. Nate Robinson. Isaiah Thomas. Dejounte Murray. Tony Wroten. The list of Sea-Tac athletes who attended UW goes on and on. Romar had a knack for recognizing future NBA talent right in his own backyard and convincing them to stay. All of these players bought into his system and all of them benefited. This led to an outsized number of Huskies making the leap to the NBA at a rate that outpaced their college peers on the West Coast—and even some of the blue bloods back east.

"Traditionally, college basketball on the West Coast never gets much attention," Schrempf says now, reflecting on Washington's talent pool. "An 8 PM Pacific start time is eleven o'clock at night on the East Coast. But then you look at the history of players who have come out of the state at the college level and pro level who are all from the area, and it's impressive. It definitely has scouts and recruiters saying that they have to spend more time in Washington."

While Schrempf is the only modern Emerald City Hoops Triple Crown winner (having played high school ball in Seattle, college ball at Washington and NBA ball with the Sonics), there are over a dozen players in the last twenty years from Washington who form a veritable pipeline to the NBA. It's partly due to the competition in the region and partly due to the camaraderie of the players who go to the school.

"When I was in college, we had a great basketball scene at Washington," Schrempf says. "I played pick-up ball all summer long at courts all over the area. Some of the pros would come back and play pick-up games. The guys that have come out of UW, I just want them to succeed. I offer to help as needed. It's amazing how many of them have had long careers and come back to work with the younger players. It's a testament to the community."

Spencer Hawes, who went to Seattle Prep for high school, was a second-generation Husky who chose to follow in his father's and uncle's footsteps and play for Washington. Once again, the appeal was the family and local pride of representing the purple and gold, and Romar locked in the commitment.

Nate Robinson, who was the Washington state player of the year in both football and basketball as a high school senior at Rainier Beach, was being recruited by everyone from Michigan to the University of Southern California for football, but there was only one school he truly wanted to attend: Washington

"People don't know this, but I never really had an official visit with Washington," Robinson says. "I knew all about the team from growing up around it, and when my recruiting was wrapping up, I set up a meeting with Coach Romar, who hadn't recruited me because he thought I was going to play football somewhere else. I'd definitely seen him at local high school all-star games and at some of our Rainier Beach playoff games, so he knew exactly who I was. When I told him I wanted to play football and basketball, he said he'd work with me to make it happen and I got to stay home."

Nearly every Washington-native, five-star high school player who stayed in state has a similar story: They rooted for the program growing up, they knew about Romar's ability to spot NBA talent and get players to the next level, and they loved the Husky culture that was handed down from one class to another like a secret handshake.

"I was really happy when the talented basketball players in Seattle started staying in Seattle for college ball," Karl says. "That wasn't the case in the '90s. When I was there, Washington was primarily a football program. Now it's a mutual partnership between football and basketball. It started with Coach Romar and continues with Coach Hopkins. I'd like to see it last forever."

Isaiah Thomas, the 5'8" walking bucket who scored over 1,700 points in three seasons with the Huskies (and broke Hawes' freshman scoring record only a few years after he set it), summed it up best when asked why he ultimately chose Romar and Washington over several other top colleges: "Why would I want to go somewhere else when I can do it right at home and have my friends and family watch?"

Chapter 28

Brandon Roy

Brandon Roy's mom wouldn't let him in the house. Again. She'd had enough. No, Roy wasn't in trouble for breaking curfew or skipping school or getting caught doing something dumb. That wasn't it at all. Roy, 18 years old at the time, was a respectful, mature-beyond-his-years young man who typically made smart decisions. The reason she wouldn't let him in the house was because...well...to be blunt...he stunk.

One day he'd smell like fish. Another day he'd smell like garbage. Another day he might smell like a bathroom. The list of putrid scents and filthy clothes was nearly endless while Roy worked as a utility janitor for $11 an hour at the Port of Seattle following his senior year in high school.

"I was a utility guy. Sometimes I'd go into those shipping containers with a spray and clean them out, or I'd take out trash, or I'd clean bathrooms," Roy said of his time on the port. "I was like a janitor. They also taught me how to drive the forklift, so when I got bored I'd move boxes around. It was hard work. I'd come home dirty, and I'd have to go to the porch and take off my clothes, and my mom would give me new clothes so I could come in the house. I would want my kids to go through something like that. It gives you good perspective."

Right about now you're probably thinking, *Wait. Wasn't Brandon Roy a high school state champion at Garfield in Seattle? And didn't he go on to win Pac-10 Player of the Year and then become a first-round NBA draft pick, a three-time all-star and two-time All-NBA selection?*

Yes, yes, yes, yes and yes. And yes, Roy was a star recruit after his senior year, and he even flirted with entering the NBA draft before a workout convinced him that he wasn't ready, and he committed to Washington.

So why the dock work?

Roy was diagnosed with a learning disability late in high school, which made taking timed tests like the SAT very difficult. This put Roy behind the eight ball because, when it came to NCAA eligibility, a baseline SAT score was as critical as a pulse. The first time Roy took the test, he did poorly. But Roy dug in. After months of studying and working almost daily with tutors, he took the test again toward the end of his senior year and passed with flying colors—only the flying colors were so bright, the NCAA didn't believe his score and flagged it. Right about the time he was supposed to begin his freshman year at Washington, he was notified that he was ineligible, and he'd have to take the SAT a third time.

Way to buckle down, Brandon, but you did too well, and we don't believe your score. Mind taking the test again?

In what felt like an instant, Roy went from maybe declaring for the NBA Draft to accepting a scholarship to be a Husky to…nothing. No pro career. No college career. It was as if Roy was about to sit in his first-class seat for a flight to Hawaii but then he was suddenly escorted off the plane, given a paddle and dinghy and told to start rowing. Brutal.

This scenario hit close to home for another reason. Brandon's older brother Ed was an elite high school athlete as well who had scholarship offers from major Division I schools in both football and basketball. He also had a learning disability, only his went undiagnosed and he gave up college and pro aspirations, something Brandon wanted desperately to avoid.

Roydell Smiley, a teammate of the Roy brothers, said, "I think the guy with the biggest upside was Ed Roy. He was better than all of us at a young age."

Instead of sulking, Brandon Roy got studying. His parents provided the motivation, telling him, basically, "you go out and do so well that the NCAA has to flag you again." And this brings us back to his job at the Port of Seattle.

"After I graduated [high school], I was sitting at home on the couch," Roy told ESPN as his star began to rise in the NBA. "I knew I'd be missing the autumn quarter, so I told my parents I wanted to get a part-time job. I never wanted to be that guy just sitting around. And my parents didn't have a lot of money, so I didn't want to just live off them. I wanted to make my own way. So, I went to my old AAU coach to see if he knew somebody who could give me a job. He gave me a few options.

> The job I decided on was working down in the Seattle docks. It was a great experience for me. I was there with people who worked extremely hard and didn't get paid like basketball players. It was a chance to get to know the everyday working guy. In talking to them, they told me that when I pass that test and get

> into college, I have to make the most of my opportunity. I try to keep that mentality with me today.

At the time, the job was a day-to-day reminder of how fleeting the opportunity for success could be. Roy admits that after all the accolades and attention he received from playing basketball, the anonymity and the grind of the job at the docks got to him.

"I was a nobody," he said. "I was that guy they said, 'What happened to Brandon Roy? He's another guy who failed.'"

Each morning Roy would head to the docks, and each night he'd come home, change clothes and prep for the SAT. His friend Cole Allen said he'd come by to see if Roy wanted to hang out, but he wasn't having any of it. He was a man on a mission. For years, an unspoken theme hung around the Garfield High basketball team like a heavy winter coat: *Nobody from Garfield goes to college.*

"A lot of these guys didn't like school; they flat out told me," Garfield coach Wayne Floyd said. "But they realized it was part of the puzzle. I'm really proud of them."

Roy studied and studied, and after he finally took the test, the waiting game began. August turned to September and September to October and still nothing. Roy's new Washington teammates were about to start their season and all Roy could do was watch and wait.

And wait.

And wait.

And wait.

Warm summer mornings turned into crisp fall nights, and then full-on winter set in and still, no word from the NCAA.

On January 16, 2003, Coach Romar asked Roy to come to the Huskies facilities because the NCAA was due to send its verdict. Pass or fail. Could Roy play or not? His whole future hung in the balance.

As he sat in the players' lounge and fidgeted, he wondered what he'd do if all the work didn't...work. What if he missed his whole freshman year? What if he never got a chance to play?

Finally, Coach Romar called him into his office.

When Roy walked in it seemed like Romar was trying to put off telling him the bad news. Seconds felt like semesters, and then finally he said, "I'm trying to figure out if we can get you a uniform for tonight." Sweet relief. He embraced his coach for what felt like an eternity. His third SAT score was his highest yet. Brandon Roy could start his college basketball career.

"That was probably the most special day of my life," Roy said.

***

Long before Brandon Roy became All-NBA and three-time all-star BRANDON ROY, he was Ed Roy's little brother at Garfield High School, where he played both junior varsity and varsity and was known for one thing: an otherworldly leaping ability.

In a feature in *Washington Monthly* magazine, Cole Allen, Roy's best friend since high school, commented on his 42-inch vertical leap: "Brandon could jump higher than any other person I've seen on the floor. The day after the 2000 NBA Dunk Contest, Brandon was in the gym during lunchtime, duplicating those dunks in front of the whole school."

If you'll recall, 2000 was the year that Vince Carter changed the contest forever by throwing his arm down to the elbow through the rim and hanging there. Not sure if Roy did that exact dunk, but even if he came close as a high school sophomore, that's closer than most fully developed NBA players will ever get.

"I played against Brandon's brother Ed," Jamal Crawford says. "I knew about him. Will Conroy was telling me how good he was. And I kept hearing about it, and I saw him when he was about fifteen. He had unbelievable athleticism and he had such a coolness about the way he played. You just knew he'd be a stud. He had no weaknesses in his game, and I wasn't surprised by his ascent at all."

Later that sophomore year, he'd have what was his highlight of the season, a two-handed dunk in the state playoffs over one of Seattle's most vicious shot blockers. By the time Roy was a junior, he'd gone from being Ed's little brother to B-Roy, a high school star in his own right who averaged 19 points per game and led his team to a 27-2 record. He'd also come to fully believe that becoming an NBA player was his destiny. When Dan Raley of the *Seattle Post-Intelligencer* sat down with Roy and his high school teammates and asked them who had the best chance of making the NBA, Brandon's answer was simply, "besides me?"

Perfect.

"I remember talking to Jamal Crawford and he was telling me, 'There's a kid here you have to watch. He's a freak and he's really special'. So next time I was in Seattle, I went to watch him, and that kid was Brandon Roy," Doug Christie said.

Physically, Roy had the frame and the physique to go pro. Mentally, he was a basketball wunderkind, like one of those gifted people who pick up a guitar for the first time and start playing Hendrix by ear. While his teammates saw the zeroes and ones of the hoops Matrix, Roy could actually see the full picture.

"I've always kind of had that in my game, that maturity," Roy said in his first *Dime* magazine cover story. "Even in high school, my coach would pull me aside and say, 'You've gotta be more patient with your teammates. Things will come faster to you than it will to them.' I had to learn that at an early age, 'cause I would get mad and get on 'em. I always *thought* the game, while most players react. It's kind of been a gift of mine. In college, Coach Lorenzo Romar would say, 'Just because a play comes easy to you, it may not come as easy to your teammates. You gotta learn to trust your teammates and be patient with them.' I learned to be more patient and think the game. It's worked for me all my life, and it's not gonna change now."

Romar recognized that Roy had a hard-court super computer in his head about an hour after he gave Brandon the news that he was eligible to play. During Roy's first practice, he was able to virtually master an offense that had taken most of the Husky players a few months to merely become familiar with.

"We took him up to the gym and he learned our offense in forty-five minutes," Romar said. "High basketball IQ."

As a true freshman, Roy came off the bench and scored about 6 points in roughly seventeen minutes per game. During his sophomore year he fought through injuries and played excellent basketball while future three-time NBA Slam Dunk Champion (and fellow Seattle native) Nate Robinson grabbed the headlines. The Huskies were 19-12 that year and Roy averaged 12.9 points, 5.3 rebounds and 3.3 assists. It was perhaps during the '04-'05 season when Roy truly endeared himself to Husky fans and lovers of unselfish basketball everywhere.

After having knee surgery for a torn meniscus in November 2004, Roy returned to the court after missing only three weeks (he was supposed to miss four to six) for a game against 12th-ranked NC State. The applause he got upon entering the game belongs in a *Remember the Titans*-type sports movie—and true to form, Roy delivered. In only eighteen minutes of play, Roy shot 5-for-5 from the field, scored 10 points, had 3 rebounds, a block and two steals, helping the team to victory. At the time of Roy's return, the team was 7-1 and guards Robinson and Tre Simmons were playing lights-out basketball. Bobby Jones and Will Conroy were also playing well. Not wanting to disrupt the team's chemistry, Roy came off the bench for the remainder of the season as the team went 29-6 and earned a number one seed in the NCAA tournament (where they lost to Louisville in the Sweet Sixteen).

Finally, as a senior, Roy was fully healthy and fully ready to be the leader of the team. It had been a long time coming—the SAT setbacks, the injuries, the timing with the line-up. It felt like ten years had passed since he graduated high school, but it was worth the wait. In no uncertain terms, from the fall of 2005 to the spring of 2006, Brandon Roy put together one of Washington's all-time greatest basketball seasons.

"There's not too many things he didn't do," Romar said. "You go back and check every year of every player who has ever put on a Husky uniform. None had the year Brandon Roy had. Brandon Roy separated himself from any era. You can't match what he did. Brandon's in a class by himself."

Roy's rock-solid per game totals tell only half the story of his season: 20.2 points, 5.6 rebounds, 4.1 assists and 1.4 steals. The other half is a mash-up of his lethal efficiency (he shot 50% from the floor, 40% from three-point range and 80% from the foul line) and his leadership, which was recognized league-wide—and nationwide—after the Huskies finished their season 26-7. In short order, Roy won the Pac-10 Player of the Year, was First-Team All Pac-10, was a Consensus All-American, and a finalist for the Oscar Robertson, Naismith, Wooden and Adolph Rupp awards. In 2009 he became only the second Washington player to have his number retired. The culmination of his senior year was his selection as the sixth overall pick in the 2006 NBA Draft by the Minnesota Timberwolves (who quickly traded him to the Portland Trail Blazers).

Once in Portland, Roy continued his ascent to basketball prominence by winning the Rookie of the Year award in 2007, being named an all-star in '08, '09 and 2010, All-NBA Second Team in 2009, and All-NBA Third Team in 2010. In 2011, Roy was forced to retire after only four and a half seasons due to his bad knees. He tried a brief comeback in 2012 after receiving platelet-rich plasma treatment, but once again injured his knee after five games.

"Any time you walk away from the game, you have 'what-ifs,'" he said reflecting on his comeback attempt. "I feel like I was able to answer those questions…by going out and giving it a try."

Like nearly all of the NBA players who come out of Seattle, Roy's first thought post-career was to go back to his hometown and make a difference, which he did by becoming the head basketball coach at Nathan Hale High School. In his second season he coached the team to an impeccable 29-0 record and won the Naismith National High School Coach of the Year award and a state championship for Nathan Hale.

Then, in a move to truly bring his life full circle, he signed on to coach at his alma mater, Garfield High School, in 2018, where he has already won two state championships (2018 and 2020). The journey from Garfield High JV player to varsity star to all-time Husky great to NBA franchise player and back to Garfield High as the state championship-winning head coach took less than two decades but has created a legacy that will last forever. For Roy, it's all part of what being a member of the Seattle basketball brotherhood really means.

Chapter 29

Nate Robinson

I wonder if I can jump and touch that countertop...
I wonder if I can jump and touch that cabinet...
I wonder if I can jump and touch that windowsill...
Or that doorway...
Or that street sign...
Or that tree branch...

To live inside the mind of a young Nate Robinson is to be in constant wonder of how far your legs can take you off the ground. Such is the case when you're born with spring-loaded coils in your legs instead of the usual calf muscles. As a toddler, Robinson's family swears that he was jumping before he was walking. For most kids, the stages of mobility are crawling, walking, running. For Robinson, it was crawling, hopping, walking, jumping, running, leaping.

"When I was a little kid and I'd be around adults, they looked at me like I was from another planet or something," Robinson says. "Here I was, this little kid, getting a foot or two off the ground."

The adults had a point. How many four-year-olds have a twelve-inch vertical?

By middle school, Robinson could dunk a volleyball on a ten-foot hoop. By eighth grade, even with small hands that couldn't palm a ball (something that would carry over into adulthood) he was able to dunk a basketball.

It's important at this point to note that Robinson stood about 5'1" in middle school and entered his freshman year at about 5'4". Ninety-nine percent of basketball players at that height never dunk a ball, let alone as a fourteen-year-old. But Robinson had a gift: raw, unfettered, explosive leaping ability. Couple that with an uncanny knack for getting to the basket and a jump shot he worked on tirelessly, and Robinson played about a foot taller and five years older than he really was. It took one practice with the freshman basketball team for Rainier Beach Head Coach Mike Bethea to realize it was a joke for Robinson to compete with kids in his own grade.

"Guys would mock me and call me every name in the book for being short, but I really didn't let it bother me," Robinson says. "I think what allowed me to get through it was how I carried myself. I knew I was better than every single guy on the freshman team and that my real competition was with the older guys. Coach Mike put me with the freshmen and that didn't last long because I was too good to play with them."

Bethea then bumped Robinson up to the junior varsity squad and he dominated there as well, forcing his coach's hand to put Nate on varsity as a fourteen-year-old. In order to stay eligible for varsity, he could play only two quarters of JV and then he'd have to be pulled, so he treated the two quarters as a warm-up, often scoring twenty or thirty points while barely breaking a sweat. As a varsity-playing freshman, he made a small contribution off the bench, but come sophomore year, Robinson was ready to go full tilt, play huge minutes and, of course, start dunking on everyone.

"My first in-game dunk happened my sophomore year on an out-of-bounds, alley-oop play, and the gym exploded," Robinson says. "Nobody expected it. Even the other team's fans went crazy. It was awesome."

By the time Robinson became a senior and was averaging nearly twenty points a game as the smallest guy on the floor, it was clear to everyone, especially Bethea, that they had a uniquely talented athlete on their hands.

"You can be anything you want to be," Bethea told Nate. "You have something that nobody else has. I see it in your eyes. I've never seen anyone with the eye of the tiger that you have."

If you know Robinson from The Big 3 or as a three-time NBA Slam Dunk champion or from his epic showdown with LeBron James in the second round of the 2013 NBA Playoffs, then the story so far makes sense. Obviously, Robinson was a gifted high school basketball player before he became an exceptional college player and an eventual NBA starter. What you might not know is that for most of his high school career he was known around Seattle and the state of Washington for his football prowess.

"Nate was a better football player than basketball player in high school," Doug Christie says. "Nate had that dog in him in a way that not a lot of people do. I knew he'd make it once he chose basketball. But he was better at football back then."

As a shutdown corner and running back for Rainier Beach, Robinson ran for 1,264 yards on 111 carries and scored 28 touchdowns. He helped Beach win the Metro League title and was the *Seattle Times* Class 3A State Player of the Year and an all-state pick. He got recruiting letters and offers from nearly every top football school in the country: Notre Dame, Texas, Texas A&M, Tennessee, Mississippi State, UCLA, Arizona. During his official visit to the University of Southern California, Pittsburgh Steelers legend and USC star Troy Polamalu was his host, showing him around Los Angeles and taking him to the best spots on campus. He hung out with then-Trojan stars Reggie Bush and LenDale White and spent time with head coach Pete Carroll, who assured Robinson that he was recruiting him to be the all-around athlete on offense that he'd been in high school.

Robinson also visited Arizona State and was hosted by future Pro Bowler and Super Bowl champion Terrell Suggs. Both schools appealed to Robinson, and the idea of playing big-time college football was tempting, but something inside told him to keep his college options open until after he played his senior year of high school basketball.

Smart move.

In Robinson's words, the Rainier Beach high school basketball team during the 2001-02 season was a "freight train."

"We only lost one game all year and we were unstoppable," Robinson says. "Between me and the twins, Lodrick and Rodrick Stewart, nobody could match up with us. Somewhere in the middle of the season, the basketball recruiters who were going to the games to look at the twins started to look at me. I was known mostly as a football guy, but one of the scouts who recruited Jamal Crawford remembered me as a freshman and came to see how I was doing. The first basketball offer I got was from Michigan."

Robinson went on to win MVP of the Class 3A state tournament, where he'd average 25.8 points per game and help the Vikings win the title (and finish as the eighth-ranked team in the nation by *USA Today*). He was also named the *Seattle Times* 3A State Player of the Year and all-state, making him the State Player of the Year in both football and basketball.

And we can't leave out his feats on the track. Before he left high school, he broke the state record in the 110-meter hurdles at the Metro League Championships to wrap up his high school athletic career.

"I first saw Nate in eighth grade when he was running track," Jamal Crawford says. "He was an unbelievable high school athlete. Nate is so different than everybody else. He had football and basketball and track records. He can dance. This guy could do anything. Without a doubt he could have played professional football. I don't think we'll ever see an athlete like him again."

But when it came time to pick a school, he had one major decision to make. *Should he play college football or college basketball?*

How about both?

When assessing his options, Nate had full-ride offers for football from all of the schools previously mentioned, but full-ride basketball offers only from Santa Clara, the University of San Francisco and Gonzaga. After being recruited in football by the USCs of the world, those smaller schools just wouldn't do. Robinson wanted to play at a bigger program in a major conference, which led him back to his hometown Washington Huskies.

"Since I was local, both the head football coach, Rick Neuheisel, and the basketball coach, Lorenzo Romar, knew who I was," Robinson says. "When I talked to Washington's assistant head football coach Keith Gilbertson, he just asked me, 'What do you want to do here at Washington, Nate?'"

Nate told him he wanted to do three things.

"I want to play offense and defense in football, and I want to play basketball," he said.

The Huskies' coaches conferred and said they'd work with Robinson to play both sports, and he committed the next day. The decision to become a Husky was important on several fronts. First, he was excited to be able to stay near home, and second, his father was a star running back at Washington who rushed for over 2,300 yards in his career.

***

It's one thing to play two ways in college football; it's quite another to play two ways in college football and also play college basketball. Robinson's typical day at Washington began at 6 AM with mandatory study hall before his weight-lifting session, which was followed by breakfast and classes all morning. After lunch, Robinson would attend the meetings for all the different roles he played on the football team. He was in the defensive meetings, the offensive meetings, the punt and kick return meetings, the hands team meetings, and on and on. Then he'd have football practice until seven or eight at night, after which he'd force himself to the basketball gym to get shots up to keep pace with the basketball team.

"Every night, no matter how exhausted I was, I made myself grab a ball and work on my game, because I knew the rest of the basketball team was going through full practices and I had to keep my game solid," Robinson says. "Most nights I wouldn't get to the gym until 8 PM or 9 PM and I'd just take off my shoulder pads, put my helmet in the corner and start shooting and working on moves until ten at night."

The Husky football team was ranked 11th to start the season and lost to 13th-ranked Michigan by two points in the first game. The Huskies won their next three games before losing to Cal by a touchdown, beating Arizona, and then getting blown out by Robinson's almost-team, USC. After the blowout, Robinson was named the team's starting corner as a true freshman and he started the next six games. In the team's rivalry game against Washington State, known as the Apple Cup, Robinson had a crucial interception in the fourth quarter to give his team the ball, down three with a few minutes left. The Huskies tied the game on a field goal and then won in triple overtime. When the regular season ended, Robinson played two games with the basketball team (fouling out of the first one), then played in the Sun Bowl with the football team before joining the basketball team for the rest of the season.

It was all uncharted territory. In a world where sports specialization was becoming king, Robinson was bouncing between two sports that were essentially each full-time jobs—all while attending school. Playing in just thirteen basketball games, Robinson led the team in scoring with 13 points per game and was named to the All-Pac 10 Freshman Team.

That off-season, after Washington fired head coach Rick Neuheisel, Robinson had a bad feeling about where the team was headed, and it made him think long and hard about whether he wanted to continue playing two sports. After talking with his mom, his dad, his friends and his teammates, he decided it was time to focus on one sport. To his own surprise, that sport was basketball.

"Up until that decision, if you would have asked me which sport I was going to drop I would have said basketball for sure," Robinson says. "But I was feeling so positive about basketball, and something was telling me that basketball was the way. We had so many talented players and I had so much success just playing for a few months, I wondered how good I could be if I played hoops full-time, which was something I had never done in my life. It was time to find out."

When summer rolled around and his ex-football teammates were about to start two-a-days and training camp, Robinson was firmly planted in the gym, determined to make the most of being "just a basketball player." All he did as a full-time basketball player for the first time in his life was lead the team in scoring with 13.2 points per game, to go along with 3.9 rebounds and 2.7 assists. The team also qualified for the NCAA tournament but lost in the first round.

The next season, however, was both Robinson's and Washington's coming out party. He began the regular season by winning the Most Outstanding Player in the Great Alaska Shootout tournament and finished it by helping the team win the Pac-10 tournament and a number one seed in the NCAA tournament. Along the way he led the team in scoring for a third straight year with over 16 points per game. Early in his college career, the headlines he received often mentioned his height or his size as a novelty:

Little Big Dawg

Washington's Little Big Man

'Little Kid' is a Big Time Player

Small in Size, Large in Heart, Big Time in Games

Somewhere in the middle of his senior year, the buzz around Robinson went from talking about his size to discussing his legitimate chance of making it to the NBA. When the season-ending awards were announced, he was an Associated Press third-team All-American and made first-team All-Pac 10 for the second year in a row. He was no longer a curiosity. He was a bona fide NBA prospect.

After the NCAA tournament, in which the Huskies suffered a disappointing loss in the Sweet Sixteen, Robinson went home, chilled at his mom's house for a few days, and emerged with a decision: He was declaring for the NBA Draft.

"Instead of going to class that spring I got myself a trainer and began getting ready to work out for NBA teams," Robinson said. "I worked with Washington basketball icon Steve Gordon. Gordon worked with pretty much every Seattle-area basketball legend at one point and was on the staff of the Sonics. He knows every single thing about basketball."

By the time of the draft, Robinson had worked out for twenty-three of the thirty NBA teams, the last of which was the New York Knicks, which required a cross-country overnight flight from Sacramento and a near 36-hour sleepless streak before his workout. No matter. When the time came to perform, he was ready.

"I didn't miss a shot for about the first hour," he said. "Every single drill or test they put me through, I aced. I even recorded the highest vertical of my life with 48 inches. I didn't know at the time, but that trip would change my life."

On June 28, 2005, Robinson's last workout in New York paid off when the Knicks selected him as the 21st overall pick in the first round. Jamal Crawford, his fellow Rainier Beach star and Seattle native, was already on the Knicks roster and they'd become the first two high school teammates to play together on the same team in the NBA. Legendary Detroit Pistons point guard Isiah Thomas was the president of the Knicks and he called to personally congratulate Robinson.

"Watching Nate play, you're drawn to him because of his size," Thomas said about his initial thoughts on Robinson. "But also, for me, because of his heart and his freakish athleticism."

Larry Brown was the head coach of the Knicks at the time and he notoriously ignored rookies, even first-rounders with Robinson's energy-in-a-bottle capability. The Washington native played about twenty minutes per game and averaged nine points on 40% shooting. However, one thing Brown couldn't keep Robinson from was participating in the 2006 NBA All-Star Slam Dunk Competition, with an assist from Crawford.

Leading up to the competition, his high school buddy called him and shared with him an idea: Why not pay homage to another great little-man dunker in 5'7" Spud Webb, who won the contest twenty years earlier, by jumping over him for a dunk? Nate loved the idea, and when they finally got in touch with Spud, he loved it too.

"The way Nate plays gives me a little pride," Webb said. "You feel like it's your brother out there or your son because you want him to do well."

When the time came, Robinson cleared Webb by several inches and it was the signature dunk of the contest, which he won over Andre Iguodala. It was the first of three Slam Dunk titles for Robinson, including one when he jumped over 6'10" Dwight Howard (dressed as Superman) in a green jersey and green shoes as his alter-ego, Krypto-Nate.

He played four years with the Knicks, almost two with the Celtics (which included several iconic moments in the playoffs), and then parts or full seasons with the Thunder, Bulls, Warriors, Nuggets, Clippers and Pelicans. During his NBA run, he scored 45 points in a game, was named NBA Eastern Conference Player of the Week in February 2013, and outdueled LeBron James and the Miami Heat in a few games during the playoffs.

After his last NBA stop in New Orleans, Robinson played for several teams overseas and then for Ice Cube's three-on-three league, The Big 3. But between all the seasons and all the NBA stops, he kept his house in Seattle and is sending his kids to Rainier Beach schools. His son is already a future star for the Vikings, just like his dad was. Staying in Seattle and giving back to the Emerald City was the one constant in his always moving pro basketball career.

"We were blessed to have the Sonics growing up," Robinson says. "We go to watch our heroes like Gary Payton and Shawn Kemp and Detlef Schrempf and Hersey Hawkins and Nate McMillan and that whole squad. The coolest part was that we'd not only see our heroes on TV but we'd see their faces in the community. That really meant everything. They'd always show their faces at events and things. They'd come down to the Rainier Community Center and they were always giving back. They gave kids like me the dream that we could one day make it, that we could do what they do."

In Robinson's case, he not only used the Sonics players to motivate himself but he also took pieces of their game—the brashness of Gary Payton, the explosiveness of Shawn Kemp, the leadership of Nate McMillan. He emulated the best traits of his favorite players and added them to his personal skill set.

The result was something that very few high school athletes get to experience. He not only enjoyed the on-court accolades and recognition, but the actual players he patterned his game after got to see him play on a regular basis.

"When I started getting recognition in high school it made it that much more fun," Robinson says. "They used to come to our games, and then write-ups in the paper about our team were right next to stories about their team, and it was great. It's hard to explain now how much it meant, because you'd see these guys at your high school game, and they were there to watch you, and you'd get butterflies. You were in the presence of greatness."

That feeling of having the stars of your hometown hoops team watch you play is something that, unfortunately, his son Nahmier, a budding star at Rainier Beach, will likely never have. He was four years old when the Sonics last played a game in Seattle. When Robinson heard the rumors that his beloved Sonics might be gone, it hit him hard.

"It made me sad and angry and it hurt," he says. "They mean so much to the city, and it was like a strange reality. Like, 'You can just take our team?' It was something that nobody wanted to believe was happening. The Sonics are such a part of our history and our life here."

Ever the optimist, he says that with the Sonics gone, it has opened the door for fans to cheer for other teams, including the WNBA's Seattle Storm, which has already won two titles since the Sonics have been gone.

"There are so many teams here now that people can support," he says. "Soccer is big now with the Sounders. And the Storm are doing such a great job by winning championships and attracting fans. They're always in the Finals now. They're great for the state of Washington. It's been difficult without the Sonics, but at the same time, it's been great to see these other teams step up. One day we'll get the Sonics back, and it's gonna be rocking."

Chapter 30

Isaiah Thomas

Jason Terry drove down from Seattle to hang out with his dad and brother and…

Bounce.

He was just trying to watch some TV and catch up and…

Bounce

As he talked, all he heard from outside was…

Bounce. Bounce. Bounce.

Finally, he looked out the window and confirmed his suspicion. The small kid who was friends with his little brother Curtis in grade school was getting shots up. Again. Terry's dad was a renowned AAU coach so the family was used to kids playing basketball, but *this one* was different. He was the littlest kid on the team, but he was also the toughest.

"My dad had a hoop in the back of his house and we'd just hear a ball bouncing," Terry says. "And you'd look out there, and there was this little figure shooting. You knew he could hoop. He was always feisty, and you knew if he grew any he'd be a star. You saw it in him even as a young kid. Well, he grew just enough to be a star."

Who was that "small figure" shooting in the back?

Future two-time NBA all-star Isaiah Thomas.

"I was always chilling with Curtis, and when Jason came to town it meant everything to me to hang out with him," Thomas says. "He was the first professional athlete I'd ever been around and I looked up to him right away. He'd rebound for me and talk to me about the league, and it really kicked off my dream of wanting to be an NBA player. He helped me out in so many ways. I soaked up everything he said. Then to be able to have things come full circle and play against him in the NBA at the end of his career… It was special."

Terry's father coached Thomas from the fourth to the eighth grade, and despite the twelve-year age difference there were some similarities to his oldest son. They were both on the small side but blessed with eye-popping speed and quickness. They were also both gym rats with an innate work ethic and desire to constantly improve. Hence, Thomas getting shots up at all hours at a friend's house. They both also borrowed from the NBA legends they looked up to.

Jason Terry co-opted Slick Watts' headband look and Thomas borrowed Terry's unique habit of wearing the opposing team's shorts the night before a game.

"Jason was a shorts collector, and he had shorts from every NBA team," Thomas explains. "Once I got into the NBA and people started respecting my grind, I started getting shorts. I have two or three pairs of NBA shorts from every team, and I put that in my repertoire because I wanted to be like Jason."

In addition to shortness (relative to NBA standards) and the shorts obsession, Terry and Thomas both also had iconic high school careers with moments that have lived on in Washington hoops lore long after their senior proms.

Thomas played most of his high school basketball at Curtis Senior High in University Place, just east of Sunset Beach. Like Nate Robinson of Rainier Beach a few years earlier (and thirty miles north), he began his high school hoops career known for three things: his short stature, his explosiveness and his ability to put up Pop-A-Shot-level numbers in organized basketball. Game after game during his freshman year, parents and fans of the teams he played against would wonder who the "little kid" on the floor was, only to be amazed when that same little kid would pump twenty or thirty points into the box score with a dizzying array of drives, hesitation moves, deep threes, crossovers and floaters.

Did he really just do that? This question seemed to fill an omnipresent thought bubble wherever he played. As the season wore on, his ascension from local curiosity to regional phenomenon seemed to happen at warp speed. He went from "have you heard of him" to "you have to see him" in about two seconds.

"The buzz started around my ninth-grade year," Thomas says. "For my sophomore season, you'd have to show up at halftime of the JV game just to get a place to sit. It was packed. As a kid, it was a surreal feeling. It was like I wanted to put on a show and have fun. I just thought the success and attention was normal. I wanted to be Kobe Bryant. I wanted to be Allen Iverson. So, I carried myself like those guys. Being small was definitely a factor. The arena would be filled and people would say, 'How is this little boy doing all of this?' And I was only about 140 pounds back then, so I looked like I was maybe ten or twelve years old."

By the end of his sophomore year, he was the go-to guy on the Vikings offense in crunch time and the focal point of the opposing team's defense. By his junior year, he was averaging over 30 points per game, with regular outbursts of 40 or more in front of packed gyms. He was, in a word, electric.

"The bigger the game, the better he played," his coach at Curtis, Lindsay Bemis, said. "He just had that confidence. But a lot of people didn't call it confidence when he was sixteen."

Cockiness. Brashness. Boldness. Tenacity. Whatever you want to call it, Thomas exuded it, and when the 2006 Washington State Tournament rolled around, he summoned all of his powers and put on a record-breaking show in the state semi-final against Franklin. The performance is so revered and so much a part of Seattle basketball lore that on its ten-year anniversary in 2016, Jayson Jenks of the *Seattle Times* compiled an oral history of the game that included several memorable quotes.

"Before the game, they [Franklin] were just talking. Everybody was talking. But once I got going, it was like Michael Jordan stuff that no matter what they did, they weren't going to stop me that night," Thomas said. "Those were all guys I had played against from the AAU days, so we already had a little battle. I was talking stuff to the bench, to the players on the court, to the coaches. That was me. I learned that from Gary Payton. But they definitely got the last laugh."

"The first play of the game, he came down and shot a three like he was Steph Curry, and once he did that, it was like, 'Oh, man, this is going to be a tough game,'" Daniel Vasquez, a Franklin player, recalled.

After draining the initial three-pointer, Thomas made back-to-back threes, each from farther away than the first, and it brought to mind a classic scene from Jordan's video *Come Fly With Me*, in which he talks about what it's like to be in the zone and describes it as, "the hoop looks like a big old bucket." For Thomas, the hoop seemed larger than a bucket; it was more like a full-sized above-ground pool, and he couldn't miss. By halftime he had scored 32 points.

The entire Franklin team had thirty-three.

"We re-inserted a game plan that we had used against Brandon Roy his senior year, which was: We're going to let him be alone, but when he puts it down, we're going to come at him," Franklin Coach Jason Kerr said. "That, and we told our guys they had to stay mentally in the game even when shots went down. Much of the prep was on how we were going to try to take the ball out of his hands and make somebody else beat us. We did not anticipate that we were going to send two—and then in the second half send three—defenders at him. And he'd still pull up and bang a shot in our face."

Thomas hit shot after shot after shot on his way to a state record 51 points. And this wasn't one of those performances where a guy chucks it fifty times in a high school game to hang a fifty burger. No. Thomas was an efficient 16-for-30 from the floor, including 8-for-16 from three and 11 free throws on 17 attempts. (Thomas is still bothered by the missed free throws to this day, knowing he should have had 55 or 56 points.)

"This was one of those games that everyone remembers because it was the number one and number two teams in the state facing each other. It should have been the finals," Thomas says. "You had all of Seattle on one side of the Tacoma Dome and all of Tacoma on the other. And those were all kids that I'd been competing against in AAU my whole high school career. This was some real rivalry stuff on several levels. They had a freshman on their team, Peyton Siva, who went on to win a national championship at Louisville. There was a lot of talent on that floor. Everyone in the state of Washington wanted to see it."

Unfortunately, the Curtis defense all but collapsed in the final quarter and Franklin was able to win, 80-76. Thomas was crestfallen. He scored 40 in the consolation game, but it was no consolation. He'd come for a state title and he wasn't leaving with one. When the season ended, he committed to the University of Washington and planned on getting revenge in the playoffs as a senior. Then he was thrown a proverbial curveball and had to make a quick decision.

"I was enrolled at Curtis for the first few months of my senior year, but Washington called me and my parents and said I had to change some things for me to be eligible," Thomas says. "It was around November of my senior year, and we decided that it would be best if I went to a prep school to get my grades up and get away from being a local celebrity. I was sixteen and on the front page of the newspaper just like the Sonics. It was a lot for me."

As it turned out, the 91-point combined effort in the playoffs was Thomas' last hoops performance in the city of Seattle until he returned to attend the University of Washington a few years later. The newspaper headlines treated his departure like it was the loss of a relative.

"Guard Isaiah Thomas has taken his amazing talent back East, leaving Vikings confident they can cope," blared the *News Tribune* headline from Tacoma, Washington in December 2006. Thomas was matriculating at the South Kent School in Connecticut and reclassifying for the 2008 graduating class, making him a junior and giving him more time to get his grades right and his basketball ready. It also allowed him to spend more quality time with one of his mentors, Jamal Crawford.

"I first heard of Isaiah when he was a sophomore and I wanted to meet him," Crawford says. "And we were bound to meet, because I heard he wanted to meet me and I was like, 'Who is this little guy'? When he was thinking of going to the prep school, I told him that if he comes, I'll look out for him because I was in New York with the Knicks. Once he went there, he came and stayed with me and my wife on the weekends. He was always so respectful and hard working. We'd drive out to see him play and be the only ones in the stands. He's my brother. He had a plan and he's truly an inspiration."

On the flip side, Thomas really needed Crawford at that point in his life. He was sixteen and living thousands of miles from home and away from his family and his friends for the first time. He was only allowed to go home twice a year, and Connecticut was a completely different environment and atmosphere than the Pacific Northwest.

"I was depressed, honestly," Thomas says. "Luckily, Jamal and Nate Robinson were on the Knicks. I'd take the train to Jamal's condo and get away from everything, and I could feel like I was home and could be with someone who was from where I was from. I got to watch him play and go to Madison Square Garden, and it reinforced the plan that I was on."

The plan worked.

Following his first year at South Kent, he moved up to a four-star prospect, and over the summer attended a whirlwind tour of camps and tournaments before his senior year, including the U.S. Reebok team in Europe, the NBA camp in Virginia, the Steve Nash Skills Academy, the Philly RBK camp, the Peach Jam

Tournament in Georgia, the Nike Main Event in Las Vegas, and then finally to Portland for the Nike Global Challenge.

After a successful senior season at South Kent, when he averaged 31.6 points per game and got his grades up to par, and then after another summer filled with camps, he made his official Husky debut at Saint Martin's University in Lacey, Washington on October 17, 2008. While he was in Connecticut, he received offers from UConn, Louisville, Kentucky and other big-time East Coast schools, and Thomas admits to being tempted to check them out.

"At one point I thought of getting out of my commitment to Washington and opening up my recruitment, but I'd been away for two years and my parents are really big on your word mattering," Thomas says. "So, if I said I was going to Washington, that's what I was going to do. And that's when I decided to go back home for good and play there. Guys like Brandon Roy and Nate and Will Conroy, they put Washington back on the map to where it was cool to stay home, so that's what I did."

When the time came for his Emerald City return, the hype was off the charts.

Dan Raley of the *Seattle Post-Intelligencer*, in a charmingly dated intro to his piece on Thomas' debut, wrote, "These days, everything that's new and cool and compact has a similar brand name—iPod, iPhone, iTouch—and that includes the Washington men's basketball team's latest product line. The Huskies...will pull the wraps off "I.T.," as in Isaiah Thomas, someone counted on to fill up the basket and the seats, if not restore the buzz that's been missing around Lorenzo Romar's team the past two seasons."

Thomas was no longer a high school star spending his summers hopping from all-star team to all-star team. He was now the face of a major college program. There were expectations. There were responsibilities. There were ample opportunities for overwhelming pressure. Not to mention the fact that he'd be tackling all of this in his own backyard. He'd either win big in front of his family and friends or...well...with Thomas there was no "or."

"The only pressure you have in your life is the pressure you hold over your own head," Thomas said in the Raley piece. "Pressure shouldn't be used in your head at any time. There is no pressure. I can't wait until the season starts to show people who I am. People know me around here. I want to be a national name."

Declaring your desire for national recognition is gutsy under any circumstances, but considering that the Huskies were coming off a 16-17 season and an eighth-place finish in the Pac-10, the statement didn't just take guts, it took a vision. This wasn't a team in the middle of a Final Four hot streak; rather, they were on a two-year hiatus from even making March Madness. It's tough to become a national name if you're not even on national television. Athletes aren't signing shoe deals from NIT performances.

No matter.

Hard work? Focus? Will? These were traits Thomas had in buckets. Like his favorite rapper Nipsey Hussle said:

Out the garage is how you end up in charge
It's how you end up in penthouses, end up in cars
It's how you start off a curb server, end up a boss
It's how you win the whole thing and lift up a cigar
With sweat drippin' down your face 'cause the mission was hard

Step one to national stardom went as follows: On the individual side, lead the Huskies in scoring as a freshman with 15.5 points per game and 447 points (the most ever for a freshman); win the Pac-10 Freshman of the Year award and make the All-Freshman team with fellow future NBA all-stars Klay Thompson and DeMar DeRozan. On the team side, help Washington to a 24-7 record and its first outright conference title since winning the Pacific Coast Conference in 1953, while lifting your coach, Lorenzo Romar, to a Coach of the Year award and your team back into March Madness.

Step two was to continue to improve year over year. During his sophomore season his scoring average jumped to 16.9 points per game to go along with 3.9 rebounds and 3.2 assists. He'd also help the Huskies to a 26-10 season, a Pac-10 Tournament title, and he'd pick up a Pac-10 Tournament MVP award and first-team All-Pac 10 honors along the way. Following the season, Thomas was named to the preseason John R. Wooden award list for 2010-11, officially marking the moment he was ejected from the Washington orbit and put into the national conversation, just as he'd planned.

The Thomas train continued to roll into his junior year, when he again averaged 16-plus points per game, again helped the Huskies win 20-plus games, again was First-Team All-Conference, again helped the Huskies win the Pac-12 Tournament, and again won the tournament's MVP award. The only difference was that this time, Thomas did all of the above in legendary fashion—including perhaps the most memorable finish to the Pac-12 Tournament of all time. In order to properly appreciate the moment, the scene at the Staples Center in Los Angeles on March 12, 2011 must be properly set.

There were eighteen seconds left on the clock in overtime of the Pac-12 Tournament final. Number one seed Arizona (ranked 16th nationally) had been in a battle with the third-seeded, but not nationally ranked, Washington squad. Derrick Williams, the future number two overall pick in the NBA Draft that year, led the Wildcats in scoring while Thomas paced the Huskies. The two schools traded baskets all game and forced overtime, and then continued to trade baskets during overtime to set up a tie score at 75-75. With less than twenty seconds left, Thomas dribbled the ball up the floor for the game's final possession—and we'll just let the great Gus Johnson take it from here.

> *Isaiah! Shot clock turned off! Game clock at eight! He's gonna do it himself! Thomas! Shake! Crossover! Step baaaaaaack! Ohhhhhhhh!!!! At the buzzer!!! And Washington! Wins it on a last-second J! Coooold Bloooded!!*

The call. The shot. The timing. All of it was vintage Thomas and was a sign of things to come in his professional career.

"When I saw IT knock down that shot, I said, 'oh, buddy! Here we go,'" Doug Christie says. "He was a bona fide killer on the court."

With the hype surrounding the shot and all of the end-of-year awards, Thomas had a choice to make: to enter the NBA Draft or not enter the NBA Draft?

"When I was making my decision to go to the NBA, a lot of people were telling me, 'Isaiah, you should stay. You can be the all-time leading scorer. The all-time leader in assists, the all-time this and that,'" Thomas says. "But my mindset was that I went to college to get to the NBA. People looked at me different because I was so focused on that goal. And when I hit that shot to win the Pac-12 Tournament, I realized there was nothing else I could do to raise my stock. I mean, I could have chased a national championship the next year, but I didn't know how realistic it was. When I took that shot at the Staples Center, where I'd watched Kobe make so many shots like it, and it went in, I knew it was time to go to the NBA. I wanted to bet on myself."

In a twist of fate that wouldn't reveal itself for several years, Kyrie Irving was selected as the number one overall pick in the 2011 NBA Draft and Thomas was taken as the last pick, number 60, by the Sacramento Kings. That day, Thomas' unshakeable confidence almost wobbled as he watched name after name that wasn't his get called. As the minutes passed and he waited for that oh-so-sweet call from his agent to tell him that he'd been selected, he ran through all of the workouts he had done in his mind.

"The Lakers had four picks in the second round and their last pick was at 58," he recalled. "I totally forgot about Sacramento being my first workout. It was a while before. I thought then that, 'I might not get drafted.' It was really the very first time that I let myself think that, that it was a possibility. Two picks later while the Lakers were on the clock, my agent called me and said the Kings would take me with the 60th pick. Some people thought I was disappointed, but I was fine. I always told myself that all I ever wanted was a chance. It didn't matter if I was drafted first or last, I just wanted to get drafted because I knew if I got the opportunity with a team, I'd take advantage of it."

Unfortunately, at that time in the NBA's history, rookies entering the league weren't just behind the eight ball, they were on the outside of the billiard room and across the street at the gas station. The 2011 draft class entered the league amidst a lockout, a canceled summer league, a shortened training camp—pretty much everything except the plague. So Thomas, who was selected by the Kings behind their first-round potential star Jimmer Fredette and their second-round pick Tyler Honeycutt, would need all the reps he could get to impress the front office and earn minutes. After squeezing in about two weeks of workouts with Tyreke Evans in Sacramento, he signed a three-year rookie minimum deal on the eve of camp.

It's time, he told himself.

Knowing he'd be in the third row of the Kings' rookie SUV behind Fredette and Honeycutt, who were comfortably in the middle, Thomas braced himself mentally to seize any opportunity he'd get at camp. In order to shine in the brief moments he'd have on the court, he turned every minute into the final possession of game seven of the NBA Finals.

Full-court pressure.

Following every shot.

Sprinting back on defense.

Thomas was in fifth gear the second his laces were done being tied.

"Every time I was put on the floor, I had a cutthroat mentality. I had to be a killer," Thomas says. "It was a situation where I had to fight for my job. It was literally every day. I knew I had limited chances to show everyone I could play. I came up with a strategy where I thought of my practices as my games. That was the way I looked at practices."

Despite a stressful rookie season that featured erratic playing time, strings of DNPs (did not play) and the frustration of going from college stardom to the end of an NBA bench, Thomas averaged 11.5 points on 45% shooting in just under twenty-six minutes per game. The next year his minutes stayed relatively the same, but his scoring jumped to 13.9 points per game with his assists hitting 4 per game. In year three, Thomas heard the whispers that he shot too much and that he was a scoring point guard and not a pass-first point guard, and he just had a sense the Kings didn't want him. It was like being in a relationship where all your partner does is point out things they don't like. *Oh, you made me a steak with potatoes au gratin from scratch for dinner tonight? So what. You didn't get my favorite salad dressing.*

Thomas' third year in Sacramento proved two things: One, he could be an offensive force in the NBA; two, he probably wasn't going to play for the Kings much longer. As his minutes steadily increased, so did his production. He went from 11.5 points per game to 13.9 to 20.3 in the 2013-14 season. Not only that, he was averaging 6.3 assists per game, shooting at a 45% clip, and had become a fan favorite. And yet, the Kings seemed dead set on focusing on Thomas' perceived weaknesses.

"It was clear to me that they didn't believe in me," Thomas says. "They made it really obvious by bringing in different guards. It was always something. I just knew they didn't want me."

On July 11, they traded him to the Phoenix Suns, where he'd play in only forty-six games before another trade in mid-February sent him to the Boston Celtics, a move that would ultimately change his life.

The 2014-15 Celtics were in transition mode under new coach Brad Stevens. They were now several years removed from the Paul Pierce-Kevin Garnett-Ray Allen championship team and were reshuffling the deck. They had already traded Rajon Rondo, the fourth piece to the Celtics title run, and Jeff Green, a scorer they'd hoped would fill the void of Pierce's departure. It was a team in no-man's land, with a very young Marcus Smart, a still-solid Avery Bradley, Evan Turner and Jae Crowder. With Thomas' arrival, they'd finally have someone they could rely on to score in bunches. But he was hesitant.

"When I got traded there, I wasn't happy about going to a rebuilding team after being close to the playoffs with Phoenix," Thomas says. "I'm a fan of the NBA and I watch what's happening around the league. The Celtics had signed about thirty players that year. But when I did my research, I saw that they were one game out of the playoffs. Then when I got home to my house in Phoenix, Isiah Thomas called me and pumped me up and said, 'You guys are a game and a half out of the eighth spot. You can take this team to the playoffs. You can be the most liked person in Boston.' I slept on that and my mindset shifted right then. I thought, *I think I can make the playoffs for the first time with these guys.*"

Thomas scored 21 points off the bench in his debut with the team, and then led them to a 20-10 record to close out the season, including a six-game win streak that secured a playoff berth. The Celtics were ultimately swept in the first round by the Cavaliers led by LeBron James, Kyrie Irving and Kevin Love, but Thomas led the Celtics in scoring and proved to Stevens and the organization that he was capable of running a team. Not only that, but once again the fans fell in love with him.

"The fans in Boston loved me for who I am. They loved that I was a scorer,"

Thomas says. "They loved me for what I bring to the court night in and night out and that I was small. All of it. I never heard things like, 'He can't do this or can't do that or here's what his negatives are.' It felt like I was back at Washington. There is no other feeling like Boston. My teammates and my coaches loved me for who I am."

What was not to love?

In two full seasons Thomas made two all-star teams, garnered a third-team All-NBA selection, and led the team to three playoff appearances and a run to the Eastern Conference Finals in 2017, where he averaged 28.9 points per game.

He had a signature, legendary nickname with the "King of the Fourth."

He had a signature move that kids could copycat on playgrounds everywhere, pointing to his imaginary wristwatch when crunch time came.

He had it all, and it was glorious.

On the court.

Off the court, however, in April 2017 he lost his sister Chyna in a car accident and his world was turned upside down. They were as close as siblings could be, and while he played through it and was embraced and supported by his new city, the pain was always there.

"I didn't really understand how special I was playing because I was going through the loss of my sister," he says. "My body was there and I was performing, but my mind wasn't. Everything was raw and it was tough, and I didn't have my sister to lean on, who had been there for me my whole life. But those were genuine moments between me and the city of Boston. I'll never forget how much love they showed me."

To this day, Jamal Crawford takes pride in what Thomas accomplished while wearing Celtics green.

"Watching his journey of going from the last pick in the draft to the epicenter of the playoffs in Boston made me so proud," Jamal Crawford says. "That was my brother, right there. Knowing everything he was going through off the court. To reach that point. To be an all-star and have the city wrap their arms around him. He is truly an inspiration."

From the outside looking in, it was the perfect match for a city and a coach and a style of play and a system, but Celtics general manager Danny Ainge thought differently. In his mind, there was always a move to make, and when Kyrie Irving and LeBron James began having troubles in Cleveland, Ainge saw an opening. Ignoring the fact that the entire city of Boston backed Thomas and looked forward to watching him for years to come, Ainge pulled the trigger on a controversial trade that sent Thomas, the most popular Celtic since Paul Pierce, packing.

The trade hurt.

It hurt the fans in Boston, and it hurt Thomas. To the city, it felt like a disapproving parent swooping in to break up a young couple about to go on their honeymoon. To Thomas, it felt like he was finally on the doorstep of achieving the NBA legacy he'd dreamed of, when it was suddenly and heartlessly yanked away at the last minute.

"We had so much success and it came together organically," Thomas says. "That's why I think it hurt people so much. That was arguably the most fun time in my career, and then it was done."

You put a sub-.500 team on your back and brought them to the Conference Finals in three years. Your teammates love you. Your coaches love you. Your city loves you. Too bad. You're gone.

The NBA, like all professional sports, is a business first. But in this case, to the diehard Boston fans, the trade felt cruel and unnecessary. They were just getting started!

Thomas, after a brief period of frustration, knew his future was once again uncertain. An added wrinkle was that Thomas had injured his hip but gutted through it during the Celtics' playoff run, and he wasn't able to get back to 100%.

After stops in Cleveland, Los Angeles, Denver and Washington, Thomas finally had the proper surgery to repair the issue and continue his NBA career. But regardless of his highest highs and his lowest lows, he's always drawn inspiration from the team he grew up rooting for, the Sonics.

"I remember my first Sonics game like it was yesterday," Thomas says. "It was in 1997 against the Timberwolves, and they had Kevin Garnett and Stephon Marbury. We had Payton and Kemp. My dad took me, and the funny thing was that he was a Lakers fan, so I was a forced Lakers fan, and I went to the Sonics versus Wolves game wearing a full Lakers warm-up."

The purple-and-gold tear away aside, Thomas' dad made sure that when they went to games his son experienced the full treatment. They went early so Isaiah could hang out by the tunnel and slap the players high-five on their way to the floor. They stayed late to ask for autographs by the players' parking lot. Thomas was the ultimate NBA fanboy, and every run-in with an NBA player fueled his dream of playing in the league more and more.

By the time Thomas made it to the NBA, the Sonics had been out of the league for three years. When he first heard that the team might be leaving, he was distraught. It was like someone was stealing a part of his childhood.

"The Sonics are a huge part of who I am," he says. "I went to one or two games that last season and it was such a negative, sad energy. It was just a countdown to leave and it sucked. And the worst thing for the city was that kids growing up after 2008 wouldn't have the Sonics in their lives. That's tough for our basketball culture. Seeing the Sonics around town and at camps and schools growing up was so inspirational for me. I built relationships with these guys and I looked up to them. It makes the dream real. And we've produced so many pros since then. I think at some point the Sonics will be back. I'd love to play for them. That would be a dream."

Acknowledgments

I am in my favorite chair holding the 1974-75 Don Watts base set Topps basketball rookie card. He's not wearing his signature headband in the card for some reason, which is travesty number one, and travesty number two is that Topps went with "Don" on the card instead of the name an entire city chanted when he performed: "Slick." I am also holding the 1973-74 Fred Brown Topps basketball rookie card. Once again, a gross injustice has occurred, as Topps chose "Fred" over "Freddie" or, more accurately, "Downtown" Freddie as a first name.

Prior to starting this book, I wouldn't have had much of an opinion about either of these choices by Topps. Yes, I knew the nicknames of Watts and Brown, but having grown up in Boston before the internet and the NBA League Pass and any semblance of West Coast NBA ball being televised on the East Coast, I didn't know their stories. In fact, I could say the same for "the Wizard" Gus Williams, "the Wichert Wonder" Jack Sikma, "the X-Man" Xavier McDaniel, "the Glove" Gary Payton, "the Reign Man" Shawn Kemp and really, the whole of Seattle, "the Emerald City." Of course, I was a huge fan of those '90s Sonics teams (who wasn't) and I'd always been fascinated with Seattle through movies and Ken Griffey Jr. and the Seahawks and Pearl Jam, but that's a far cry from really *knowing* anything.

But after immersing myself in the history of basketball in the Pacific Northwest, reading every book I could find, combing through thousands of articles and interviews and clippings and programs, and having countless hours of conversations with the hoops icons from the city, I have far more than an understanding of what basketball and the Sonics have meant to Seattle—I have a great appreciation for it.

When we dive into a new subject, we naturally try to find ties to things we're familiar with. In this case, I became fascinated with the connections between my hometown Celtics and the Sonics. You've got the big connections: Bill Russell coaching both teams... Dennis Johnson being a critical part of both teams' championship runs... the Ray Allen trade making a Celtics title in

2008 possible... and the smaller connections with guys like Xavier McDaniel and Dana Barros and Vin Baker.

And of course, my personal out-of-the-blue e-mail to Nate Robinson many years ago that led to an article, then a book, then introduced me on a first-hand basis to Rainier Beach, the incredible Sea-Tac high school basketball scene, the insane Washington-to-NBA pipeline, and so many more connections that led to this book. To be able to tell the story of Seattle and the Sonics and the legendary players from the Pacific Northwest has been an honor.

First off, I have to thank Isaiah Thomas and T.J. Regan for believing in me that I could properly tell this story—which is really their story—of growing up and loving the Sonics and the basketball culture in their city. Their confidence, conversations, connections and belief in this book from Day 1 have made it all possible. The rest of the Slow Grind Media team has also been sensational. Sharmila Sahni has done the great work of helping us plan and announce this project properly, and Ashton Owen has designed, in my opinion, one of the all-time coolest sports book covers. And I will forever be indebted to the Gary Payton and Shawn Kemp of research and ideas, my guys Vincent Doherty and Danny Priest, who came with me deep into the archival abyss to grab the nitty gritty newspaper articles, write-ups, interviews and details that make books like this possible. Joe McLean and the team at Intersect Capital have been terrific as well. I also have to thank editing ace Jared Evans for taking his eagle eye to the manuscript and, as always, helping my words sound like the best version of how I intended. Also, a big shout out to Rachel Shuster for organizing the chaos of the references and to Scott Bedgood for the ever-crucial fresh-eyes read to wrap things up.

And of course, my heartfelt thanks to the Seattle hoops legends who were gracious with their time to help me tell this story and set up interviews with their peers: Shannon Allen, Ray Allen, Mike Bethea, Doug Christie, Jamal Crawford, Kevin Durant, Bobby Jones, George Karl, Rich Kleiman, Shawn Kemp, Gary Payton, Nate Robinson, Brandon Roy, Detlef Schrempf, Jason Terry, Isaiah Thomas and so many more.

I also have to give a shout out to the staffs and writers of the *Seattle Times*, the *Seattle Post-Intelligencer*, and *Seattle Weekly* for their stellar work covering their hometown team over the years. Especially in the '70s and '80s, their accounts of the players and big games and moments helped piece together the picture of their city and their team.

On a personal note, I wrote this book through eight months of a pandemic that started for my family in Dallas, Texas and ended up with a move to South Florida. Throughout all the working from home and virtual learning and getting a new puppy and driving across the country and writing in hotel rooms, and with moving boxes all around, I had two constants: the story of Seattle basketball and my family.

Thank you to my two kids, Reese and Grant, for their daily question: "Daddy, are you writing tonight?" which was answered for hundreds of days on end with "yes," but followed up with them asking, "Can we shoot hoops/swim/bike ride/hike first?" The answer to that, as always, was "yes" as well.

Writing a book like this is an immersive, all-encompassing project where your mind is constantly on a manuscript being written in your head. I am grateful for the balance my kids provided and the dozens of hours of hikes/rides/dog walks we took to give my mind (and posture) a break from the work. They're the best. And I'm also grateful for my wife, Steph, who is always supportive and has gracefully endured too many random stories about Seattle to count (like the time I came out of our office after talking to Jason Terry for an hour and told her how excited I was to discover that Slick Watts was Terry's grade school gym teacher. "Great!" she said. "Who's Slick Watts and Jason Terry?") Such is the life of a mostly non-sports fan wife married to someone like me. To be fair, while I was writing this book, she was busting her butt getting an MBA, so there are only so many new critical facts one brain can handle.

As always, the support of my parents and my brother have never waivered in my nearly two decades of being a writer (or typist, as my brother jokingly says). My brother, Craig, gets the brunt of my midnight texts about Gus Johnson's incredible Pac-12 game calls or screen shots of Xavier McDaniel's Costacos Bros. poster. And he's always my first reader.

This is also the first book I've ever written that my grandfather, Jacob Gettleman, will not be able to read. He was a champion of every word I wrote from the time I learned to write, and he passed away at the end of 2019. He had every article I ever wrote saved in his house. He printed up all of my online work that even I didn't print up. He lived an awesome life and I miss him, especially the call I'd get after he'd finish a new book of mine.

Papa, this one's for you.

Finally, thank you, the reader. To paraphrase Jay-Z, you could be reading any book in the world, but you chose to read this one.

Thank you! It means everything!

— Jon

References

Chapters 1-9

Almond, Elliott. "The Original 'Hardship' – Spencer Haywood, The First Player To Bolt Early For The Pros, Waits For History To Remember Him," *The Seattle Times*, Oct. 29, 1997, https://archive.seattletimes.com/archive/?date=19971029&slug=2569018.

Andriesen, David. "Sonics ushered Seattle into the big time 40 years ago Saturday," *Seattle Post-Intelligencer*, Oct. 12, 2007, https://www.seattlepi.com/news/article/Sonics-ushered-Seattle-into-the-big-time-40-years-1252457.php.

Arnold, Mark. "Bob Rule-The Passing of a Sonics Legend," From A Native Son, Sept. 8, 2019, http://fromanativeson.com/2019/09/08/bob-rule-the-passing-of-a-sonics-legend-by-mark-arnold/.

Associated Press. "'25 Years Enough,' Says Bill Russell," July 31, 1969, https://www.newspapers.com/image/251506561/?terms=Bill%2BRussell%2Bleaves%2BCeltics.

Associated Press. "Bill Russell Is SuperSonics New Coach, General Manager," May 12, 1973, https://www.newspapers.com/image/267596375/?terms=Bill%2BRussell%2BSupersonics.

Associated Press. "Bill Russell leaves Sonics," May 5, 1977, https://www.newspapers.com/image/188466513/?terms=Bill%2BRussell%2Bleaves%2BSonics.

Associated Press. "Celtics' Bill Russell Retires," July 31, 1969, https://www.newspapers.com/image/200575251/?terms=Bill%2BRussell%2Bleaves%2BCeltics.

References

Associated Press. "Coaching Plan Told By Russell," May 16, 1973, https://www.newspapers.com/image/436835354/?terms=Bill%2BRussell%2Bpractice.

Associated Press. "Klein buys Chargers," Feb. 25, 1972, https://www.newspapers.com/image/412555829/?terms=Sam%2BSchulman%2Bbuys%2BChargers.

Associated Press. "Loughery Spurs Baltimore To Win Over SuperSonics," Oct. 25, 1967, https://www.newspapers.com/image/576005496/?terms=Sonics%2Bfirst%2Bseason.

Associated Press. "Russell Will Try To Lose Chip," June 6, 1973, https://www.newspapers.com/image/58843742/?terms=Bill%2BRussell%2Btrades%2Bplayer.

Associated Press. "Sonics make playoffs, Russell smiles," Mar. 31, 1975, https://www.newspapers.com/image/435943407/?terms=Sonics%2Bmake%2Bplayoffs.

Associated Press. "Tucker Wins MVP Award," Mar. 20, 1967, https://www.newspapers.com/image/36603198/?terms=Al%2BTucker%2Bbasketball.

Associated Press. "Youthful Sonics 'Submit', Belong to Coach Russell, Feb. 24, 1976, https://www.newspapers.com/image/198349297/?terms=Bill%2BRussell%2BSonics.

BasketballRealGM.com. "Seattle SuperSonics All-Star Game Selections," https://basketball.realgm.com/nba/teams/Seattle-SuperSonics/27/Awards/All_Stars.

BasketballReference.com. "1967-68 Seattle SuperSonics Roster and Stats," https://www.basketball-reference.com/teams/SEA/1968.html.

BasketballReference.com. "Bill Russell," https://www.basketball-reference.com/coaches/russebi01c.html.

Bell, Jim. "Kansas City Hasn't Seen Last of OBU," *The Daily Oklahoman*, Mar. 15, 1965, https://www.newspapers.com/image/451631801/?terms=Al%2BTucker%2Bbasketball.

Boggs, Frank. "One 'Uh Oh' and Bunch of Specialists," *The Daily Oklahoman*, Mar. 7, 1967, https://www.newspapers.com/image/452022123/? terms=Al%2BTucker%2Bbasketball.

Burns, Bob. "Sport is only part of Tom Meschery's rich life," *The Sacramento Bee*, Apr. 9, 1995, https://www.newspapers.com/image/627099312/?terms=Tom%2BMeschery.

Carroll, Tom. "Tucker Brothers Again Starring," *Dayton* (OH) *Daily News*, Dec. 19, 1965, https://www.newspapers.com/image/404292670/?terms=Al%2BTucker%2B%2BOklahoma%2BBap-tist%2BUniversity.

The Daily Oklahoman. "Tucker Snaps Scoring Mark In OBU Romp," Feb. 13, 1966, https://www.newspapers.com/image/451526496/?terms=Al%2BTucker%2Bbasketball.

Eaton, Nick. "From Beatles to Sonics to Storm: Timeline of Seattle Center Coliseum and KeyArena," *The Seattle Times*, Jan. 11, 2017, https://www.seattletimes.com/sports/nba/from-beatles-to-sonics-to-storm-timeline-of-seattle-center-coliseum-and-keyarena/.

Eig, Jonathan. "The Cleveland Summit and Muhammad Ali: The true story," The Undefeated, June 1, 2017, https://theundefeated.com/features/the-cleveland-summit-muhammad-ali/.

Elderkin, Phil. "Bill Russell Is Moody, Controversial Person," *The Christian Science Monitor*, June 4, 1973, https://www.newspapers.com/image/68460893/?terms=Bill%2BRussell%2Bcolumn%2BSeattle.

Encyclopedia.com. "The Basketball Club of Seattle, LLC," https://

www.encyclopedia.com/books/politics-and-business-magazines/basketball-club-seattle-llc.

Engstrom, John. "Bill Russell an Enigma — Many of Many Faces," UPI, May 8, 1977, https://www.newspapers.com/image/653261023/?terms=Bill%2BRussell%2Bcolumn%2BSeattle.

Eskanazi, David S. "Seattle Raiders, 1938-1964 — A Slideshow," HistoryLink.org, Nov. 6, 2004, https://www.historylink.org/File/7123.

Eskenazi, David. "Wayback Machine: Two Trojans Who Changed Seattle," SportspressNW.com, May 24, 2011, http://sportspressnw.com/2118184/2011/wayback-machine-two-trojans-who-changed-seattle.

Eskenazi, Stuart. "First Sonics owner brought passion, title to Seattle," *The Seattle Times*, June 14, 2003, https://archive.seattletimes.com/archive/?date=20030614&slug=schulman14m.

Facebook.com. "Woodland Cemetery and Arboretum," Jan. 7, 2015, https://www.facebook.com/108257459235508/posts/died-on-this-date-albert-tucker-sr-when-albert-was-a-child-and-money-was-scarce-/834130999981480/.

Hall, Jane. "Hall Marks," *The* (Raleigh, NC) *News & Observer*, Jan. 14, 1962, https://www.newspapers.com/image/652144887/?terms=Paul%2BThiry.

Himmelsbach, Adam. "Why was Boston Garden nearly empty when Bill Russell's number was retired in 1972?" *The Boston Globe*, Oct. 7, 2017, https://www.bostonglobe.com/sports/celtics/2017/10/07/why-was-boston-garden-nearly-empty-when-bill-russell-number-was-retired/f2hGuHb1tEJiirpOOBeqcP/story.html.

JackGordon.org. "Sam Schulman—the key to the merger," Apr. 23, 1971, http://www.jackgordon.org/Sports/SuperSonicSpencerHaywood.htm.

Jenks, Jayson. "'Is John really dead?'; The mysterious disappearance of John

Brisker, the Sonics legend who never was," *The Seattle Times*, Sept. 13, 2018, https://www.seattletimes.com/sports/nba/the-mysterious-disappearance-of-john-brisker-the-sonics-legend-who-never-was/.

Johnson, Frank. "Bill Russell on Hard Times at the Boston Celtics," YouTube, Apr. 23, 2017, https://www.youtube.com/watch?v=ZAR_aeJu1ss.

Johnson, Martenzie. "Bill Russell, activist for the ages," The Undefeated, July 12, 2019, https://theundefeated.com/features/bill-russell-activist-for-the-ages/.

Kossen. "Thunder And The Glory – An Era When The Hydros Reigned Supreme – In The '60a, Seattle Was In Love With Rooster Tails; Then A Series Of Deaths Helped Cool The Ardor," *The Seattle Times*, Aug. 4, 1991, https://archive.seattletimes.com/archive/?date=19910804&slug=1298026.

Last, Bill. "Tucker Follows Hoop Tradition," *Dayton* (OH) *Daily News*, Feb. 14, 1960, https://www.newspapers.com/image/402773673/?terms=Albert%2BTucker%2BJr.%2Bbasketball.

Lyons, Gil. "Supers Name4d Sonics," YouTube, Apr. 30, 2013, https://www.youtube.com/watch?v=jwZMfbaSGfg.

McLellan, Dennis. Am Schulman, 93; Original Owner of Seattle SuperSonics Who Changed NBA's Draft Policy," *Los Angeles Times*, June 14, 2003, https://www.latimes.com/archives/la-xpm-2003-jun-14-me-schulman14-story.html.

Nesgoda, Kevin. "The Original Seattle Supersonic: Al Tucker," SonicsRising.com, Mar. 4, 2013, https://www.sonicsrising.com/2013/3/4/4162194/the-original-seattle-supersonic-al-tucker.

The New York Times. Russell Is Signed as Sonics' Coach," May 12, 1973, https://www.nytimes.com/1973/05/12/archives/russell-is-signed-as-sonics-coach-exceltic-great-also-to-be-general.html.

OBUBison.com. "Albert A. Tucker, Jr.," https://obubison.com/hof.aspx?hof=100&kiosk=true.

Olympia Time. "The Los Angeles Sonics and the lies of legacy," Feb. 9, 2013, http://www.olympiatime.com/2013/02/the-los-angeles-sonics-and-lies-of.html.

Owen, John. "Franchise in NBA Pending," *Seattle Post-Intelligencer*," Dec. 16, 1966, https://blog.seattlepi.com/seattlesports/files/library/P-I_Sonics_clips_(300_dpi).pdf.

Padwe, Sandy. "A Sensitive Tour of NBA With Tom Meschery," *The Philadelphia Inquirer*, Feb. 28, 1970, https://www.newspapers.com/image/167907656/?terms=Tom%2BMeschery.

Padwe, Sandy. "Tom Meschery: The court poet," *The Philadelphia Inquirer*, Mar. 8, 1966, https://www.newspapers.com/image/154729879/?terms=Tom%2BMeschery.

Quinton, Sean. "50 years ago today, the Sonics played their first game. Here's a look back," *The Seattle Times*, Oct. 17, 2017, https://www.seattletimes.com/sports/nba/50-years-ago-today-the-sonics-played-their-first-game-heres-a-look-back/.

The Seattle Times. "Homes of the Sonics," July 15, 2008, https://www.seattletimes.com/sports/nba/homes-of-the-sonics/.

The Seattle Times. "Memories from Sonics fans," July 10, 2008, https://www.seattletimes.com/sports/nba/memories-from-sonics-fans/.

SmallCollegeBasketball.com. "Al Tucker," https://www.smallcollegebasketball.com/altucker.

SonicsCentral.com. "1973-74: The Dictator," http://www.sonicscentral.com/7374.html.

Spears, Marc J. "From Russell to KG to today's Celtics: Being a black player in Boston," The Undefeated, Feb. 29, 2020, https://theundefeated.com/features/celtics-being-a-black-player-in-boston/.

Spears, Marc J. "What's in a name? Walt Hazzard's struggle with Islam & identity in the NBA," The Undefeated, Dec. 15, 2016, https://theundefeated.com/features/whats-in-a-name-walt-hazzards-struggle-with-islam-identity-in-the-nba/.

Strode, George. "Tucker All-Star Story At Jeff May Continue," *Dayton* (OH) *Daily News*, Mar. 3, 1963, https://www.newspapers.com/image/404347110/?terms=Albert%2BTucker%2BJr.%2Bbasketball.

SuperSonicSoul.com. "Supersonicpedia: Al Tucker," Sept. 10, 2008, http://blog.supersonicsoul.com/2008/09/mark-your-calendars.html.

The Town Talk (Alexandria, LA). "Hawks Look to Kron For Game Leadership," Sept. 27, 1966, https://www.newspapers.com/image/215832082/?terms=Tommy%2BKron.

Villigan, Tiffany. "Bob Rule: Second Greatest Sonic?" Sonics Rising, Jan. 20, 2014, https://www.sonicsrising.com/2014/1/20/5321364/bob-rule-second-greatest-sonic.

YouTube. "Underrated: Spencer Haywood," June 2, 2013, https://www.youtube.com/watch?v=xrwRfZTnePc.

YouTube. "What was Bill Russell like as a head coach for the Seattle Sonics?" July 23, 2017, https://www.youtube.com/watch?v=V1gOln6hLwg.

Wikipedia.com. "Paul Thiry (architect)," https://en.wikipedia.org/wiki/Paul_Thiry_(architect).

Zofkie, Jim. "May, Tucker Win Berths For Games," *The* (Dayton, OH) *Journal Herald*, Apr. 10, 1967, https://www.newspapers.com/image/394587443/?terms=Albert%2BTucker%2BJr.%2Bbasketball.

Aron, Jaime. "Even 20 years later, Mavs-Sonics game still sheer madness,"

Associated Press, Apr. 24, 2004, https://www.myplainview.com/news/article/Even-20-years-later-Mavs-Sonics-game-still-sheer-8901934.php.

Associated Press. "All Sonics on block, says owner," Jan. 14, 1983, https://www.newspapers.com/image/571972942/?terms=Seattle%2BSupersonics.

Associated Press. "Williams fuels rally as Sonics top Suns," Nov. 2, 1983, https://www.newspapers.com/image/572000456/?terms=Seattle%2BSupersonics.

BasketballReference.com. "1982-83 Seattle SuperSonics Roster and Stats," https://www.basketball-reference.com/teams/SEA/1983.html.

BasketballReference.com. "1983-84 Seattle SuperSonics Roster and Stats," https://www.basketball-reference.com/teams/SEA/1984.html.

BasketballReference.com. "1984-85 Seattle SuperSonics Roster and Stats," https://www.basketball-reference.com/teams/SEA/1985.html.

BasketballReference.com. "1985-86 Seattle SuperSonics Roster and Stats," https://www.basketball-reference.com/teams/SEA/1986.html.

BasketballReference.com. "1986-87 Seattle SuperSonics Roster and Stats," https://www.basketball-reference.com/teams/SEA/1987.html.

BasketballReference.com. "1987-88 Seattle SuperSonics Roster and Stats," https://www.basketball-reference.com/teams/SEA/1988.html.

BasketballReference.com. "1988-89 Seattle SuperSonics Roster and Stats," https://www.basketball-reference.com/teams/SEA/1989.html.

BasketballReference.com. "Lonnie Shelton," https://www.basketball-reference.com/players/s/sheltlo01.html.

BasketballReference.com. "Scooter McCray," https://www.basketball-reference.com/players/m/mccrasc01.html.

Cour, Jim. "Sonics to improve Chambers, Wood," Associated Press, Sept. 2, 1983, https://www.newspapers.com/image/571985001/?terms=Seattle%2BSupersonics%2Blosing.

Craig, Jack. "SuperSonics will headline new regional cable channel," *The Boston Globe*, June 26, 1983, https://www.newspapers.com/image/572670279/?terms=Seattle%2BSupersonics.

Longview (WA) *Daily News*. "SuperSonics sign trio," Sept. 7, 1983, https://www.newspapers.com/image/576710134/?terms=Seattle%2BSupersonics.

The (Spokane, WA) *Spokesman-Review*. "Suns, Celts swap; Shelton to Cavs," June 28, 1983, https://www.newspapers.com/image/572670497/?terms=Seattle%2BSupersonics.

Weaver, Dan. "Images and thrills are large for impressionable ball boys," *Spokane Chronicle*, Oct. 26, 1983, https://www.newspapers.com/image/568016104/?terms=Jack%2BSikma.

Allen, Percy. "41 most memorable Sonics," *The Seattle Times*, July 10, 2008, https://www.seattletimes.com/sports/nba/41-most-memorable-sonics/.

The Association for Professional Basketball Research. "NBA/ABA Home Attendance Totals," http://www.apbr.org/attendance.html.

Baker, Geoff. "Kingdome debt to be retired 15 years after implosion," *The Seattle Times*, Mar. 26, 2015, https://www.seattletimes.com/sports/seahawks/kingdome-debt-to-be-retired-15-years-after-implosion/

Baker, Geoff. "Steve Gordon, Sonics special assistant, charged with federal wire fraud," *The Seattle Times*, Apr. 20, 2015, https://www.seattletimes.com/sports/nba/steve-gordon-former-sonics-special-assistant-charged-with-federal-wire-fraud/.

Banel, Feliks. "Remembering Seattle's Historic NBA Moment 35 Years

Ago," KUOW Radio, May 30, 2014, https://kuow.org/stories/remembering-seattles-historic-nba-moment-35-years-ago/.

BasketballRealGM.com. "Washington 95, Seattle 105," May 27, 1979, https://basketball.realgm.com/nba/boxscore/1979-05-27/Washington-at-Seattle/186545.

BasketballReference.com. "1977-78 Seattle SuperSonics Roster and Stats," https://www.basketball-reference.com/teams/SEA/1978.html

BasketballReference.com. "1978-79 Seattle SuperSonics Roster and Stats," https://www.basketball-reference.com/teams/SEA/1979.html.

BasketballReference.com. "1979-80 Seattle SuperSonics Roster and Stats," https://www.basketball-reference.com/teams/SEA/1980.html.

BasketballReference.com. "1980-81 Seattle SuperSonics Roster and Stats," https://www.basketball-reference.com/teams/SEA/1981.html.

BasketballReference.com. "1981-82 Seattle SuperSonics Roster and Stats," https://www.basketball-reference.com/teams/SEA/1982.html

BasketballReference.com. "1982-83 Seattle SuperSonics Roster and Stats," https://www.basketball-reference.com/teams/SEA/1983.html.

BasketballReference.com. "1983-84 Seattle SuperSonics Roster and Stats," https://www.basketball-reference.com/teams/SEA/1984.html.

BasketballReference.com. "1984-85 Seattle SuperSonics Roster and Stats," https://www.basketball-reference.com/teams/SEA/1985.html.

Broussard, Chris. "Downtown Freddie Brown Is Still a Man to Bank On," *The New York Times*, Nov. 30, 2003, https://www.nytimes.com/2003/11/30/sports/basketball-downtown-freddie-brown-is-still-a-man-to-bank-on.html.

Churaisin, Max. "Ranking the Greatest Coaches in SuperSonics History, Part IV: Lenny Wilkens," SonicsRising.com, Mar.

20, 2014, https://www.sonicsrising.com/2014/3/20/5517048/ranking-greatest-coaches-in-supersonics-history-part-iv-wilkens.

Daniels, Chris. "Sonics legend Lenny Wilkens to end foundation this year," KING-TV, June 24, 2019, https://www.king5.com/article/news/sonics-legend-lenny-wilkens-to-end-foundation-this-summer/281-01702ef8-ec09-4105-a2da-14db94a4f4a3.

DuPree, David. "Forever Linked," NBA.com, http://archive.nba.com/encyclopedia/finals/sonics_bullets_78-79.html.

DuPree, David. "NBA's Surprising SuperSonics New Heart-throbs of Northwest," *The Washington Post*, Apr. 25, 1978, https://www.washingtonpost.com/archive/sports/1978/04/25/nbas-surprising-super-sonics-new-heartthrobs-of-northwest/c69aa8e1-25ea-483b-89dd-3d005cb81df1/.

Hickey, Justin. "Reliving the 1978 NBA Finals: Bullets vs Sonics," BasketballForever.com, Apr. 3, 2020, https://basketballforever.com/2020/04/03/reliving-the-1988-nba-finals-bullets-vs-sonics.

Hughes, Chase. "Game 6 of the 1978 NBA Finals between the Bullets and SuperSonics," NBC Sports Washington, Mar. 18, 2020, https://www.nbcsports.com/washington/wizards/vault-looking-back-bullets-sonics-game-6-1978-nba-finals.

Levesque, John. "Photo: 300,000 People Celebrate NBA Champion SuperSonics in Downtown Seattle in 1979," *Seattle Business*, December 2017, http://seattlebusinessmag.com/retail-services/photo-300000-people-celebrate-nba-champion-supersonics-downtown-seattle-1979.

Luzer, Daniel. "Seattle's Kingdome Debts Finally Paid Off—15 Years After Stadium's Destruction," Governing.com, Mar, 27, 2015, https://www.governing.com/topics/finance/seattles-stadium-debts-finally-paid-off15-years-after-buildings-implosion.html.

MacIntosh, Heather. "Kingdome: The Controversial Birth of a Seattle Icon (1959-1976)," HistoryLink.org., Mar. 1, 2000, https://www.historylink.org/File/2164.

Museum of History & Industry. "Super Sonics inaugural game reception invitation, October 20, 1967," https://digitalcollections.lib.washington.edu/digital/collection/imlsmohai/id/11822.

NBA.com. "Legends profile: Lenny Wilkens," https://www.nba.com/history/legends/profiles/lenny-wilkens.

NBAHoopsOnline.com. "Gus Williams – a Man of Principle," https://nbahoopsonline.com/Articles/2018-19/GusWilliams.html.

The New York Times. "Wilkens Out as Coach," Apr. 25, 1985, https://www.nytimes.com/1985/04/25/sports/sports-people-wilkens-out-as-coach.html.

NorthwestPrimeTime.com. "Seattle SuperSonics," June 1, 2019, http://northwestprimetime.com/news/2019/jun/01/seattle-supersonics/

Papanek, John. "Add Super to the Sonics," *Sports Illustrated*, Jan. 9, 1978, https://vault.si.com/vault/1978/01/09/add-super-to-the-sonics.

Pittman, Travis. "Stadium's debts paid off—15 years after implosion," KING-TV, Mar. 27, 2015, https://www.usatoday.com/story/money/2015/03/27/seattle-kingdome-financing-bonds/70529912/.

Redtfeldt, Cotton. "Lenny Wilkens shares message of believing, achieving," *Yakima* (WA) *Herald*, Mar. 28, 2015, https://www.yakimaherald.com/unleashed/meet_the_staff/colton_redtfeldt/lenny-wilkens-shares-message-of-believing-achieving/article_ebe0e9ef-9009-55be-9ebc-626c231b3fe4.html.

Robinson, Brian. "Appreciating Lenny Wilkens," SonicsRising.com, June 24, 2019, https://www.sonicsrising.com/2019/6/24/18713276/appreciating-lenny-wilkens.

Rosenberg, I.J. "Lenny Wilkens was exceptional as a player and as a coach," *The Atlanta Journal-Constitution*, Sept. 23, 2016, https://www.ajc.com/sports/basketball/lenny-wilkens-was-exceptional-player-and-coach/zMLKVKy5wa0PWoL9FYSt3N/.

SeattleSportsHell.com. "2008: A Seattle Sports Apocalypse," Sept. 22, 2012, https://www.seattlesportshell.com/featured-article/2008-a-seattle-sports-apocalypse/.

Spokane Chronicle. "Coaches Depart," Dec. 1, 1977, https://www.newspapers.com/clip/51789134/.

SportsEncyclopedia.com. "Seattle SuperSonics," https://sportsecyclopedia.com/nba/seattle/sonics.html/.

Thiel, Art. "Lenny Wilkens Honored for Lifetime NBA Achievement," SportspressNW.com, June 5, 2011, http://sportspressnw.com/2118733/2011/lenny-wilkens-honored-for-lifetime-nba-achievement.

WeAreBasket.net. "Jack Sikma – A Player with Dutch Heritage in the NBA's Hall of Fame," https://www.wearebasket.net/jack-sikma-a-player-with-dutch-heritage-in-the-nbas-hall-of-fame/

Wilkens, Lenny. "Lenny Wilkens: Whether at Key or Sodo, together, let's bring back our Sonics," *The Seattle Times*, Jan. 24, 2017, https://www.seattletimes.com/opinion/whether-at-key-or-sodo-lets-bring-back-our-sonics-together/.

YouTube. "1980 NBA Playoffs: Sonics at Lakers, Gm 5," Sept. 10, 2007, https://www.youtube.com/watch?v=BfLBEkWx9KA.

YouTube. "Lenny Wilkens: Son of the City," Mar. 25, 2015, https://www.youtube.com/watch?v=wYGBG_kh3_s.

Allen, Percy. "'You either adapt or die': How Sonics legend Jack Sikma carved his path to the Basketball Hall of Fame, *The Seattle Times*, Sept. 6, 2019, https://www.seattletimes.com/sports/nba/

sonics-legend-jack-sikma-ready-to-cement-legacy-in-naismith-basketball-hall-of-fame/.

Associated Press. "Brown savors crown," June 3, 1979, https://www.newspapers.com/image/634632199/?terms=Freddie%2BBrown%2BDrafted%2BSonics.

Associated Press. "Bullets' inside play difference," June 9, 1978, https://www.newspapers.com/image/571673662/?terms=Supersonics.

Associated Press. "If Sonics win 1st title it's because Sikma grew up," May 29, 1979, https://www.newspapers.com/image/281676815/?terms=Sonics%2Bwin%2BTitle.

Associated Press. "Johnson tenacious in Sonics victory," May 29, 1978, https://www.newspapers.com/image/571669483/?terms=Supersonics.

Associated Press. "Johnson with Seattle," July 15, 1976, https://www.newspapers.com/image/57449809/?terms=Dennis%2BJohnson%2BPepperdine.

Associated Press. "Seattleites Go Wild," June 2, 1979, https://www.newspapers.com/image/564889838/?terms=Supersonics%2BNBA%2BChampionship.

Associated Press. "Sonics confident they'll win title," May 16, 1979, https://www.newspapers.com/image/590376120/?terms=Sonics%2Bwin%2BTitle.

Associated Press. "Sonics Respected Now," June 2, 1979, https://www.newspapers.com/image/312639403/?terms=Sonics%2Bfans%2Bcelebrate.

Associated Press. "Sonics Seek Victory for NBA 'Best' Coach," May 17, 1978, https://www.newspapers.com/image/578449098/?terms=NBA%2BFinals.

Associated Press. "Sonics Sign Johnson to

Four-Year Pact," July 14, 1976, https://www.newspapers.com/image/578459759/?terms=Dennis%2BJohnson%2BPepperdine.

Associated Press. "Sonics win title without the help of 'star system,'" June 4, 1979, https://www.newspapers.com/image/244309732/?terms=Sonics%2Bwin%2BTitle.

Associated Press. "Sonics win Western Conference title," Apr. 27, 1979, https://www.newspapers.com/image/350086080/?terms=Sonics%2Bwin%2BWes.

Associated Press. "SuperSonics put it together, defeat Suns," May 18, 1979, https://www.newspapers.com/image/149458575/?terms=Sonics%2Bdefeat%2BSuns.

Associated Press. "With an NBA title in their grasp, the Sonics celebrate, June 3, 1979, https://www.newspapers.com/image/109439086/?terms=Sonics%2Bcelebrate.

Banel, Feliks. "Seattle's ill-fated Stanley Cup run of 1919," MyNorthwest.com, Apr. 3, 2019, https://mynorthwest.com/1331813/seattle-stanley-cup-run-1919/.

BasketballReference.com. "1979 NBA Finals SuperSonics vs. Bullets," https://www.basketball-reference.com/playoffs/1979-nba-finals-supersonics-vs-bullets.html.

BasketballReference.com. "1977-78 NBA Season Summary," https://www.basketball-reference.com/leagues/NBA_1978.html.

BasketballReference.com. "1978-79 NBA Season Summary," https://www.basketball-reference.com/leagues/NBA_1979.html

BasketballReference.com. "1979 NBA Western Conference Finals Suns vs. SuperSonics," https://www.basketball-reference.com/playoffs/1979-nba-western-conference-finals-suns-vs-supersonics.html.

BasketballReference.com. "1979 NBA Western Conference Semifinals Lakers vs. SuperSonics," https://www.basketball-reference.com/playoffs/1979-nba-western-conference-semifinals-lakers-vs-supersonics.html.

BasketballReference.com. "Fred Brown," https://www.basketball-reference.com/players/b/brownfr01.html

BasketballReference.com. "Dennis Johnson," https://www.basketball-reference.com/players/j/johnsde01.html.

BasketballReference.com. "Jack Sikma," https://www.basketball-reference.com/players/s/sikmaja01.html.

Brigham, Joel. "Still Walking Tall," *Illinois Wesleyan Magazine*, Spring 2008, https://www.iwu.edu/magazine/2008/spring/Sikma.html.

Broussard, Chris. "Downtown Freddie Brown Is Still a Man to Bank On," *The New York Times*, Nov. 30, 2003, https://www.nytimes.com/2003/11/30/sports/basketball-downtown-freddie-brown-is-still-a-man-to-bank-on.html.

Caviezel, Jim. "St. Anne wins 19th straight," *The Daily Leader* (Pontiac, IL), Mar. 14, 1973, https://www.newspapers.com/image/18245952/?terms=Jack%2BSikma.

Cronin, Don. "Sonics Win Title In Five Over Bullets," UPI, June 2, 1979, https://www.newspapers.com/image/17383644/?terms=Sonics%2Bwin%2BTitle.

Derrick, Merle. "Something to Sell," *Spokane Chronicle*, May 18, 1978, https://www.newspapers.com/image/578450870/?terms=Championship%2Bfavorites%2Bfor%2BNBA%2Bseason.

El Paso Times. "Sonics, Suns expect rugged game," May 17, 1979, https://www.newspapers.com/image/435833539/?terms=Sonics%2BSuns.

Frandsen, Mike. "Seattle's Last Title: SuperSonics' 1979 NBA Finals Win over Washington Bullets," Bleacher Report, Feb. 1, 2014, https://bleacherreport.com/articles/1945151-seattles-last-title-supersonics-1979-nba-finals-win-over-washington-bullets.

Gierasimczuk, Mark. "How a Team in Seattle, of All Places, Changed Hockey Forever," *The New York Times*, Mar. 27, 2017, https://www.nytimes.com/2017/03/27/sports/hockey/seattle-metropolitans-stanley-cup-seattle-ice-arena.html.

Junkert, Glenn. "A shooter's mentality: Freddy Brown III," GoGriz.com, Nov. 30, 2018, https://gogriz.com/news/2018/11/30/mens-basketball-a-shooters-mentality-freddy-brown-iii.aspx.

Kerns, Josh. "Former Sonics great Wally Walker remembers Seattle's last big parade," MyNorthwest.com, Feb. 4, 2014, https://mynorthwest.com/23628/former-sonics-great-wally-walker-remembers-seattles-last-big-parade/.

Kirkpatrick, Curry. "Down to One Last Collision," *Sports Illustrated*, June 12, 1978, https://vault.si.com/vault/1978/06/12/down-to-one-last-collision-the-bullets-blew-out-the-sonics-in-game-6-and-the-whole-nba-playoff-show-headed-west-one-more-time.

KIRO-TV. "Seattle once had a hockey team and it changed the game forever," Mar. 25, 2019, https://www.kiro7.com/news/local/seattle-once-had-a-hockey-team-and-it-changed-the-game-forever/660430545/.

LandofBasketball.com. "NBA 1978-79 Regular Season and Playoff Summary," https://www.landofbasketball.com/yearbyyear/1978_1979_nba.htm.

Levesque, John. "Photo: 300,000 People Celebrate NBA Champion SuperSonics in Downtown Seattle in 1979," *Seattle Business*, December 2017, http://seattlebusinessmag.com/retail-services/photo-300000-people-celebrate-nba-champion-supersonics-downtown-seattle-1979.

Mann, Gordon. "Successful plan sends Sikma to Hall," D3Hoops.com, Sept. 4, 2017, https://www.d3hoops.com/notables/2017/09/sikma-hall-of-fame.

Moore, Jim. "Bill Scott, 1949-2007: 'Beerman' lifted everyone's spirits," *Seattle Post-Intelligencer*, Mar. 26, 2007, https://www.seattlepi.com/sports/article/Bill-Scott-1949-2007-Beerman-lifted-1232359.php.

NBA.com. "Legends profile: Dennis Johnson," https://www.nba.com/history/legends/profiles/dennis-johnson.

Powers, John. "NBA playoff preview," *The Boston Globe*, Apr. 9, 1978, https://www.newspapers.com/image/436990364/?terms=NBA%2Bseason%2Bpreview.

Ryan, Bob. "The inimitable Celtic," *The Boston Globe*, Aug. 13, 2010, http://archive.boston.com/sports/basketball/celtics/articles/2010/08/13/the_inimitable_celtic/.

Robinson, Brian. "Happy 40th Anniversary Sonics Fans," SonicsRising.com, June 1, 2019, https://www.sonicsrising.com/2019/6/1/18648485/happy-40th-anniversary-sonics-fans.

Rorden, David. "It made no sense, but it was fun," *Longview* (WA) *Daily News*, June 5, 1979, https://www.newspapers.com/image/576642723/?terms=Sonics%2Bchampionship%2Bparade.

Sachare, Alex. "Bullets Subdue Sonics to Claim NBA Crown," Associated Press, June 8, 1978, https://www.newspapers.com/image/349993813/?terms=Sonics%2Blose%2BNBA%2Bfinals.

Saskatoon Daily Star. "Canadiens Lose Third Game and the World's Hockey Championship," Mar. 25, 1919, https://www.newspapers.com/image/508202845/?terms=Seattle%2BMetropolitans.

SonicsGate.com. "The Greatest Weekend in Seattle Sports History," Feb. 6, 2014, http://sonicsgate.com/blog/?p=63.

Sports Illustrated. "New Stripes, Same Old Slick Tiger," Mar. 19, 1973, https://vault.si.com/vault/1973/03/19/new-stripes-same-old-slick-tiger.

SportsReference.com. "Fred Brown," https://www.sports-reference.com/cbb/players/fred-brown-1.html.

Stearns, Steve. "The Ten Greatest Players In Supersonics History – #5," SonicsRising.com, Apr. 13, 2013, https://www.sonicsrising.com/2013/4/13/4202456/the-ten-greatest-players-in-supersonics-history-5.

Tanos, Lorenzo. "NBA Season Recaps: 1977-1978 NBA Season," TheBestSportsBlog.com, http://www.thebestsportsblog.com/nba-season-recaps-1977-1978-nba-season.html.

Thompson, Lynn. "Here we go again: Seahawks parade to rival Sonics in '79," *The Seattle Times*, Feb. 5, 2014, https://special.seattletimes.com/o/html/localnews/2022837179_seahawksparadexml.html.

Ticen, Kevin. "Seattle Metropolitans win the Stanley Cup on March 26, 1917, HistoryLink.org, Jan. 28, 2020, https://www.historylink.org/file/20915.

UPI. "Seattle Fans Celebrate NBA Championship," June 5, 1979, https://www.newspapers.com/image/468789470/?terms=Sonics%2Bfans%2Bcelebrate.

UPI. "Sonics defeat Suns in series inaugural," May 3, 1979, https://www.newspapers.com/image/533902326/?terms=Sonics%2Bdefeat%2BSuns.

UPI. "Sonics Defeat Suns to Take 2-Game Advantage," May 6, 1979, https://www.newspapers.com/image/13915985/?terms=Sonics%2Bdefeat%2BSuns.

Van Dusen, Randy. "Dennis Johnson Leads the Sonics to Ring, Takes Home Finals MVP (1979)," Dec. 10, 2019, https://www.youtube.com/watch?v=Yj9YZfJpR4Y.

Washington Secretary of State Blog. "The Day the Sonics Won the NBA Title," June 1, 2016, https://blogs.sos.wa.gov/fromourcorner/index.php/2016/06/the-day-the-sonics-won-the-nba-title/.

YouTube. "The 1979 Seattle SuperSonics return home to celebrate their 40-year anniversary," Feb. 6, 2019, https://www.youtube.com/watch?v=E5t8axXwcNE.

YouTube. "CityStream: Seattle's Stanley Cup Story," June 13, 2019, https://www.youtube.com/watch?v=1_TE78iS9x4.

YouTube. "Jack Sikma's Basketball Hall of Fame Enshrinement Speech," Sept. 6, 2019, https://www.youtube.com/watch?v=a4xFOo1Gk7E.

Chapters 9 - 22

Agness, Scott. "'He was the guy who made the machine go': How Nate McMillan was molded into a coach," The Athletic, Apr. 30, 2020, https://theathletic.com/1779394/2020/04/30/he-was-the-guy-who-made-the-machine-go-how-nate-mcmillan-was-molded-into-a-coach/.

Anstine, Dennis. "Shawn Kemp sparkplug for Sonics," United Press International, Nov. 12, 1989, https://www.newspapers.com/image/535369628/?terms=Sonics%2Bdraft%2BShawn%2BKemp.

Araton, Harvey. "Perkins Has a Pair of Proud 'Dads,'" *The New York Times*, June 7, 1991, https://www.nytimes.com/1991/06/07/sports/basketball-perkins-has-a-pair-of-proud-dads.html.

Associated Press. "All signs point to Sonics picking Gary Payton," June 27, 1990, https://www.newspapers.com/image/575583527/?terms=sonics%2Bdraft%2Bgary%2Bpayton.

Associated Press. "Bulls say draft couldn't have been better," June 29, 1989, https://www.newspapers.com/image/417312757/?terms=Fans%2Breaction%2Bto%2BShawn%2BKemp%2Bdraft%2Bpick.

Associated Press. "Lakers trade Sam Perkins," Feb. 23, 1993, https://www.newspapers.com/image/553052354/?terms=Sonics%2Btrade%2Bfor%2BSam%2BPerkins.

Associated Press. "Sonics: Derrick-for-Detlef deal done," Nov. 2, 1993, https://products.kitsapsun.com/archive/1993/11-02/288426_sonics__derrick-for-detlef_deal.html.

Associated Press. "Sonics expect Payton to provide immediate leadership," June 28, 1990, https://www.newspapers.com/image/575583676/?terms=sonics%2Bdraft%2Bgary%2Bpayton.

Associated Press. "Sonics plan to keep top draft picks," June 28, 1989, https://www.newspapers.com/image/566594751/?terms=Sonics%2Bdraft%2BShawn%2BKemp.

Associated Press. "Sonics see Perkins as instant impact guy," Feb. 24, 1993, https://www.newspapers.com/image/636249894/?terms=Sonics%2Btrade%2Bfor%2BSam%2BPerkins.

Associated Press. "Team-by-Team Look at the NBA for the 1993-94 Season," Oct. 31, 1993, https://www.latimes.com/archives/la-xpm-1993-10-31-sp-51656-story.html.

Associated Press. "Trade's timing miffs Schrempf," Nov. 3, 1993, https://www.newspapers.com/image/251175664/?terms=Schrempf%2Btalks%2Babout%2BSeattle.

Associated Press. "Youngest Sonic meets the press," July 8, 1989, https://www.newspapers.com/image/572976068/?terms=Sonics%2Bdraft%2BShawn%2BKemp.

Baker, Chris. "When He Needs Assist, Oregon State Is There: Gary Payton's

Performance Makes St. John's Regret Turning Him Down," *Los Angeles Times*, Feb. 2, 1989, https://www.latimes.com/archives/la-xpm-1989-02-02-sp-2526-story.html.

Coble, Don. "Barkley has the hardware, now he wants the ring," Gannett News Service, Oct. 31, 1993, https://www.newspapers.com/image/223643946/?terms=nba%2Bseason%2Bpreview.

Dickau, Dan. "Catching up with Detlef Schrempf, former Centralia High School and NBA star," Scorebook Live, Feb. 6, 2019, https://scorebooklive.com/washington/2019/02/06/wayback-wednesday-catching-up-with-detlef-schrempf-former-centralia-high-school-and-nba-star/.

Evans, Richard. "Payton Was A Yapper In High School, Too," *Deseret News*, June 2, 1996, https://www.deseret.com/1996/6/2/19246048/payton-was-a-yapper-in-high-school-too.

The Everett (WA) *Herald*. "A tale of two Sonics: young and talented," Nov. 4, 1990, https://www.newspapers.com/image/200765462/?terms=Gary%2BPayton%2Bdraft.

Goldstein, Alan. "Perkins, Divac to be dealt? Sonics, Mavericks involved in deal," *The Baltimore Sun*, Feb. 22, 1993, https://www.baltimoresun.com/news/bs-xpm-1993-02-22-1993053022-story.html.

Hamar, Jake. "Better Call Detlef," SonicsRising.com, Sept. 8, 2015, https://www.sonicsrising.com/2015/9/8/9242805/why-detlef-schrempf-mattered.

Hatch, Brooks. "Payton's 58-point fury unravels USC," *Corvallis* (OR) *Gazette-Times*, Feb. 22, 1990, https://www.newspapers.com/image/383864066/?terms=gary%2Bpayton%2Bcollege.

Henderson, James. "McMillan: 'I Was Always a Wolfpack Fan,'" 247Sports.com, Apr. 13, 2007, https://247sports.com/college/north-carolina-state/Article/McMillan-I-Was-Always-a-Wolfpack-Fan-104412186/.

Kirkpatrick, Curry. "'Gary Talks It, Gary Walks It,'" *Sports Illustrated*, Mar. 5, 1990, https://vault.si.com/vault/1990/03/05/gary-talks-it-gary-walks-it-oregon-states-gary-payton-a-loose-jawed-kid-from-the-city-has-quietly-become-the-premier-college-basketball-player-of-the-season-up-in-the-woodsy-precincts-of-corvallis.

Kirkpatrick, Curry. "A Towering Twosome," *Sports Illustrated*, Nov. 28, 1983, https://vault.si.com/vault/1983/11/28/a-towering-twosome

Kurz Jr., Hank. "NBA Preview Package: Team Capsules for 1994-95," Associated Press, Oct. 29, 1994, https://apnews.com/2f25fb66c0d2386440c96e91f5d1a999.

Lewis, Adam. "20 years later, Sonics fans will never forget '96 Finals squad," *Seattle Post-Intelligencer*, June 7, 2016, https://www.seattlepi.com/sports/article/Remembering-the-1995-96-Seattle-SuperSonics-20-7964765.php.

Matthews, Bob. "NBA Season Preview," Gannett News Service, Oct. 29, 1995, https://www.newspapers.com/image/279353731/?terms=nba%2Bseason%2Bpreview.

Montieth, Mark. Schrempf-McKee deal good: Walsh," *The Indianapolis News*, June 12, 1996, https://www.newspapers.com/image/313261303/?terms=Sonics%2Btrade%2Bfor%2BDetlef%2BSchrempf.

Nanaimo (British Columbia) *Daily Free Press*. "NBA/Season Preview," Oct. 26, 1994. https://www.newspapers.com/image/324519053/?terms=nba%2Bseason%2Bpreview.

Nelson, Glenn. "Easy Does It – Sam Perkins: Selfless, Sacrificial Sonic," *The Seattle Times*, May 2, 1993, https://archive.seattletimes.com/archive/?date=19930502&slug=1699047.

Nelson, Glenn. "Man-Child – Seattle's Shawn Kemp Is Anything But A Little

Kid On The Basketball Court," *The Seattle Times*, May 3, 1991, https://archive.seattletimes.com/archive/?date=19910303&slug=1269263.

Ott, Matt. "SuperSonics will dethrone Phoenix in Pacific Division," *The Daily Utah Chronicle*, Nov. 4, 1993, https://www.newspapers.com/image/430282922/?terms=Supersonics%2Bseason%2Bpreview.

The Palm Beach Post. "NBA 1993-94 Preview," Oct. 31, 1993, https://www.newspapers.com/image/133048214/?terms=Supersonics%2Bseason%2Bpreview.

Plunkett, Bill. "Without Jordan, title 'up for grabs,'" Gannett News Service, Nov. 4, 1993, https://www.newspapers.com/image/179320953.

Powell, Shaun. "Two newest teams show shaky moves in draft strategy," *The Miami Herald*, June 2, 1989, https://www.newspapers.com/image/634769072/?terms=Fans%2Breaction%2Bto%2BShawn%2BKemp%2Bdraft%2Bpick.

The Sacramento Bee. "Words of praise for Payton," Mar. 6, 1990, https://www.newspapers.com/image/624806365/?terms=Gary%2BPayton%2Bfeature.

The Sante Fe New Mexican. "Going nowhere fast," Feb. 11, 1988, https://www.newspapers.com/image/583193218/?terms=Shawn%2BKemp%2Bhigh%2Bschool.

The Seattle Times. "Flashback: Centralia H.S. took magical ride with Schrempf in 1981," Mar. 22, 2005, https://www.seattletimes.com/sports/high-school/flashback-centralia-hs-took-magical-ride-with-schrempf-in-1981/

Sidiqqi, DJ. "Jason Kidd says that Gary Payton made him cry in high school," 247Sports.com, Sept. 4, 2018, https://247sports.com/nba/golden-state-warriors/Article/Jason-Kidd-says-that-Gary-Payton-made-him-cry-in-high-school-121418657/.

Spander, Art. "Gary Payton learned plenty in Corvallis," *The San Francisco Examiner*, June 22, 1990, https://www.newspapers.com/image/461960277/?terms=Gary%2BPayton%2Bdraft.

The (Spokane, WA) *Spokesman-Review*. "Kings surprise of NBA draft," June 28, 1990, https://www.newspapers.com/image/572886613/?terms=Gary%2BPayton%2Bdraft.

Tucker, Kyle. "'It got so out of control': Shawn Kemp's Kentucky career ended before it began," The Athletic, Apr. 16, 2020, https://theathletic.com/1750656/2020/04/16/it-got-so-out-of-control-shawn-kemps-kentucky-career-ended-before-it-began/?redirected=1.

Underwood, Roger. "Just who is Shawn Kemp?" Scripps Howard News, July 1, 1989, https://www.newspapers.com/image/572263138/?terms=Sonics%2Bdraft%2BShawn%2BKemp.

The Vancouver Sun. "NBA Season Preview," Nov. 3, 1995, https://www.newspapers.com/image/495931017/?terms=nba%2Bseason%2Bpreview.

Winderman, Ira. "Sundvold's success proves Rice may be good gamble," *Sun-Sentinel*, July 2, 1989, https://www.newspapers.com/image/237877176/?terms=Sonics%2Bdraft%2BShawn%2BKemp.

YouTube. "Kendrick Perkins shares hilarious story about Gary Payton during his rookie year," June 20, 2019, https://www.youtube.com/watch?v=yvP1AyuxLw0.

Chapter 11

Arace, Michael. "Sonics, Spurs Join Celtics in Disarray," *The Hartford Courant*, June 12, 1994, https://www.courant.com/news/connecticut/hc-xpm-1994-06-12-9406120354-story.html.

Associated Press. "Cavaliers' Karl Enjoys 'Pressure,'" Oct. 25, 1985, https://www.newspapers.com/

image/285906694/?terms=George%2BKarl%2BCleveland%2BCavaliers%2Bplayoffs.

Associated Press. "George Karl named as Spurs assistant," Apr. 15, 1978, https://www.newspapers.com/image/512056910/?terms=George%2BKarl%2BSan%2BAntonio%2Bassistant.

Associated Press. "Karl is Fired as the Cavaliers Coach, and Little Gets the Job on Interim Basis," Mar. 17, 1986, https://www.latimes.com/archives/la-xpm-1986-03-17-sp-22418-story.html.

Associated Press. "Karl likely to become Cavs' coach," July 26, 1984, https://www.newspapers.com/image/295202036/?terms=George%2BKarl%2BCleveland%2BCavaliers.

Associated Press. "Nuggets' Karl is top coach," Apr. 15, 1981, https://www.newspapers.com/image/349664686/?terms=George%2BKarl%2BMontana%2BGolden%2BNuggets.

Associated Press. "Perkins, Lakers top Sonics 116-110," Jan. 21, 1992, https://www.newspapers.com/image/132374969/?terms=George%2BKarl%2BSeattle%2BSupersonics.

Associated Press. "Report: Karl will coach Sonics," Jan. 20, 1992, https://www.newspapers.com/image/201660610/?terms=George%2BKarl%2BReal%2BMadrid.

Associated Press. "Supersonics Fire Coach George Karl," May 27, 1998, https://apnews.com/e16b39a0be136fa1c3ec5e0225638494.

Beslic, Stephen. "Jordan Gave His Blessing for a Pippen Trade: 'Scottie can make your other players better,'" BasketballNetwork.net, May 5, 2020, https://www.basketballnetwork.net/jordan-gave-his-blessing-for-a-pippen-trade-scottie-can-make-your-other-players-better/.

CBS News. "Sonics Bid Adieu to Coach Karl," May 26, 1998, https://www.cbsnews.com/news/sonics-bid-adieu-to-coach-karl/.

Fortner, Larry. "Stopping George Big Problem," *The Indianapolis News*, Mar. 30, 1974, https://www.newspapers.com/image/312571190/?terms=George%2BKarl%2BSan%2BAntonio.

Gelb, Zach. "George Karl reflected on the 1996 NBA Finals, which Michael Jordan and the Bulls won in six games," CBS Sports Radio, May 12, 2020, https://cbssportsradio.radio.com/articles/george-karl-on-gary-payton-michael-jordan-1996-nba-finals.

Gustafson, Brandon. "Former Sonics HC George Karl says he'd love to coach another Seattle team," MyNorthwest.com, Jan. 30, 2020, https://sports.mynorthwest.com/764044/sonics-george-karl-love-coach-seattle-team/?.

Kahn, Mike. "Sonics need commitment to land talented coach," McClatchy News Service, Jan. 19, 1992, https://www.newspapers.com/image/573677104/?terms=George%2BKarl%2BReal%2BMadrid.

Kitsap Sun (Bremerton, WA). "Doug Christie, Sonics' top draft pick, wants a trade," Nov. 6, 1992, https://products.kitsapsun.com/archive/1992/11-06/248904_doug_christie__sonics__39__top_.html.

May, Peter. "Who's minding the hardware store?" *The Hartford Courant*, Apr. 12, 1987, https://www.newspapers.com/image/245969913/?terms=George%2BKarl%2BGolden%2BState%2BWarriors.

MyNorthwest.com. "Former Sonics coach George Karl on his new book," Jan. 19, 2017, https://sports.mynorthwest.com/category/podcast_player/?a=10014710&sid=1014&n=Bob,%20Groz%20and%20Tom.

Naab, Bill. Pride Spurs George Karl Off His Seat," *Pittsburgh Press*, Mar. 22, 1977, https://www.newspapers.com/image/147215185/?terms=George%2BKarl%2BSan%2BAntonio.

NBA.com. "April 20, 1985: Karl's Comeback Cavs Fall to Heavily-Favored Celtics," https://www.nba.com/cavaliers/news/features/date-history-160420.

Nelson, Glenn. "Coach-In-Your-Face – The Methods and Madness of George Karl," *The Seattle Times*, Nov. 7, 1993, https://archive.seattletimes.com/archive/?date=19931107&slug=1730378.

Nelson, Glenn. "Karl Comes of Age in Seattle," *The Seattle Times*, May 10, 1992, https://www.chicagotribune.com/news/ct-xpm-1992-05-10-9202110752-story.html.

Smith, Phil. "CBA teams names Karl head coach," *Great Falls (MT) Tribune*, Sept. 4, 1980, https://www.newspapers.com/image/239823991/?terms=George%2BKarl%2BMontana%2BGolden%2BNuggets.

Smith, Sam. "Loose Lips Sink Karl," *Chicago Tribune*, May 27, 1998, https://www.chicagotribune.com/news/ct-xpm-1998-05-27-9805270086-story.html.

Smith, Sarah E. "George Karl Adjusts To Life On Edge As Sonics' Coach," Feb. 25, 1996, https://www.newspapers.com/image/142499177/?terms=George%2BKarl.

SonicsRising.com. "Greatest of All-Time: A Look at the 1991-92 Seattle SuperSonics," Mar. 11, 2014, https://www.sonicsrising.com/2014/3/11/5410622/greatest-of-all-time-a-look-at-the-1991-92-seattle-supersonics.

Taylor, Phil. "Peerless in Seattle," *Sports Illustrated*, May 2, 1994, https://vault.si.com/vault/1994/05/02/peerless-in-seattle-with-the-voluble-george-karl-in-control-the-relentless-sonics-are-the-team-to-beat.

Truthandbasketball.com. "Truth and Basketball with George Karl," Feb. 12, 2020, https://truthandbasketball.libsyn.com/sonics-summit.

UPI. "Karl resigns post at Golden State," Mar. 24, 1988, https://www.newspapers.com/image/285336449/?terms=George%2BKarl%2BGolden%2BState%2BWarriors%2Bresigns.

WSCR Radio. "Karl: Krause Was 'Committed' To Trading Pippen," May 14, 2020, https://670thescore.radio.com/chicago-bulls-jerry-krause-trade-scottie-pippen-1994-seattle-supersonics-george-karl.

Yuscavage, Chris. "George Karl Confirms He Spoke With Michael Jordan About Possibly Trading Shawn Kemp For Scottie Pippen," Complex.com, Dec. 28, 2016, https://www.complex.com/sports/2016/12/george-karl-confirms-spoke-with-michael-jordan-about-trading-shawn-kemp-scottie-pippen.

Associated Press. "All systems go," May 4, 1996, https://www.newspapers.com/image/574761660.

Associated Press. "Bulls complete an amazing season," June 17, 1996, https://www.newspapers.com/image/575902453/?terms=Sonics%2BBulls.

Associated Press. "'Embarrassment' may cost Seattle's Karl his job," May 6, 1995, https://www.newspapers.com/image/134235222/?terms=Seattle%2BSupersonics%2Bseason%2Bpreview.

Associated Press. "Fans celebrate after 'torture' ends," June 3, 1996, https://www.newspapers.com/image/574825913/?terms=Sonics%2BJazz%2Bseries.

Associated Press. "Finals final act in drama," June 5, 1996, https://www.newspapers.com/image/340970529.

Associated Press. "Gary Payton pushes SuperSonics past the Utah Jazz, 94-93," Jan. 27, 1996, https://www.newspapers.com/image/575651252/?terms=Gary%2BPayton%2Bscores%2B38.

Associated Press. "Payton gives

Sonics a lift," Dec. 23, 1996, https://www.newspapers.com/image/574867596/?terms=Gary%2BPayton%2Bscores%2B38.

Associated Press. "Payton keys Sonics victory," Nov. 27, 1995, https://www.newspapers.com/image/574762732.

Associated Press. "Payton outguns Kidd in victory," Jan. 22, 1996, https://www.newspapers.com/image/574779186/?terms=Gary%2BPayton%2Bscores%2B38.

Associated Press. "Perkins buries Jazz with late 3-pointer," Mar. 31, 1996, https://www.newspapers.com/image/574788859/?terms=Sonics%2Bwinning%2Bstreak.

Associated Press. "Playing in the shadows," May 18, 1996, https://www.newspapers.com/image/428564012/?terms=Sonics%2BJazz%2Bseries.

Associated Press. "Seattle Finally Reaches Round 2," May 3, 1996, https://www.latimes.com/archives/la-xpm-1996-05-03-sp-65489-story.html.

Associated Press. "Sonics finish off Rockets; Magic now lead 3-0," May 13, 1996, https://www.newspapers.com/image/413212083/?terms=Sonics%2Badvance%2Bpast%2BRockets.

Associated Press. "Sonics hear the clamor," Apr. 30, 1996, https://www.newspapers.com/image/574785095/?terms=Sonics%2BKings%2Bseries.

Associated Press. "Sonics-Jazz series pits Kemp, Malone," May 18, 1996, https://www.newspapers.com/image/200772619/?terms=Sonics%2BJazz%2Bseries.

Associated Press. "Sonics make good argument to shed image as chokers," May 2, 1996, https://www.newspapers.com/image/246810014/?terms=Sonics%2Beliminate%2BKings.

Associated Press. "Sonics open playoffs with, what else,

a win," Apr. 27, 1996, https://www.newspapers.com/image/575700505/?terms=Sonics%2BKings%2Bseries.

Associated Press. "Sonics thump Kings," Apr. 11, 1996, https://www.newspapers.com/image/574756556.

Associated Press. "Sonics trounce Kings, live to see second round," May 3, 1996, https://www.newspapers.com/image/574758574.

Associated Press. "Sonics win 64th, stop Timberwolves," Apr. 20, 1996, https://www.newspapers.com/image/574781389/?terms=Sonics%2Bfinish%2Bregular%2Bseason.

Associated Press. "SuperSonics march by 3s," Mar. 19, 1995, https://www.newspapers.com/image/574372632/?terms=Sonics%2Bwin%2Bfirst%2Bgame%2Bof%2Bthe%2Bseason.

Azzerad, Michael. "Grunge City: The Seattle Scene," *RollingStone*, Apr. 16, 1992, https://www.rollingstone.com/music/music-news/grunge-city-the-seattle-scene-250071/.

Barker, Kim. "A thirst for thrills," *The* (Spokane) *Spokesman-Review*, June 3, 1996, https://www.newspapers.com/image/574825844.

BasketballReference.com. 1995-96 Seattle SuperSonics Roster and Stats," https://www.basketball-reference.com/teams/SEA/1996.html.

Boling, Dave. "Karl guarding against early-season burnout," *Tacoma News Tribune*, Nov. 2, 1996, https://www.newspapers.com/image/574837288/?terms=Sonics.

Chicago Tribune. "Bulls-Sonics Head-to-Head," June 5, 1996, https://www.newspapers.com/image/167816387/?terms=Sonics%2BBulls.

Chicago Tribune. "Killer 'Ds' make matchups moot," June 5, 1996, https://www.newspapers.com/image/167810949.

Cour, Jim. “Olajuwon: They have a championship team,” Associated Press, May 14, 1996, https://www.newspapers.com/image/574759548.

Cour, Jim. “Sonics: No need to panic,” Associated Press, Oct. 30, 1995, https://www.newspapers.com/image/574774664/?terms=NBA%2Bseason%2Bpreview.

Howard-Cooper, Scott. “Bulls Finally Get Uncorked,” *Los Angeles Times*, June 17, 1996, https://www.newspapers.com/image/159301022.

Cour, Jim. “Sonics rocket to victory in Game 1,” Associated Press, May 6, 1996, https://www.newspapers.com/image/575970594/?terms=Sonics%2Bvs.%2BRockets%2Bplayoffs.

Cour, Jim. “Sonics win 9th straight, close in on West’s best record,” Apr. 6, 1996, https://www.newspapers.com/image/575692254/?terms=Sonics%2Bwin%2Bin%2Bovertime.

Cour, Jim. “SuperSonic future looks bright if both Payton and Karl stay,” Associated Press,”https://www.newspapers.com/image/575902601/?terms=Sonics%2BBulls.

Howard-Cooper, Scott. “Why it will/won’t work out for Sonics,” *Los Angeles Times*, June 5, 1996, https://www.newspapers.com/image/574830140.

Isola, Frank. “Air to Throne,” (New York) *Daily News*, June 17, 1996, https://www.newspapers.com/image/491763950.

Jenks, Jayson and Bob Condotta. “Oral history of Seattle’s last great NBA team: The 1995-96 Sonics,” June 11, 2016, https://www.seattletimes.com/sports/nba/oral-history-of-seattles-last-great-nba-team-the-1995-96-sonics/.

Kragthorpe, Kurt. “Dream Ends – For Now,” *The Salt Lake Tribune*, June 3, 1996, https://www.newspapers.com/image/612633016/?terms=Sonics%2BJazz%2Bseries.

Kreidler, Mark. "Richmond felled by twist of fate; Kings sent packing," *The Sacramento Bee*, May 3, 1996, https://www.newspapers.com/image/627271564/.

KRT News Service. "Seattle sweeps Houston," May 13, 1996, https://www.newspapers.com/image/300804687/?terms=Sonics%2Badvance%2Bto%2BConference%2BFinals.

Lawrence, Mitch. "The Finals: Sonics try Hersey first, prayer next," (New York) *Daily News*, June 5, 1996, https://www.newspapers.com/image/473634967/?terms=Sonics%2BBulls.

Lincicome, Bernie. "Sonics Nothing More Than Bridesmaids?" *Chicago Tribune*, June 3, 1996, https://www.newspapers.com/image/612633100/?terms=Sonics%2BJazz%2Bseries.

Luhm, Steve. "Jazz Looking Like Odd Team In," *The Salt Lake Tribune*, May 18, 1996, https://www.newspapers.com/image/612917983/?terms=Sonics%2BJazz%2Bseries.

Lyke, M.L. "Sonics winners at No. 2," *Seattle Post-Intelligencer*, June 18, 1996, https://www.newspapers.com/image/574835550.

May, Peter. "Bulls climb back on top," *The Boston Globe*, June 17, 1996, https://www.newspapers.com/image/441025322/.

May, Peter. "Finals are fit for a king," *The Boston Globe*, June 5,1996, https://www.newspapers.com/image/442010342/?terms=Sonics%2BBulls.

McGrath, John. "Sonics gain very useful experience," June 17, 1996, https://www.newspapers.com/image/574834323.

McNeal, Martin. "Kings have Sonics' attention," *The Sacramento Bee*, Apr. 30, 1996, https://www.newspapers.com/image/627316592/?terms=Sonics%2BKings%2Bseries.

McNeal, Martin. "Richmond will need help," *The*

Sacramento Bee, Apr. 23, 1996, https://www.newspapers.com/image/627279135/?terms=Sonics%2BKings%2Bseries.

Moore, Jim. "Sonics vindicate past flops," *Seattle Post-Intelligencer*, June 3, 1996, https://www.newspapers.com/image/574826279.

Nadel, Mike. "Sonics: Now hear this — Bulls beatable," Associated Press, June 4, 1996, https://www.newspapers.com/image/574827693/?terms=Sonics%2BBulls.

Nelson, Glenn. "Sonics brace for Utah," *The Seattle Times*, May 18, 1996, https://www.newspapers.com/image/574770309.

Nelson, Glenn. "Rockets-Sonics: a saga good to the last shot," *The Seattle Times*, May 5, 1996, https://www.newspapers.com/image/356811093/?terms=Sonics%2Bvs.%2BRockets%2Bplayoffs.

Nelson, Glenn. "Sweep dreams," *The Seattle Times*, May 13, 1996, https://www.newspapers.com/image/574759076.

Roof Pig. "Why 10 Has 11: Grunge and Basketball," Apr. 10, 2013, https://roofpig.wordpress.com/2013/04/10/why-10-has-11-grunge-and-basketball/.

Schumacher, John. "Little time for sonics to celebrate," *The Sacramento Bee*, May 3, 1996, https://www.newspapers.com/image/627272907/?terms=Sonics%2BKings%2Bseries.

Smith, Sam. "Beware, Seattle's no slouch," *Chicago Tribune*, June 4, 1996, https://www.newspapers.com/image/167799679.

Smith, Sam. "Sonics might have grand future if they can keep team together," *Chicago Tribune*, June 17, 1996, https://www.newspapers.com/image/167743033/?terms=Sonics%2BBulls.

Smith, Theresa. "Can we just all get along?" *Tacoma News Tribune*, Nov. 1, 1996, https://www.newspapers.com/image/574834050/?terms=Sonics'.

Smith, Theresa. "Facing a first-round jinx," *Tacoma Morning News Tribune*, Apr. 26, 1996, https://www.newspapers.com/image/627296118/?terms=Sonics%2BKings%2Bseries.

The (Spokane) *Spokesman-Review*. "Kemp keys Sonics' win," Nov. 5, 1995, https://www.newspapers.com/image/574751495/?terms=Sonics%2Bbeat%2BLakers.

The (Spokane) *Spokesman-Review*. "Sonics opener not super," Nov. 4, 1995, https://www.newspapers.com/image/574750021.

The (Spokane) *Spokesman-Review*. "Sonics respectful of Utah," May 18, 1996, https://www.newspapers.com/image/574771186/?terms=Sonics%2Bfinish%2Bregular%2Bseason.

The (Spokane) *Spokesman-Review*. "Sonics' streak hits nine," Feb. 25, 1996," https://www.newspapers.com/image/574768393/?terms=Kemp%2Bleads%2BSonics.

Tacoma News Tribune. "Karl will split the difference," Mar. 24, 1996, "https://www.newspapers.com/image/574771578/?terms=Sonics%2Bwinning%2Bstreak.

Vecsey, Laura. "Kemp's come a long way," *Seattle Post-Intelligencer*, Dec. 31, 1995, https://www.newspapers.com/image/574929107/?terms=Kemp%2B20-20.

Vorva, Jeff. "Four-closure," June 17, 1996, https://www.newspapers.com/image/203630765/?terms=Sonics%2BBulls.

Allen, Percy. "1996: When Sonics fans went crazy," *The Seattle Times*, June 9, 2011, https://www.seattletimes.com/sports/nba/1996-when-sonics-fans-went-crazy/.

Armour, Terry. "Bulls' goal: Don't allow SuperSonics to get into a zone," *Chicago Tribune*, June 5, 1996, https://www.newspapers.com/image/167811069.

Associated Press. "Now Kemp says he'll talk to owner," July 16, 1997, https://www.newspapers.com/image/584501928/?terms=Shawn%2BKemp%2Breflects%2Bon%2B-time%2Bin%2BSeattle.

Associated Press. "Payton no-show at media day," Oct. 1, 2002, https://www.newspapers.com/image/575834617/?terms=Gary%2BPayton.

Associated Press. "Vin Baker vows to show SuperSonic fans he's a big-time player," Sept. 27, 1997, https://www.newspapers.com/image/584780439/?terms=Shawn%2BKemp.

Blanchette, John. "End of era: Sonics trade Payton," *The* (Spokane) *Spokesman-Review*, Feb. 21, 2003, https://www.newspapers.com/image/575855337.

Boling, Dave. "For Kemp, money measure of manhood," *Tacoma News Tribune*, Oct. 29, 1997, https://www.newspapers.com/image/156845820/?terms=Shawn%2BKemp%2Breflects%2Bon%2B-time%2Bin%2BSeattle.

Brockway, Kevin. "'Last Dance' evokes memories for Pacers coach McMillan," *Commercial-News* (Danville, IL), May 5, 2020, https://www.commercial-news.com/sports/last-dance-evokes-memories-for-pacers-coach-mcmillan/article_161fc1a8-8f30-11ea-aa10-d7f99563f3dc.html.

CBS News. "Sonics Bid Adieu To Coach Karl," May 26, 1998, https://www.cbsnews.com/news/sonics-bid-adieu-to-coach-karl/.

Condotta, Bob. "Sonics' future sits in Walker's hands," *Tacoma News Tribune*, May 28, 1998, https://www.newspapers.com/image/575237700

Condotta, Bob. "Walker runs Karl out of Seattle," *Tacoma News Tribune*, May 27, 1998, https://www.newspapers.com/image/575235222.

Conn, Jordan Ritter. "From Ground Beans to Grounded: Meet the Man Who Tried to Run the SuperSonics Like Starbucks," TheRinger.com,

Oct. 10, 2019, https://www.theringer.com/2019/10/10/20907621/sonic-boom-episode-2-supersonics-seattle-starbucks-howard-schultz.

Cour, Jim. "Payton's Seattle Era Ends With Trade," Associated Press, Feb. 20, 2003, https://www.ourmidland.com/news/article/Payton-s-Seattle-Era-Ends-With-Trade-7084598.php.

Cour, Jim. "Supersonics Fire Coach George Karl," Associated Press, May 27, 1998, https://apnews.com/e16b39a0be136fa1c3ec5e0225638494.

Demasio, Nunyo, "For Ackerley, 'NBA Champions Has Nice Ring To It – Owner of Sonics Hoping For Title This Year," *The Seattle Times*, Apr. 24, 1998, https://archive.seattletimes.com/archive/?date=19980424&slug=2747026.

Dwyer, Kelly. "Gary Payton is still irked by his 2003 departure from Seattle," Yahoo! Sports, Sept. 17, 2013, https://sports.yahoo.com/gary-payton-still-irked-2003-departure-seattle-184430100--nba.html?y20=1.

ESPN. "Bucks acquire Payton from Sonics," Feb. 20, 2003, http://www.espn.com/nba/news/2003/0220/1511870.html.

Hughes, Frank. "Why Schultz tuned out and sold out the Sonics," ESPN, July 20, 2006, https://www.espn.com/nba/columns/story?columnist=hughes_frank&id=2525634.

Kelley, Steve. "Return of the Reignman," *The Seattle Times*, Oct. 8, 2011, https://www.seattletimes.com/sports/return-of-the-reignman/.

Kelley, Steve. "Trade makes Sonics better," *The Seattle Times*, Sept. 27, 1997, https://www.newspapers.com/image/574877895/?terms=Shawn%2BKemp.

Lewis, Adam. "20 years later, sonics fans will never forget '96 Finals squad," *Seattle Post-Intelligencer*, June 7, 2016, https://www.seattlepi.com/sports/article/Remembering-the-1995-96-Seattle-SuperSonics-20-7964765.php.

Nesgoda, Kevin. "George Karl Talks '96 Finals," Cascadia Sports Network, Feb. 19, 2020, https://www.cascadiasn.com/blog/seattle-supersonics/george-karl-talks-96-finals.

Pluto, Terry. "Kemp's spin move looking positive," *Akron* (Ohio) *Beacon-Journal*, Sept. 28, 1997, https://www.newspapers.com/image/574880534/?terms=Shawn%2BKemp.

Roberts, Selena. "Sonics' Kemp Gets Wish and Is Traded, to Cavs," *The New York Times*, Sept. 26, 1997, https://www.nytimes.com/1997/09/26/sports/pro-basketball-sonics-kemp-gets-wish-and-is-traded-to-cavs.html.

Sheridan, Chris. "Chicago wraps up title series," Associated Press, June 17, 1996, https://www.newspapers.com/image/574834323/?terms=George%2BKarl.

Smith, Sam. "Loose Lips Sink Karl," *Chicago Tribune*, May 27, 1998, https://www.chicagotribune.com/news/ct-xpm-1998-05-27-9805270086-story.html.

Smith, Sam. "Sonics Owner Kills Deal," *Chicago Tribune*, June 30, 1994, https://www.chicagotribune.com/news/ct-xpm-1994-06-30-9406300177-story.html.

Smith, Theresa. "Can we all just get along?" *Tacoma News Tribune*, Nov. 1, 1996, https://www.newspapers.com/image/574832459/?terms=Supersonics.

SonicsCentral.com. "1996-97: Talent, But More Turmoil," http://www.sonicscentral.com/9697.html.

Springer, Steve. "Karl's Reign Is Over in Seattle," *Los Angeles Times*, May 27, 1998, https://www.newspapers.com/image/159065310/?terms=George%2BKarl%2Bfired.

Stecker, Brent. "Kevin Calabro, voice of the Sonics, looks back at the 1996

NBA Finals," MyNorthwest.com, May 11, 2020, https://sports.mynorthwest.com/841407/kevin-calabro-sonics-1996-nba-finals/?.

Stecker, Brent. "Sonics legend Detlef Schrempf: 'I didn't realize we were such an 'underdog' vs Bulls in 1996 NBA Finals," MyNorthwest.com, May 14, 2020, https://sports.mynorthwest.com/841848/sonics-detlef-schrempf-underdog-vs-bulls-96-finals/?.

Tillery, Ronald. "Seattle job goes to Westphal," *The* (Spokane) *Spokesman-Review*, June 18, 1998, https://www.newspapers.com/image/575269322.

The Washington Post. Kemp Is Traded to Cavaliers in Three-way Deal," Sept. 26, 1997, https://www.washingtonpost.com/archive/sports/1997/09/26/kemp-is-traded-to-cavaliers-in-three-way-deal/a505e303-422b-4c21-ba05-1a135fccedc3/.

YouTube. "Gary Payton on the 1996 Finals vs. Chicago and Michael Jordan," Mar. 14, 2010, https://www.youtube.com/watch?v=s9ryMgGogyo.

YouTube. "Gary Payton on Seattle Sonics fans," Apr. 11, 2020, https://www.youtube.com/watch?v=qclbZASlHdw.

YouTube. "George Karl talks 'The Last Dance', 1996 NBA Finals, coaching against Jordan, Kobe," May 5, 2020, https://www.youtube.com/watch?v=RiBVXWxhD-4.

YouTube. "George Karl Relives His Fondest NBA Memories," Mar. 23, 2020, https://www.youtube.com/watch?v=fyQ3ntcYpjo.

YouTube. "Shawn Kemp Return Game Back to Seattle after Trade 97-98 Season," Nov. 25, 2018, https://www.youtube.com/watch?v=tTmEgWKeQR0.

Washburn, Gary. "Departure from Seattle bad memory for Gary Payton," *The Boston Globe*, Sept. 13, 2015, http://www.bostonglobe.com/sports/2013/09/14/

nba-notes-departure-from-seattle-bad-memory-for-new-hall-famer-gary-payton/ExM0g5KAqwmgB7ksuWRziI/story.html?s_campaign=sm_tw.

Bogage, Jacob. "' I know it's been a rough 10 years': Kevin Durant and the NBA return to Seattle for a night," *The Washington Post*, Oct. 6, 2018, https://www.washingtonpost.com/sports/2018/10/06/i-know-its-been-rough-years-kevin-durant-nba-return-seattle-night/.

Booth, Tim. "Sonics put on show in victory," Associated Press, Apr. 14, 2008, https://www.newspapers.com/image/610723207/?terms=durant.

Conn, Jordan Ritter. "The Final Days of the Sonics: Lawsuits, Backroom Politics, and a confused Kevin Durrant," TheRinger.com, Nov. 21, 2019,

https://www.theringer.com/2019/11/21/20975531/seattle-supersonics-final-days-sonic-boom.

Friedell, Nick. "With Kevin Durant Visiting First NBA Hometown, Warriors Star Advocates for Seattle Franchise," ESPN, Oct. 3, 2018, https://www.espn.com/nba/story/_/id/24882858/kevin-durant-pushes-nba-team-seattle-once-again.

Letourneau, Connor. "Kevin Durant readies for emotional Seattle homecoming," *San Francisco Chronicle*, Oct. 4, 2018, https://www.sfchronicle.com/warriors/article/Kevin-Durant-readies-for-emotional-Seattle-13279581.php.

Made, Taylor. "Kevin Durant talks Seattle; "they should have a basketball team," SonicsRising.com, Sept. 23, 2016, https://www.sonicsrising.com/2016/9/23/13036060/kevin-durant-seattle-should-have-basketball-team.

Allen, Percy. "'It was indescribable': An oral history of Sonics' final game at KeyArena as the NBA returns a decade later," *The Seattle Times*, Oct. 6, 2018, https://www.seattletimes.com/sports/nba/

it-was-indescribable-as-kevin-durant-and-the-nba-return-to-seattle-an-oral-history-of-the-final-game/.

Chapter 23

Associated Press. "Rainier Beach wins AA crown," Mar. 14, 1988, https://www.newspapers.com/image/577339869/?terms=rainier%2Bbeach%2Bbasketball%2Bcoach.

Associated Press. "Spending by Schools Hit," Mar. 19, 1959, https://www.newspapers.com/image/25369475/?terms=rainier%2Bbeach.

Basketball.RealGm.com, "Rainier Beach High School, Seattle (WA) Players, https://basketball.realgm.com/highschool/teams/1/Rainier-Beach-High-School.

Basketball.RealGM.com, "Washington Gatorade Player of the Year," https://basketball.realgm.com/highschool/awards/1/94.

BasketballReference.com, "NBA and ABA Players Who Attended High School in Washington," https://www.basketball-reference.com/friv/high_schools.cgi?country=US&state=WA.

Curto, Mike. "Garfield ends rival Rainier Beach's 3A reign with late run to claim title," *The* (Tacoma, WA) *News Tribune*, Mar. 7, 2015, https://www.thenewstribune.com/sports/high-school/article26263801.html.

HistoryLink.org. "Seattle Public Schools, 1862-2000: Rainier Beach High School,"

https://www.historylink.org/File/10577#:~:text=Rainier%20Beach%20Junior%2DSenior%20High,class%20entered%20the%20first%20year.

Jenks, Jayson. "Garfield vs. Rainier Beach boys' basketball is the best rivalry in Seattle," *The Seattle Times*, Mar. 4, 2016, https://www.seattletimes.com/sports/high-school/garfield-rainier-beach-best-rivalry-in-the-city/.

Johansson, Anna. "Rainier Valley: One of America's Most Diverse Neighborhoods," Curbed Seattle, June 10, 2013, https://seattle.curbed.com/2013/6/10/10234520/rainier-valley-one-of-americas-most-diverse-neighborhoods.

The Johnson Partnership. "Seattle Public Schools built between 1945 and 1965," August 2012, https://www.seattle.gov/Documents/Departments/Neighborhoods/HistoricPreservation/Landmarks/CurrentNominations/SeattlePublicSchoolsbuiltbetween1945and1965.pdf.

Lee, Greg. "Rogers girls bid for title in Saturday Pasco meet," *Spokane Chronicle*, Apr. 17, 1987, https://www.newspapers.com/image/569558723/?terms=rainier%2Bbeach%2Btrack%2Bchampions.

Liebeskind, Josh. "Bethea builds champions and bonds at Rainier Beach," *The Seattle Times*, Mar. 1, 2014, https://www.seattletimes.com/sports/high-school/bethea-builds-champions-and-bonds-at-rainier-beach/.

MaxPreps.com, "Garfield Basketball Rival," https://www.maxpreps.com/high-schools/garfield-bulldogs-(seattle,wa)/basketball/rival.htm.

MaxPreps.com, "Rainier Beach Basketball Rival," https://www.maxpreps.com/high-schools/rainier-beach-vikings-(seattle,wa)/basketball/rival.htm.

Miles, Todd. "Most years for the Rainier Beach boys, prominence is like clockwork. But this was an entirely new path to the Tacoma Dome: 3 observations," SBLive Washington, Feb. 29, 2020, https://washington.scorebooklive.com/2020/02/29/29997/.

Oxley, Dyer. "'Warning: Entering Rainier Valley' signs posted in South Seattle neighborhoods," MyNorthwest.com, Oct. 8, 2015,

https://mynorthwest.com/18268/warning-entering-rainier-valley-signs-posted-in-south-seattle-neighborhoods/?.

Peterson, Matt. "Boys Basketball: Rainier Beach is No. 1 in the nation,"

The Seattle Times, Dec. 17, 2002, .https://archive.seattletimes.com/archive/?date=20021217&slug=beach17.

RainierValleyHistory.org. "Rainier Valley Historical Society Preserving the Past," http://www.rainiervalleyhistory.org/.

Raley, Dan. "Nate, a Hoops Lifer: 'Until the Day I Die, I'll Keep Playing Basketball," *Sports Illustrated*, Dec. 28, 2019,

https://www.si.com/college/washington/legends/robinson-is-retired-from-the-nba-or-is-he.

Seattle Public Schools. "Annual Enrollment Report," 2018-2019, https://www.seattleschools.org/UserFiles/Servers/Server_543/File/District/Departments/Enrollment%20Planning/Reports/Annual%20Enrollment/2018-19/Section%206%20w%20ADA.pdf.

The (Spokane, WA) Spokesman-Review. "State Championships," May 26, 1985, https://www.newspapers.com/image/572514988/?terms=rainier%2Bbeach%2Bstate%2Bchampions.

Stalwick, Howie. "Late bloomer wins Masters road race," *The* (Spokane, WA) *Spokesman-Review*, Aug. 13, 1989,https://www.newspapers.com/image/572856135/?terms=rainier%2Bbeach%2Bboys%2Btrack%2Band%2Bfield.

Taylor, Kevin. "Colville, WV lose close ones," *Spokane Chronicle*, Mar. 11, 1988, https://www.newspapers.com/image/567238825/?terms=rainier%2Bbeach%2Bstate%2Bchampions.

Uitti, Jacob. "Rainier Beach Coach Bethea Looks Toward Next Championship," South Seattle Emerald, Nov. 19, 2018, https://southseattleemerald.com/2018/11/19/rainier-beach-coach-bethea-looks-toward-next-championship/.

Wikipedia, "Rainier Beach High School," https://en.wikipedia.org/wiki/

Rainier_Beach_High_School#:~:text=Rainier%20Beach%20has%20won%20the,2013%2C%202014%2C%20and%202016.

Wilma, David. "Rainier Valley — Thumbnail History," HistoryLink.org., Mar. 13, 2001, https://historylink.org/File/3092.

Chapter 24

Associated Press. "State team beats City, Class A stars top B's in all-state basketball," June 22, 1988, https://www.newspapers.com/image/577312690/?terms=doug%2Bchristie%2Brainier%2Bbeach.

The Baltimore Sun. "LSU's O'Neal to skip final year," Apr. 4, 1992, https://www.baltimoresun.com/news/bs-xpm-1992-04-04-1992095106-story.html.

Chortkoff, Mitch. "Can't-miss Christie missing out," *The Daily Breeze* (Torrance, CA), Jan. 10, 1993, https://www.newspapers.com/image/608214560/?terms=doug%2Bchristie%2Bnba%2Bdraft.

Dickau, Dan. "Throwback Thursday: 7 questions with Doug Christie, former Rainier Beach High School star," Scorebook Live, Feb. 14, 2019, "https://sblivewa.com/2019/02/14/throwback-thursday-7-questions-with-doug-christie-former-rainier-beach-high-school-star/.

Fernas, Rob. "Actually, Pressure Is Off for the Waves," *Los Angeles Times*, Mar. 16, 1992, https://www.newspapers.com/image/177365580/?terms=Doug%2BChristie%2BPepperdine.

Fernas, Rob. "Streaking Pepperdine Lacks Stars," *Los Angeles Times*, Mar. 5, 1992, https://www.newspapers.com/image/177283941/?terms=Doug%2BChristie%2BPepperdine.

Kugiya, Hugo. "Accolades for Christie – Rainier Beach Retires No. 25," *The Seattle Times*, Apr. 23, 1992, https://archive.seattletimes.com/archive/?date=19920423&slug=1488227.

Mathieu, Stephanie. "Home Grown: NBA's Doug Christie recalls MM ties," *The Daily News* (Longview, WA), Sept. 23, 2006, https://tdn.com/business/local/home-grown-nbas-doug-christie-recalls-mm-ties/article_b24f9b5e-9e04-5184-a45f-98caec6f508c.html.

May, Mark. "Doug Christie is happy to be going home again," *The Daily News* (Longview, WA), June 25, 1992, https://www.newspapers.com/image/577324293/?terms=doug%2Bchristie%2Bnba%2Bdraft.

Nelson, Glenn. "Doug Christie Comes Home – Draft Brings Newest Sonic Back To Seattle," *The Seattle Times*, June 25, 1992, https://archive.seattletimes.com/archive/?date=19920625&slug=1498971.

Ramos, Kyle. "Christie and Jordan's Little-Known Connection," Sacramento Kings, Oct. 31, 2015, https://www.nba.com/kings/blog/doug-christie-and-montell-jordans-little-known-connection.

Ripton, Ray. "After Its Young Team Finished 22-9, Pepperdine Believes the Best Is Yet to Come," *Los Angeles Times*, Mar. 28, 1991, https://www.latimes.com/archives/la-xpm-1991-03-28-we-1427-story.html.

SPS Athletic Hall of Fame. "Doug Christie," http://spsathletichalloffame.org/doug-christie-bio.htm.

Taylor, Kevin. "Christie, Jones top selections for state team," *The* (Spokane) *Spokesman-Review*, Apr. 7, 1988, https://www.newspapers.com/image/572874976/?terms=doug%2Bchristie%2Brainier%2Bbeach.

Chapter 25

Associated Press. "Ellerbe denies guard told him he was going pro," Feb. 14, 2000, https://www.newspapers.com/image/210282539/?terms=Jamal%2BCrawford%2BRainier%2BBeach.

Conner, Shannon. "Seattle is refuge for prep star Crawford," *St.*

Louis Post-Dispatch, Dec. 9, 1998, https://www.newspapers.com/image/139556510/?terms=Jamal%2BCrawford%2BRainier%2BBeach.

Dickau, Dan. "Coaches Spotlight: Craig Jackson Franklin HS," Scorebook Live, Jan. 16, 2019, https://sblivewa.com/2019/01/16/coaches-spotlight-craig-jackson-franklin-hs/.

EtanThomas.com. "Jamal Crawford," Apr. 14, 2011, https://www.etanthomas.com/fatherhood-1/2018/3/8/jamal-crawford.

MGoBlue.com. "1999-2000 Men's Basketball Roster: Jamal Crawford," https://mgoblue.com/sports/mens-basketball/roster/jamal-crawford/876.

Newnham, Blaine. "Young and restless," *The Sacramento Bee*, July 2, 2000, https://www.newspapers.com/image/628806591/?terms=Jamal%2BCrawford%2BRainier%2BBeach.

O'Neil, Danny. "Crawford is mapping his untraveled road," Feb. 4, 2001, https://www.newspapers.com/image/142040642/?terms=Jamal%2BCrawford%2BRainier%2BBeach.

Orsborn, Tom. "Background checks big part of NBA draft process," *San Antonio Express-News*, June 17, 2019, https://www.expressnews.com/sports/spurs/article/Background-checks-big-part-of-NBA-draft-process-14006139.php.

Sharp, Andrew. "10 Lessons From a Night in Seattle With Jamal Crawford, Baron Davis, and More," Grantland.com, Aug. 31, 2015, https://grantland.com/the-triangle/seattle-summer-hoops-lessons/.

Sharp, Drew. "Michagain: Titans bemoan loss," *Detroit Free Press*, Nov. 25, 1999, https://www.newspapers.com/image/100090436/?terms=jamal%2Bcrawford%2Bmichigan%2Bprofile.

Sherwin, Bob. "Prep Basketball – Crawford Commits to Michigan -- Rainier Beach Guard Still Needs SAT Qualifying Score,"

The Seattle Times, Oct. 29, 1998, https://archive.seattletimes.com/archive/?date=19981029&slug=2780347.

YouTube. "1998 Rainier Beach High School Basketball Championship Game Part I," Sept. 29, 2010," https://www.youtube.com/watch?v=xfSU74sUdAo.

Wise, Mike. "Jamal Crawford's long and winding road," The Undefeated, Aug. 22, 2016, https://theundefeated.com/features/jamal-crawford-of-the-clippers-long-and-winding-road/.

Chapter 26

Amacher, Ezra. "It's gotta be the socks: A look back at Jason Terry's Arizona career," Arizona Desert Swarm, May 29, 2020, https://www.azdesertswarm.com/basketball/2020/5/29/21274073/jason-terry-arizona-basketball-coach-playing-college-career-socks-hire-return-wildcats-1997-stats.

Arizona Daily Star. "Huskies' coach does not dwell on loss of Terry," Jan. 31, 1996, https://www.newspapers.com/image/167590018/?terms=Jason%2BTerry%2Bcommits%2Bto%2BArizona.

Arizona Wildcats. "Wildcats For Life: Jason Terry and Jack Murphy," June 4, 2020, https://arizonawildcats.com/news/2020/6/4/mens-basketball-wildccats-for-life-jason-terry-and-jack-murphy.aspx.

Dufresne, Chris. "Top Cats," *The Daily News* (Longview, WA), Apr. 1, 1997, https://www.newspapers.com/image/576000229/?terms=Jason%2BTerry%2BArizona%2Bbasketball.

Hansen, Greg. "Astounding team finds way to win," Arizona Daily Star," Mar. 24, 1997, https://www.newspapers.com/image/168054064/?terms=Jason%2BTerry%2BArizona%2Bbasketball.

Kelapire, Ryan. "Once a Washington commit, Jason Terry explains why he flipped to Arizona," Arizona Desert Swarm, Sept. 11, 2020, https://www.azdesertswarm.com/basketball/2020/9/11/21431511/jason-terry-arizona-committed-washington-basketball-lute-olson-seattle.

KING-TV. "Throwback Thursday: Jason Terry high school highlights," Apr. 14, 2016, https://www.king5.com/article/sports/high-school/throwback-thursday-jason-terry-high-school-highlights/133005208#:~:text=High%20School-,Throwback%20Thursday%3A%20Jason%20Terry%20high%20school%20highlights,high%20school%20highlights%20circa%201995.&text=At%20Franklin%2C%20Jason%20Terry%20helped,first%20NCAA%20championship%20in%201997.

Ortega, Tony. "Jason Terry's Last Shot," *Seattle Weekly*, Dec. 21, 2012, https://www.seattleweekly.com/news/jason-terrys-last-shot/.

Parrillo, Ray. "Arizona wins Indy race," Knight-Ridder News Service," Apr. 1, 1997, https://www.newspapers.com/image/242315354.

Raley, Dan. "Jason Terry Replays Why He Flipped from Washington to Arizona," *Sports Illustrated*, Sept. 11, 2020, https://www.si.com/college/washington/basketball/jason-terry-replays-why-he-flipped-from-washington-to-arizona.

Rosenblatt, Zack. "Terry soared from backup to star in both college, NBA," *Arizona Daily Star*, June 21, 2015, https://tucson.com/sports/basketball/college/wildcats/terry-soared-from-backup-to-star-in-both-college-nba/article_429b13af-efe0-5ee4-b802-5ed7e6dd7093.html.

Schoenfeld, Steve. "Dickerson's defense stops Mercer," *Arizona Republic*, Apr. 1, 1997, https://www.newspapers.com/image/123895970/?terms=Jason%2BTerry%2BArizona%2Bbasketball.

Tucson Citizen. "Jason Terry: The ultimate in unselfishness," Nov. 11, 2006, https://www.newspapers.com/image/580096235/?terms=Jason%2BTerry%2BArizona%2Bbasketball.

Wasser, Al. "Quakers blow away MM," *The Daily News* (Longview, WA), Mar.

11, 1995, https://www.newspapers.com/image/575818702/?terms=Jason%2BTerry%2BFranklin%2BHigh%2BSchool%2Bbasketball.

Chapter 27

Enacademic.com. "Hec Edmundson," https://enacademic.com/dic.nsf/enwiki/2311754.

Eskenazi, David and Steve Rudman. "Wayback Machine: Ace Coach Hec Edmundson," SportspressNW.com, Nov. 15, 2011, http://sportspressnw.com/2123365/2011/wayback-machine-champion-coach-hec-edmundson.

Kolloen, Seth. "The Rise and Fall of Lorenzo Romar," *Seattle Weekly*, Mar. 15, 2017, https://www.seattleweekly.com/news/the-rise-and-fall-of-lorenzo-romar/.

Pavković, Krešimir. "Detlef Schrempf: The Prototype of the modern player," BasketballNetwork.net, Sept. 22, 2018, https://www.basketballnetwork.net/detlef-schrempf-the-prototype-of-the-modern-player/.

Titus, Mark. "Lorenzo Romar's Last (Last) Chance," TheRinger.com, Sept. 30, 2016, https://www.theringer.com/2016/9/30/16042176/lorenzo-romar-washington-huskies-basketball-c288c06c881.

Chapter 28

- Another recap of a big game during B-Roy's senior year. This performance helped solidify his status as the front runner for Pac 10 Player of the Year.

- A little more in-depth breakdown from the Husky forums about what the expectations were for the squad heading into B-Roy's senior season.

Alipour, Sam. "RISE Flashback: Brandon Roy," ESPN, Mar. 4, 2010, https://www.espn.com/highschool/rise/basketball/boys/news/story?id=4964575.

Allende, Mike. "UW's Roy lands in Portland," *The Daily Herald* (Everett, WA), June 28, 2006, https://www.heraldnet.com/sports/uws-roy-lands-in-portland/.

Cacabelos, Kevin. "Brandon Roy's Top Ten Greatest Moments As A Washington Husky," SB Nation Seattle, Dec. 13, 2011, https://seattle.sbnation.com/2011/12/13/2632500/brandon-roy-top-moments-washington-huskies-portland-trailblazers.

Conroy, Denny. "NBA Dream Delayed Brandon Roy Can Play," BasketballRecruitingRivals.com, Jan. 18, 2003, https://basketballrecruiting.rivals.com/news/nba-dream-delayed-brandon-roy-can-play/printable.

Cova, Ernesto. "Kobe Bryant on Brandon Roy In 2010: 'He's The Most Difficult Player To Guard, 365 Days A Year, 7 Days A Week. Roy Has No Weakness In His Game,'" Fadeaway World, July 28, 2020,

Curry, Charles. "The Brandon Roy Story: A Career That Never Got Started," Bleacher Report, Feb. 16, 2011, https://bleacherreport.com/articles/607350-the-brandon-roy-story-a-career-that-never-got-started.

Givony, Jonathan and Mat Williams. "NBA Scouting Reports, Northwest Division (Part III), DraftExpress.com, Sept. 16, 2008, http://www.draftexpress.com/profile/Brandon-Roy-343/.

Kitsap Sun (Bremerton, WA). "State Hoops," Mar. 8, 2002, https://products.kitsapsun.com/archive/2002/03-08/0075_state_hoops.html.

Meagher, Scott. "Brandon Roy retires: NBA players react on Twitter," *The Oregonian*, Jan. 10, 2019, https://www.oregonlive.com/blazers/2011/12/brandon-roy-retires-nba-player.html.

Pelton, Kevin. "Brandon Roy calls it a career," ESPN, June 24, 2013, https://www.espn.com/blog/truehoop/post/_/id/60185/brandon-roy-calls-career.

Raley, Dan. "Garfield 'University' sends grads to big time," *Seattle*

Post-Intelligencer, Mar. 5, 2003, https://www.seattlepi.com/news/article/Garfield-University-sends-grads-to-big-time-1108986.php.

Raley, Dan. "UW's Roy emerges from layaway with total package," *Seattle Post-Intelligencer*, Mar. 14, 2006," https://www.seattlepi.com/sports/article/UW-s-Roy-emerges-from-layaway-with-total-package-1198452.php.

Seattle Sportsnet. "The Legacy of Brandon Roy," Dec. 9, 2011, https://seattlesportsnet.com/2011/12/09/the-legacy-of-brandon-roy/.

The Seattle Times. "2000-2001 Star Times basketball teams," Mar. 13, 20001, https://archive.seattletimes.com/archive/?date=20010313&slug=boycap1.

SPS Athletic Hall of Fame. "Brandon Roy," http://www.spsathletichalloffame.org/brandon-roy-bio.htm.

Uproxx.com. "The Natural: Brandon Roy's First National Cover Story," Dec. 12, 2011, https://uproxx.com/dimemag/the-natural-brandon-roys-first-national-cover-story/.

YouTube. "Ron Artest says Brandon Roy better player than Kobe," May 1, 2009, https://www.youtube.com/watch?v=fUxhwirc5OM.

Chapter 29 & 30

Associated Press. "Brockman, Thomas help UW banish Stanford," Mar. 13, 2009, https://www.heraldnet.com/sports/brockman-thomas-help-uw-banish-stanford-video/.

Boyle, John. "4A State Hoops: Curtis' Thomas no small talent," *The Seattle Times*, May 8, 2006, https://archive.seattletimes.com/archive/?date=20060308&slug=boyle08.

Divish, Ryan. "Guard Isaiah Thomas has taken his amazing talent back East, leaving Vikings confident they can cope," *Tacoma News Tribune*, Dec. 12, 2006, https://www.newspapers.com/image/673792595/.

GoHuskies.com. "Isaiah Thomas," https://gohuskies.com/sports/mens-basketball/roster/isaiah-thomas/2491.

Grippi, Vince. "First time through," *The* (Spokane) *Spokesman-Review*, Feb. 4, 2009, https://www.newspapers.com/image/578306898/?terms=Isaiah%2BThomas%2BUW.

Henderson, Brady. "Huskies' Isaiah Thomas unsure if he'll return," MyNorthwest.com, Apr. 4, 2011, https://sports.mynorthwest.com/19193/huskies-isaiah-thomas-unsure-if-hell-return/.

Jenks, Jayson. "Oral history: Isaiah Thomas was unstoppable in his 51-point state-tournament game in 2006," *The Seattle Times*, Feb. 27, 2016, https://www.seattletimes.com/sports/high-school/oral-history-isaiah-thomas-was-unstoppable-in-his-51-point-state-tournament-game-in-2006/.

Johnson, Scott M. "Doubting Thomas? No way," *Everett* (WA) *Herald*, Dec. 12, 2009, https://www.newspapers.com/image/579347261/?terms=Isaiah%2BThomas%2BUW.

Leung, Diamond. "The real reason Thomas left UW," ESPN, June 22, 2011, https://www.espn.com/blog/collegebasketballnation/post/_/id/32243/the-real-reason-isaiah-thomas-left-uw.

Mazzoncini, Zack. "Isaiah Thomas hits game-winner PAC-10 2011 Tournament Championship UW vs Arizona," Mar. 13, 2011, https://www.youtube.com/watch?v=y2TtyeXgYM8.

McCleary, Jason. "Washington Huskies Isaiah Thomas During The Prep Days!" Bleacher Report, Aug. 11, 2009, https://bleacherreport.com/articles/234561-washington-huskies-isaiah-thomas-during-the-prep-days.

The (Raleigh, NC) *News & Observer*. "Henson a Bit Too Spunky on Final Play," Mar. 21, 2011, https://www.newspapers.com/image/649472281/?terms=Isaiah%2BThomas%2BUW.

Raley, Dan. "Freshman phenom Isaiah Thomas counted on to resurrect

UW hoops," *Seattle Post-Intelligencer,* Oct. 14, 2008, https://www.seattlepi.com/sports/article/Freshman-phenom-Isaiah-Thomas-counted-on-to-1288232.php.

Raley, Dan. "Isaiah Stewart: Best UW Freshman Hoopster Ever?" *Sports Illustrated*, Jan. 21, 2020, https://www.si.com/college/washington/basketball/stewart-might-be-best-uw-freshman-ever.

Scorebook Live. "In the end, Isaiah Thomas runs away with title of best Washington high school basketball player of the 21st Century," Apr. 10, 2020, https://washington.scorebooklive.com/2020/04/10/vote-on-championship-matchup-isaiah-thomas-vs-zach-lavine/.

Stone, Larry. "Isaiah Thomas deserved his ceremony — and after the past year, he needed it, too," *The Seattle Times*, Feb. 17, 2018, https://www.seattletimes.com/sports/uw-husky-basketball/huskies-retire-isaiah-thomas-no-2-jersey-with-special-ceremony/.

Thomasseau, Allison. "Throwback Thursday: Isaiah Thomas high school highlights," KING-TV, Dec. 17, 2015, https://www.tennessean.com/story/sports/high-school/2015/12/17/throwback-thursday-isaiah-thomas-high-school-highlights/77485962/.

Statistics / Bios

Doug Christie

Born: May 9, 1970

Height/Weight: 6'6" / 200 pounds

Position: Small Forward / Shooting Guard

High School: Rainier Beach

College: Pepperdine University

Awards: 4-time All-NBA Defensive Team

Teams: Los Angeles Lakers, New York Knicks, Toronto Raptors, Sacramento Kings, Dallas Mavericks, Los Angeles Clippers

Career Stats

Games Played: 827

Games Started: 708

Career Per Game Averages

Points: 11.2

Rebounds: 4.1

Assists: 3.6

Steals: 1.9

Blocks: .5

Threes: 1

Jamal Crawford

Born: March 20, 1980 – Seattle, WA

Height/Weight: 6'5" / 185 pounds

Position: Point Guard/Shooting Guard

High School: Rainier Beach

College: University of Michigan

Awards: 3-time NBA 6th Man of the Year (2010, 2014, 2016)

Teams: Chicago Bulls, New York Knicks, Golden State Warriors, Atlanta Hawks, Portland Trail Blazers, Los Angeles Clippers, Minnesota Timberwolves, Phoenix Suns, Brooklyn Nets

Games Played: 1,327

Games Started: 433

Career Per Game Averages

Points: 14.6

Assists: 3.4

Steals: 0.9

Blocks: 0.2

Threes: 1.7

Nate Robinson

Born: May 31, 1984 – Seattle, WA

Height/Weight: 5'9" / 180 pounds

Position: Point Guard

High School: Rainier Beach

College: University of Washington

Awards: 3-time NBA Slam Dunk Champion, NBA Player of the Week – February 3, 2013

Teams: New York Knicks, Boston Celtics, Oklahoma City Thunder, Golden State Warriors, Chicago Bulls, Denver Nuggets, LA Clippers, New Orleans Pelicans

Games Played: 618

Games Started: 107

Career Per Game Averages

Points: 11

Rebounds: 2.3

Assists: 3

Steals: .9

Blocks: .1

Threes: 1.3

Brandon Roy

Born: July 23, 1984 — Seattle, WA

Height/Weight: 6'6" / 211 pounds

Position: Shooting Guard/Small Forward

High School: Garfield

College: University of Washington

Awards: 3-time NBA All-Star, All-NBA Second Team, All-NBA Third Team, NBA Rookie of the Year, NBA All-Rookie First Team

Teams: Portland Trail Blazers, Minnesota Timberwolves

Games Played: 326

Games Started: 300

Career Per Game Averages

Points: 18.8

Rebounds: 4.3

Assists: 4.1

Steals: 1.0

Blocks: 0.2

Threes: 1.0

Jason Terry

Born: September 15, 1977 – Seattle, WA

Height/Weight: 6'2" / 185 pounds

Position: Point Guard/Shooting Guard

High School: Franklin

College: University of Arizona

Awards: NBA All-Rookie Second Team (2000), NBA Sixth Man of the Year (2009), NBA Champion (2011)

Teams: Atlanta Hawks, Dallas Mavericks, Boston Celtics, Brooklyn Nets, Houston Rockets, Milwaukee Bucks

Games Played: 1410

Games Started: 679

Career Per Game Averages

Points: 13.4

Rebounds: 2.3

Assists: 3.8

Blocks: 0.2

Steals: 1.1

Isaiah Thomas

Born: February 7th, 1989 — Tacoma, Washington

Height/Weight: 5'9" / 185 pounds

Position: Point Guard

High School: Curtis; South Kent School

College: University of Washington

Awards: 2-time NBA All-Star, All-NBA Second Team, NBA All-Rookie Second Team

Teams: Sacramento Kings, Phoenix Suns, Boston Celtics, Cleveland Cavaliers, Los Angeles Lakers, Denver Nuggets, Washington Wizards

Games Played: 525

Games Started: 361

Career Per Game Averages

Points: 18.1

Rebounds: 2.5

Assists: 5.0

Steals: 0.9

Blocks: 0.1

Threes: 1.9

CPSIA information can be obtained
at www.ICGtesting.com
Printed in the USA
BVHW041754301120
594467BV00011B/289

9 781636 254845